AF291414

TROOPER
OF THE HOUSEHOLD CAVALRY

TROOPER
OF THE HOUSEHOLD CAVALRY

Memoir of a Piccadilly Cowboy

SIMON WALLINGTON

Pen & Sword

MILITARY

AN IMPRINT OF PEN & SWORD BOOKS LTD.
YORKSHIRE – PHILADELPHIA

First published in Great Britain in 2026 by
PEN AND SWORD MILITARY
An imprint of
Pen & Sword Books Limited
Yorkshire – Philadelphia

ISBN 978 1 03614 474 6

Typeset in Times New Roman 11/14 by
SJmagic DESIGN SERVICES, India.
Printed and bound in the UK by CPI Group (UK) Ltd.

The Publisher's authorised representative in the EU for product safety is Authorised Rep Compliance Ltd., Ground Floor, 71 Lower Baggot Street, Dublin D02 P593, Ireland.
www.arccompliance.com

For a complete list of Pen & Sword titles please contact
PEN & SWORD BOOKS LIMITED
George House, Units 12 & 13, Beevor Street, Off Pontefract Road,
Barnsley, South Yorkshire, S71 1HN, England
E-mail: enquiries@pen-and-sword.co.uk
Website: www.pen-and-sword.co.uk

or

PEN AND SWORD BOOKS
1950 Lawrence Rd, Havertown, PA 19083, USA
E-mail: uspen-and-sword@casematepublishers.com
Website: www.penandswordbooks.com

Contents

Foreword

Although there were more than 30 years between Simon and me first tipping up at Hyde Park Barracks, the emotions, challenges, and experiences we overcame are incredibly similar. While I wouldn't dream of saying I had it harder than him (after all, aren't we supposed to keep up all that nonsense about younger generations having it easier?), I will say Knightsbridge was a rough ride – for both of us – as it has been for countless others who have served there over the past fifty years.

I first got to know Simon about a year ago. The Regimental Adjutant of the Household Cavalry, Colonel Ralph Griffin, called me out of the blue to ask whether I was happy to be put in touch. His call that afternoon marked the first time the regiment had made contact with me – formally – since I left the Army 12 years earlier. I was therefore surprised and alarmed to hear one of my former Commanding Officers outline Simon's career in the regiment, although he didn't include the very worst of the reasons why Simon had been discharged in 1976.

I am, and always have been, an openly gay man. I came out at 18, in Knightsbridge, and navigated what was generally a positive experience on both the ceremonial and armoured sides of the regiment in terms of my colleagues' acceptance, with relatively few problems. Simon, on the other hand – who is not gay – was hauled over the coals three decades earlier because someone wrongly believed he was. The ins and outs, and believe me the details, of what I can only describe as scandalous – which resulted in Simon and 17 fellow members of the so-called 'Household Cavalry 18' losing their careers – are nothing short of outrageous. I won't recount that detail here; you have this excellent book to do that. But learning about this dark chapter in the Household Cavalry's semi-recent history has left me angry.

I'm writing this Foreword on what is also the final day of an inquest into the death of a young soldier in the Blues and Royals, who sadly ended his life on the base aged 18, just days after Her Late Majesty's funeral in 2022. Reports in newspapers this week have described how

Jack Burnell-Williams, who was found hanging in the block by his mates, struggled with ceremonial life in the barracks. A story in the *Daily Mail* said he was worried about being billed thousands of pounds for some lost kit; a piece in *The Mirror* included witness testimony from one of his fellow troopers, who said they were being "treated worse than the animals' during the time around Jack's death. While stories like this will have been shocking for civies to read, I'm sad to say I found none of it a surprise. I'm sure many who have also served there will have felt the same. May Jack rest in peace.

Whether it's the abuses detailed in these pages, now more than fifty years ago, or the tragic experiences that led to Jack Burnell-Williams ending his life much more recently, the fact is this: Knightsbridge was bad back then, and if these most recent matters are to be believed, it looks bad now. The question is whether or not the place can change.

I believe this book, written by a man I'm so pleased to be able to now call my friend, can have a role to play in any conversations that set out to make life better for the Troopers in that old stomping ground of ours – Hyde Park Barracks.

James Wharton
February 2026

Prologue

11 JANUARY 1972, North Camp railway station. A cold, grey winter's day greeted me as I walked out of the small, grey-stone station exit. Ahead of me, a tall, thin, blond-haired chap bounced along. He looked keen; keener than me, anyway. I was nervous, very nervous; truth be known, I didn't want to be here, but I had no choice. I could see the green canvas-covered truck waiting on the gravel car park. A tall man in khaki-coloured trousers and a green jumper was waiting. As I got closer, I noticed his red and blue hat, the peak sat flat on his face, nearly covering his eyes.

'Junior Guardsman's Wing. If you're for the Junior Guardsman's Wing get on here!' he shouted as we got to the vehicle.

There were six of us, all sat on the wooden slatted benches that ran the length of both sides of the truck. It was too noisy for much conversation, so everybody just sat looking out of the back at where we'd been. It didn't take long – about twenty minutes – to get to the Guards Depot at Pirbright, the large military camp in the Surrey countryside that was to be my home for the next two years. The vehicle stopped with a jolt. From where I was sitting, I could see strangely shaped black and white wooden buildings – there were about six of them – surrounded by well-kept grass, all connected by single-track tarmac roads. As the tailgate dropped, the soldier from the station was there again.

'Right, you lovely lot, down here and give me your name!' he shouted as we clambered down onto the tarmac. When my turn came, I gave him my name and he directed me to block C3, Lance Sergeant Ward's squad. I looked at the wooden building; there were long buildings coming out of a central block – three on each side – wide double doors welcomed us into what I can only describe as the shiniest floors I'd ever seen. These buildings and Lance Sergeant Wood's squad were my starting point for a four-year journey, from the Junior Guardsman's Wing to escorting the Queen on state occasions, carrying out the Queen's Life Guard duties at Whitehall and finally being kicked out – for something I didn't do.

Glossary

Donkey walloper	Household Cavalryman
Gobblers, Wooden Tops	Grenadier Guards
Jocks	Scots Guards
Sheep shaggers	Coldstream Guards
Micks	Irish Guards
Taffs	Welsh Guards
Barrack Room	Where squaddies live
Squaddies	Guardsmen, private soldiers, wooden tops
Troopers	Private soldiers in cavalry regiments
Piccadilly Cowboy	Household Cavalry
Cav Black	Irish-breed Household Cavalry horses
Kit	Various uniform of all types issued to the military
Bobbing or Bulling	Spit and polishing boots etc.
White sap	White Blanco used on various bits of leather state kit
Blanco	A compound used to treat canvas and some leather kit
Corporal	Two stripes with a metal crown above them; we don't have lance corporals in the cavalry
Lance Corporal of Horse	Three stripes and a cloth crown above them with two gold braids on their forage cap
Corporal of Horse	Three stripes and a metal crown above them with three gold braids on their forage cap
Staff Corporal Squadron Quartermaster Corporal	Staff Sergeant, a brass crown worn above four inverted chevrons
Squadron Corporal Major	Warrant Officer Class 2, with brass crown worn on the right wrist

Regimental Corporal Major	Laurel wreath around a crown worn on the right wrist
Regimental Corporal Major	Royal Coat of Arms worn on the right wrist
Grot or minger	Soldier who can't or doesn't keep himself or his kit clean
Taggy	Not well turned out, i.e. kit not clean or worn correctly; see minger
Shit Order	See above: grot, minger, taggy
Plug	Lazy slow black cavalry horse, normally reserved for Mussies
Mussies	Musicians
Three Bar	Lance Corporal or full Corporal of Horse
Two Bar	Corporal
Scoff or Scran	Food
Scoff rods	Knife, fork and spoon
Up Town	Hyde Park Barracks
Weapon jammed	Your weapon has jammed for some reason and won't fire; if you can't clear it yourself, hold your hand up while continuing to point weapon down range!
Apeshit	Drill Sergeants tend to lose their temper, 'going apeshit'
Webbing	Strong canvas shoulder straps attached to a belt with pouches attached to carry ammunition magazines, water and scoff; you can also attach a rucksack
GPMG	General purpose machine gun
SLR	Self-loading rifle
SMG	Sub machine gun
Bolo	Marching or any drill in fact carried out with a 'swagger'
Drill Pig	see Drill Sergeant!
Bunk	Small room attached to your barrack room for senior NCO
NCO	Non-commissioned officer
Fast Black	Young squaddie who is tasked to help senior NCO cleaning his kit (different times!)

GLOSSARY

Facing the door	On a charge, in front of the Colonel, in trouble
Jimmy the Fish	Hairdresser at Hyde Park Barracks
PTI	Physical Training Instructor; whatever you do, don't get between a PTI and a mirror!
HD jumper	Heavy duty pullover
Stable Belt	Canvas and leather 3in-wide belt; Life Guards' belts are red and blue, the other regiments in The Brigade of Guards wear the same belt but coloured red, blue, red
SD cap	Khaki Service Dress forage cap with brown leather chinstrap
Three Tonner	Bedford TL canvas 'soft skin' truck

Chapter 1

Army Selection 'Corsham'

'YOU'VE GOT TO go back, dad's going berserk downstairs.'

I sat in a rapidly cooling bath at Baugh Farm, my home, tears streaming down my face as I tried to pluck up the courage to go and face my father. It was mid-September 1971, and I'd been sent to the Army selection centre at Corsham to start the process of joining the Junior Army. I was fifteen years old. It was a short journey from Temple Meads station in Bristol to Bath Spa station, the first stop in fact, and from there a whole bunch of us were taken on the twenty-minute journey to Corsham, a small Wiltshire town set high on a hill near the village of Box. I, along with the others, were due to stay here for three days and two nights. As soon as we got there, my anxiety levels were sky high. I could barely hold back the tears and my stomach was in knots. From the get-go, I knew I couldn't go through with it. Eventually, I plucked up the courage to speak to someone in charge. I faked sickness, said I didn't feel well; I really didn't feel well – I felt terrible. Two hours later I was back at Bath railway station, waiting for a train to take me home. I knew I was in trouble – big trouble – but I also knew I couldn't go through the process that faced me back in Corsham. I thought about running away, but where would I go? I had to go home!

It was four o'clock when I walked into the large kitchen. From her chair by the range, my mother looked up in horror from her book: 'What are you doing here?'

'I couldn't go through with it; I don't know why but I couldn't.'

'Your father will go mad; you know that, don't you? He'll be home in a minute. Bloody hell, Simon, what are you playing at?'

'I'm going to have a bath.' I finished the conversation and climbed the wooden spiral staircase to the second floor of the large farmhouse.

Eventually, I let myself out of the bathroom to be confronted by my mother, arms folded, the tears in her eyes clearly visible behind her glasses. I didn't know whether it was anger or frustration; a bit of both probably.

'Your father wants to see you downstairs now' were the words that greeted me.

I suppose I was resigned to my fate. I felt empty, spent, finished; a 15-year-old failure. A mixture of fear, anger and regret filled my mind and body as I made my way back down to the kitchen. As I pushed open the door at the bottom of the stairs, I could see him below me, sat in his usual chair at the head of the large kitchen table, his suit jacket hung over the back of the chair. As I walked towards the other end of the table, he started.

'What the hell do you think you're up to?' he shouted, eyes staring with rage as he glared over his half-rimmed glasses.

I didn't say anything: I couldn't. I just stood there, staring at my feet, wishing this all would just go away. It wouldn't, though; deep down I knew that!

'You're going back. You're going back and staying there until you successfully pass and join the army, is that understood?'

I could only nod, tears welling up again, but I was determined not to cry in front of him. The only thing I could think of doing was to run, to run to the only place I felt happy, the stables. I turned and made my run for it, through the open door, through the outhouse and down the large garden, over the crumbling dry-stone wall into Alan's field. I kept running until I covered the mile or so to the stables. Climbing the gate into the small paddock that fronted the yard, I could see what I was hoping to see: Pam. Pam and I had been getting closer for some time now. She was my soul mate.

'What are you doing here? I thought you were away on that army thing,' she said with a look of surprise.

'Bottled it, couldn't do it. Came home.'

'Crikey, I bet your dad went mad.'

'Yeah, just a bit. He said I've got to go back. Don't know when, but I know he'll make it happen.'

I stood at Pam's pony's head, curling a few strands of his mane between my fingers. His head had dropped now, so it rested on my chest. We must have been there for another ten minutes, talking through the options. She gave me the confidence to try again. The truth is that she was the reason all this was going on. I couldn't bear the thought of leaving her, not seeing her. I now realised that I loved her. One slight problem though; she, as far as I knew, didn't feel the same. She was four years older than me, working full-time in a local boot factory and still living with her parents.

As I walked back home, all that occupied my mind was Pam. I had to sort this out somehow before – and if – I joined up. I had to explain my feelings, and do it before I went to Corsham again. I made my mind up to go and see her tomorrow. I knew she would be home, so I was going to sort this out, once and for all!.

The following morning, while walking to Pam's house, my head was full of 'what if's'. What if she doesn't want to go out with me? What if she says I'm too young? What would I do then? Run away and join the army? Well, I didn't have a choice over that one! Closing the rickety back gate, I glanced down the well-kept garden. It was full of different vegetables, all in neat rows. I hope her mum or dad aren't here, I thought as I turned towards the narrow path that led to the back door. As I walked, I could see Pam through the large window of their back room. Her long brown hair was wet and she held a hairdryer in her hand. She smiled when she saw me and gestured for me to come in. The house always felt, well let's say compact to me – a two up, two down end of terrace Victorian former miner's cottage. Pam was an only child, so there were just the three of them living there.

'Alright trouble,' she said with a smile as I walked into the back room. 'Are you still in trouble with your dad?'

'I guess so. He'd gone to work before I got up!'

'What are you going to do?' she continued as, strangely, she pulled a chair from beside the piano and began to climb up on it.

'What are you doing?' Curiosity had got the better of me.

'Drying my hair. Why?'

'You're drying your hair standing on a chair in the middle of the room.'

'Yeah, it plugs in the light socket,' she continued as she handed me the now redundant light bulb. 'Why don't you make a coffee.'

Placing two mugs on the small kitchen table, I sat back down in the chair, Pam was about two feet away from me. The hairdryer was whirring away, and her long brown hair seemed to dance as the warm air hit it. She was a slim, some might say 'skinny' girl, with what I thought was a beautiful body. I sat and sipped my coffee as I continued to stare; she couldn't see me, she had her back to me. I could feel slight beads of sweat forming on my forehead as I desperately tried to think of how I was going to approach this. I was fixated by her arse. I thought it was the best; she wore blue jeans, not too baggy, not too tight, just right! The blowing of the hairdryer suddenly stopped. Crooking my neck to look up, I saw Pam holding out her hand.

'Bulb,' she suddenly said. 'Bulb – hand me the bulb please.'

'Oh, sorry,' I said as I quickly stood up and handed her the bulb. I was close to her now, maybe I should make a move. I couldn't though; too shy. I just took the hairdryer from her hand, placed it on the kitchen table and sat back down. I felt like I felt yesterday while I faced my dad – inadequate.

'Shall we go out on the horses this afternoon? You could ride Snudge.'

'Yeah, love to.' As well as working at a local shoe factory, we both helped look after a local butcher's racehorses. Snudge was a particularly nice chestnut thoroughbred. Everyone enjoyed riding him; I'd taken him hunting once or twice and he was as 'safe as houses', to use a horsey term. I'd left school earlier that year. Apparently, I was gormless, according to my dad anyway. It was agreed that I would spend time at our old home, Griffin Farm, working with the horses for a couple of months before joining the army. That was the plan anyway. I was up for it – the working at the stables bit, not the army bit. I just hoped that the latter would go away.

The afternoon was unusually cold as we mounted the horses at the farm. Pam and I had bought ex-army greatcoats from a shop in Staple Hill that sold that sort of stuff. I lifted myself into the saddle to get the coat over my legs as we walked the horses through the gateway and up the short ramp to the road beyond. Pam was riding Gordena, another of the racehorses that was stabled there before he went back into training at Cheltenham. We walked the horses side by side towards Moorend, under the newly constructed concrete bridge that carried the M4 above us.

'Do you want a sweet?' Pam asked over the echoes of the horses' hooves as we walked through the tunnel-like bridge. 'They're in my pocket, help yourself.'

Reaching into her coat pocket, it was warm. The paper bag, I could feel, was full of sweets. 'What are they?' I asked before grabbing one and pulling my hand out.

'Merry Maids – my favourites.'

'Ah, nice,' I said as I put the unwrapped sweet in my mouth. The horses had loosened up now; time for work. We trotted them hard on the bit past Rutter's farm, up the hill past the old Roman fort and onwards towards Cuckoo Lane. An hour later, we were heading back down the road towards the stables. We walked the horses back on a long rein. Sweat from their efforts gently rose from their necks as they slowly cooled down. I sneaked my hand back into her large coat pocket to nick another sweet. Pam responded by putting her hand in the pocket to stop me, and suddenly we were holding hands. it was amazing. I didn't want it to stop. Looking across to her, I just said it – I still don't know where the courage came from.

'It's because of you I don't want to go, but at the same time I know I'll have to. I don't know what to do. I'll miss you so much.'

She looked me in the eye and said: 'The truth is I feel the same way.'

I thought I was going to explode with delight and excitement. Standing up in my stirrups, I leant across and kissed her; just a quick kiss, that's all I needed. When we got back to the yard, Pete Reed, our boss, was there.

'How did they go?' he asked as we dismounted.

'Fantastic, just fantastic,' I replied, with the biggest grin on my face.

'What are you so happy about? You look like you've just won the pools.'

'I have, mate. Well I haven't, but it feels like it!'

That decision changed my life. It gave me the confidence to move forward. Pam gave me the confidence to return to Corsham, go through the tests and medicals and eventually, on 13 December 1971, join the army – The Life Guards.

Chapter 2

The Spiders

IT WAS 11 JANUARY 1972. I was standing at the big white painted double doors that led into spider block C3. Darkness had fallen as five of us 'recruits' filed in. I think we were all anxious as we were confronted by a tall man in uniform, his boots like mirrors. I remember noticing the toe caps reflecting the ceiling lights above us. He was carrying a long wooden stick with various bits of highly polished brass on it; a pace stick, as I later found out.

'Name!' he shouted, barely looking up from his clipboard.

'Wallington, sir.'

'I'm not a sir – not yet anyway. You address me as sergeant, understood?'

'Yes, sir, er sorry, Sergeant.'

'Room two, first bed on the left,' he said as he pointed his pace stick to the right. The doors here were green, a pale green pair of double doors that led into a long room. The floor shone like a mirror. Metal beds lined each side, with a grey metal locker between each one, and a block of folded bedding sat on every bed. Metal-framed windows also lined both sides, looking out onto similar rooms. Twenty-three beds were lined up in the room. Twenty-two were for us – Junior Guardsmen, as we were known. The remaining bed was for the room's 'trained soldier', a professional soldier who was posted here from whatever regiment in the Brigade of Guards he was in – Coldstream Guards in his case – to 'look after us, show us the ropes'. What a joke that turned out to be, but more of that later! In the next bed to mine, a tall, gangly guy sat nervously on the edge. The room was filling up now. Lots of unfamiliar accents filled my ears as I looked around; it was a bit like the selection centre at Corsham, but that was for two nights and this was forever as far as I was concerned. Eventually, from behind several metal lockers that had been arranged into some sort of private area at the far end of the room, a plumpish man appeared. He wore green trousers with what looked like horse bandages around his ankles, joining his trousers to his boots. He also had a green jumper with a thick blue, red and blue belt over the top of it.

'Right, you lot!' he shouted. 'I'm your trained soldier, this is my room, I'm in charge, understood?'

A low muttering sound went around the room, as he made his way down the shiny lino floor towards the end of the room where I was standing. The guy sitting on the bed next to mine had his back to him. I noticed, as he came closer, that he wore an armband with a small badge on it saying 'trained soldier'. Shutting the double doors, he made his way to the middle of the room where he demonstrated how we should make up our beds and how in the morning we should strip the bed apart and make what's known as a 'bed block'. Following that, we all followed him to the toilet block, a large, cold room that sat in the middle of this strange configuration of rooms known as 'the spiders'. I noticed a bank of large white sinks in the middle – ten on each side – and the room echoed as he explained how and when we should carry out our various ablutions. Everything was sparkling clean, which made it feel quite uninviting. Next we were walked up to the canteen, which was to be the last occasion for some time that we would 'walk' anywhere. From tomorrow, we'd be marching or running nonstop, everywhere!

The next morning I was awake before the bellowing voice rang out as he crashed into the room. I was curled up like a ball, wishing I could stay there forever, also wishing I could go home. I didn't fancy this military life at all. All sorts of emotions were flying around my head: I was homesick, missing my mum, missing Pam.

'Ok you lot, hands off cocks, on with socks,' he shouted as he marched up and down the room, hitting each bed end with a 2ft length of wood that he was carrying.

'This, this is a bed stick,' he explained as he held up said piece of wood. 'You use this to measure that your bed blocks are the correct size, not too wide, not too narrow, the correct size. You've got half an hour – shit, shave and shampoo, bed blocks correctly made, and fall in outside.'

I don't think I've ever moved so fast. I had to pretend to shave; I didn't have anything to shave! But the trained soldier insisted. The bed blocks consisted of a blanket, then a sheet, followed by another blanket, another sheet, all topped off with another blanket, neatly folded into a 2ft by 2ft square. As I ran out of the barrack room to line up out on the tarmac road outside and 'fall in', I had a quick look back. The bed block looked – to me anyway – reasonable. Following breakfast, we were issued with our kit. I'd never owned so many clothes. Being the fourth of four boys, most of my clothes were hand-me-downs. Standing at a long counter in the stores, the pile of kit in front of me just kept growing. I can't carry that, I thought, as the pile was topped off with a dark blue beret and a red and blue forage cap.

'What's the problem?' the guy in the neatly pressed brown warehouse coat asked, with a cynical grin on his face.

'I don't think I can carry all this,' I sheepishly replied.

'Wait there,' he barked as he turned on his heels and made his way to the back of the enormous building. He returned a few minutes later. It felt longer; we were all standing in line and I seemed to be causing the holdup. I felt vulnerable and uncomfortable, still in civvies and the centre of attention.

'Try this,' he said as he passed a brown-green suitcase over the counter. I nodded a thanks. I could feel the heat from my cheeks as I blushed profusely.

The case was heavy as I walked – marched – back to our room in the spiders. All the beds were piled high with uniform. Some of the guys were trying some of it on; others just got on with sorting it out. Steve, the fella in the next bed, stood looking at his overflowing suitcase. His dark blue forage cap, with white band around it, was shoved roughly on the back of his head. Our trained soldier paced up and down, barking orders, as we all struggled to fit things into our standard issue metal lockers.

'You two,' he said, stopping at the foot of mine and Steve's beds. 'You two, go up to the canteen and collect the tea urn. Before you go, put the green trousers, KF shirt and your heavy-duty jumpers on. Don't worry about your putties yet, just wear your DMS boots. Understood?' DMS (or Directly Moulded Sole) ankle boots had rubber soles and leather uppers, and were standard-issue footwear in the British Army until the mid-Eighties.

He might as well have been speaking another language as far as I was concerned. I looked at Steve, shrugged my shoulders and started to hunt for some kit that looked vaguely like the stuff he'd mentioned. The trousers were new and stiff, the shirt – shirt KF, as it said on the label – was one of those you pull on over your head. It again was new and I could feel it itching as soon as I pulled it over my head. Finally, the green heavy-duty jumper. Deep down, I was enjoying this. I'd forgotten for a minute the homesickness that was trying desperately to drive me home, to drive me to give in and fail. Steve and I were walking back from the canteen, or other ranks mess as it was known, the tea urn was hot, very hot. Steve was taller than me – almost everyone was in this place – so the urn kept leaning my way. It was heavy as well, and I struggled to keep it from spilling out onto my hand as we walked!

'Put it on the wall by the entrance,' our trained soldier shouted out of the window as we waddled past.

It was eleven o'clock – NAFFI break. We weren't allowed to go to the NAFFI, but that's what they called it. I grabbed the kidney-shaped black plastic mug that I'd been issued and put it under the tap of the tea urn. The tea was sweet; it didn't matter whether you took sugar or not, that's what you got. The sweet tea tasted good. We all stood around in huddles. Most of us were smoking. I'd been told before joining that we weren't allowed to smoke, but much to my relief, that rule wasn't enforced.

'Five minutes!' a voice rang out. I was getting used to the different accents now. There was Scottish, Geordie, London, Brummie and even some like me – West Country, Bristol. This voice was Scottish. A tall man stood in the doorway, his forage cap having a band of tartan around it. Scots Guards, I thought. His peak, like the other instructors', lay flat on his face, and he had big ears which seemed to be over emphasised by his cap.

'My name's Lance Sergeant Ward,' he announced. 'I'm your squad instructor. I'm not your mother, but I'm the closest thing while you're in my squad, do you understand?'

'Yes, Sergeant,' was the muffled response.

'I can't hear you. Do you understand?' he shouted.

'Yes, Sergeant!' everybody shouted back.

'The rest of the morning you'll sort your new kit out – your trained soldier will show you how – then, this afternoon, you lucky lot, you're going on a run, a cross-country run, the PTIs [physical training instructors] want to show you the sights of this lovely place.'

* * *

It was two in the afternoon, a cold clear day, but the sun was already beginning to set in the west. We were 'fallen in' outside our spider, all in identical kit: red v-necked tee-shirts, baggy dark blue shorts and black plimsoles – 'daps' as we called them in my part of the world. Two men were striding around us. They wore dark blue tracksuit bottoms and red and blue hooped tops. All this topped off with carefully moulded khaki berets.

'They're PTIs,' somebody in front of me whispered.

'Right, you lot,' the first one said. 'We're going for a run, not any run, a race. You'll see white posts with arrows painted on them; follow them. Don't worry about getting lost, we'll be out there keeping an eye on you!'

Lining up, about eighty-five of us, at the top of the road, it was cold now. I just wanted to get going.

'Go!' the PTI shouted, and we were off. I wasn't a bad runner, but not being the biggest, I didn't think I had a chance. Yet somehow I found myself near the front. The first challenge came quickly – a hill, a hill made of sand. It looked massive as I approached. The slope was gentle to start with, then it got steep – very steep. It felt like I was taking one step forward and sliding back about two. The guy in front of me was slowing, puffing like a train. I managed to get past him and struggled to the top, lungs on fire, leg muscles burning. We were in the forest now, tall pine trees surrounding the dirt paths. At least it's relatively flat, I thought, as I tried to relax as I ran. The tracks were full of massive puddles. I couldn't run around or jump them. Only one thing for it; you're gonna get wet! I just kept running. Focusing on the red shirt I was chasing, the tracks seemed to go on forever. At one point I saw what I thought was a bush moving in the woods beside me. It was a soldier – no, two – in full camouflage. I didn't stop to look, I just kept running, running as if my life depended on it. Eventually, about an hour later, we broke out of the now darkening forest into a vast flat area. As I turned left, in the distance in front of me I could see more sand. This time it was as wide as the area we were running alongside, like a massive sand wall, and beyond that there was nothing – barren land as far as I could see. I could just make out the blue and red jerseys of the PTIs in the distance. I reckoned I was in about sixth place. Knackered, I couldn't go any faster. I needn't have worried, though, as there was plenty behind me.

Six of us stood, while some sat down in a steaming group. The steam of sweat rose in the cold air as we struggled to get our breathing back to something like a normal level. We were being joined by others all the time. I felt good; a sense of achievement swept through me. I wasn't as stupid as everyone thought. Looking around as the light faded, I worked out where we were, on one of the many rifle ranges at Pirbright.

'You lot can make your way back to your spiders,' one of the PTIs ordered. 'Form up in three ranks and march back.'

We were getting cold now, the afternoon air chilly as we marched back. Back at my locker, I unfolded one of my newly issued green towels and put it around my muddy, naked body. There was no room for shyness in this place. The showers were all open plan, like the ones you get in sports centre changing rooms. People were returning thick and fast now. Some just collapsed on their beds, some went straight to the showers. Upon returning from the shower, I realised I was starving. The thing about this place, I thought to myself, they keep you so busy you don't have time to dwell on things. You don't have time to be homesick.

After our evening meal, most of us just crashed on our beds, until, that is, our trained soldier appeared.

'See this floor,' he said, pointing at what I thought was immaculate red lino. 'This floor is minging. I'm going to show you how to clean it.'

He walked to our end of the room and opened a locker that sat in the corner. It contained various stuff that I didn't recognise. Brushes, well I knew what they were for, but that thing – what was that? It looked like a big rectangle-shaped iron weight on the end of a broom handle. It was about 12in long and 6in wide, and underneath it had what looked like a stiff-bristled base.

'This, this is a bumper. You'll learn to love this thing by the time you leave here.' He signalled a Scots guy in the opposite bed to me to join him. 'Right, hold the handle about halfway down and swing it from side to side.'

'Side to side, trained soldier, I dini get it.'

'You polish the floor by swinging it from side to side until it's gleaming.'

There were four bumpers in the locker, and they became very familiar bits of kit. We used them every day. Firstly, two of us would wax the floor, one starting at each end, then, when it was dry enough, the bumping would begin. Taking it in turns, we would swing these heavy bloody things from side to side, like the pendulum of a clock, until the floor shone. To get an extraspecial finish, we'd put an old folded blanket underneath them to get that final, mirror-like shine.

Occasionally, we were allowed an hour in the evening to go to the NAFFI. Well, not the NAFFI actually – that was at the other end of the camp. We'd go to 'Sandy's Soldiers Home', an old bungalow-type building that sat at the edge of the spiders. You could get hot drinks and various treats; also, importantly, boot polish and dusters. There was a telephone there as well, handy for phoning home. Every weeknight, between six and seven, was 'shining parade'. Everyone in all the barrack rooms would have to sit astride their beds. Agony for me; my legs weren't that long! You'd have to sit, in silence, and clean your kit. It was mostly bulling your drill boots – 'spit and polish', as it's referred to. All our kit was new. The drill boots – hobnail boots – had no give in them whatsoever, but after a couple of weeks of various techniques shown to us by our trained soldier, and a lot of elbow grease, most were in reasonable order.

While we sat there, bulling away, in total silence, we had to learn our regimental history: when it was formed, what was our motto, things like that. Like a lot of things in life, certain people were good at certain things. We had this constantly drilled into us. We were a squad, a team, and if one failed, we all failed. I remember a Scots Guards piper in our squad named Hambini. He was useless, and when I say useless, I really mean it. We literally dragged him over and around the assault course, pushed and pulled him around march and shoots. His drill was crap as was his kit cleaning, but when he picked up his bagpipes, it was amazing. I don't know whether you've tried playing those things, but I can only liken it to wrestling with an octopus! He must have had lungs like a horse; but he couldn't run! After about two weeks, the homesickness had just about gone. Regular parcels from Pam helped. She was a diamond, regularly sending stamps, cigarettes and letters.

'Are you going to the stables tonight?' a lad from another room asked as we passed in one of the spiders' many corridors.

'Yeah, are you?' I replied, while thinking you shouldn't answer a question with a question!

'I'll meet you outside after shining parade. We can walk up together.'

'Great, no problem. See you later then.'

Thus began a friendship that continues to this day. It was a Thursday evening in early April. Thursday was one of our hobby evenings, so for us going onto the mounted regiment we could go up to the stables for an hour or so. There were between eight and ten horses there. Some belonged to officers, but mostly they were military animals. For me it was the smell, that familiar smell of my childhood.

Junior Trooper Friend – 'Quiff', as he became known – and I were marching/walking up the main road/pathway that separated the old part of the depot, the spiders, and the new part. The road, Adaire Walk, formed a link between the two. The stables were about halfway along. As we walked into the rectangular yard, that familiar smell hit us. The sun was slowly going down in the west as we walked towards the tack room.

'What are you little fuckers doing here?' The voice came from the tack room; it was Sergeant Jon Ray, a Grenadier Guard. He basically ran the stables here at the depot. There were other cavalry instructors there as well – we'll meet them later though. Jon – or 'Sergeant' as we referred to him to his face – was a tall, skinny man in his forties. I say forties, but he was probably younger – he just looked that age. He had one tooth that stood out in the middle of his mouth as he cussed at whatever was happening around him.

'Now you're here, you might as well put the fucking kettle on,' he continued. As we entered the warm room, the smell of leather was intoxicating. Quiff grabbed the kettle and went to the water tap in the yard to fill it. Jon sat himself down on a large black trunk. Crossing his skinny legs, he looked over to me with a considered look on his face and asked: 'Hobbies, is it? How are you getting on down there in the spiders?'

Two questions at once. Better not take the piss, I thought. 'Er, yes, it's hobbies, and yeah, we're doing alright down there. Bit cold sometimes though.'

'Well, when you've had your tea, you can skip out [remove the dung from the loose boxes], then put their night hay nets up.'

'Yep, no problem Sergeant,' I replied as I held the hot mug of tea in my hands.

It was half past eight when we left. Just working with the horses was a tremendous tonic to me. Jon scooted his rickety old army-issue bike along as he tried to mount it, cussing as he went. Quiff and I went off in the opposite direction, back to the spiders.

'Drill tomorrow,' I mentioned as we walked.

'Yeah, that'll be a laugh – not!' Quiff chuckled as we reached the familiar big white doors.

* * *

'If you don't swing that arm to shoulder height, I'll rip it off and hit you with the soggy end.' Sergeant Ward screamed into the face of Warren, a Junior Guardsman in my squad. I was losing the battle not to laugh. I knew if I did, I'd be the next victim.

The sweat that ran down my legs caused my battle dress to itch. Soldiers wore battle dress in the Second World War, and ours was probably made for that time. The trousers – well mine anyway – were so high they were a bit tight around my chest. The blouson jacket was attached to the trousers with a combination of buttons. Khaki brown in colour, the jackets were made from a thick woollen material – very, very itchy! Combine that with a not quite so itchy KF shirt, and I can't tell you how fidgety this combination made you feel. When it got wet – and it often did – it weighed a ton. During the summer, when it was hot, it was unbearable! We had to wear it to classroom lessons and films, and I can't tell you how uncomfortable it felt, sitting there for hours.

We had advanced enough by now to be learning drill using our rifles. We used SLRs (self-loading rifles) in those days. You would have to draw it out from the armoury every time you needed it, whether that be for drill or to go on the ranges, before it was returned – though it had to be thoroughly cleaned and inspected.

There we were, twenty-two of us, Lance Sergeant Ward's squad, standing in three ranks, wearing itchy battle dress and desperately trying not to fidget. My blue and red Household Cavalry forage cap's peak stuck out so far it acted as a sunshade in the mid-morning sun.

'Drill; drill is what the Brigade of Guards is famous for, that and fighting of course,' Sergeant Ward informed us as he strode through our ranks, inspecting us. Every one of us stared straight into the blackness of our peaks as he stood before us, hoping – no, praying – he wouldn't find anything wrong as he looked us up and down. We all knew by now what would happen if any one of us wasn't turned out immaculately. 'Rifting', that's what would happen: marched at quick pace – very quick, I mean – all over the concrete parade square. Worse than that, if somebody was badly turned out, the whole squad would have to 'show' in full re-cleaned drill kit that evening. Of course, there's always the one who can't do it, who doesn't know his left from his right. In our case it was Bambini. As I said earlier, he was a brilliant piper, but as for everything else, he was useless. Sergeant Ward would scream orders directly in his face; we could see the spit hitting his face in the chilly morning air.

'Call yourself a Scots Guard? Hold that rifle above your head and run around the edge of the parade square until I tell you to stop,' he screamed. His face was red with rage as he turned, ready to continue with the remainder of us. Bambini must have run around that square dozens of times during our time in the spiders, but eventually, with everyone's help, he got it.

Talking about Bambini, one evening while we were cleaning our barrack room ahead of a big inspection the following morning, one of the lads thought it would be a good idea to play a trick on him. Our metal lockers had a polished metal mirror set in one of its doors. Being metal, they weren't that good. They weren't perfectly flat, so they gave a distorted view. Our trained soldier was at the NAFFI, so there wasn't anyone in charge.

'Hey Bambini, come over here. I'll show you what you'll look like when you're dead,' one joker said.

We all gathered around his locker as he sat Bambini in front of the mirror. Then he balanced a candle on two bedside tables that were placed on top of each other behind him. Picture the scene: Bambini sat on a chair, pillows propped him up to the height that would place his face in the metal mirror, and a candle flickered directly behind his head.

'Someone switch the lights off,' the lad shouted.

The room went into darkness; all you could see was Bambini's face glowing in the mirror's reflection. I must say it did look creepy. Dark lines etched across his face as the light moved, and coupled with the distorted mirror it did appear that he was in his coffin! After a few seconds of silence, Bambini jumped to his feet and, seeming to be possessed, ran towards a few of us with a pure look of rage in his eyes. A couple of lads managed to bring him down to the floor, where legs and arms flailed with power we'd never seen from him before. A pool of saliva was forming on our highly polished floor. Another lad got a small metal shovel from the cleaning locker and hit him on the back of the head. I, by now, had climbed up onto one of the metal beams that ran along the roof – at least I was out of the danger zone. At one point, six guys were on top of him, such was his rage. Others, like me, were trying to find safe places to hide. It took about an hour for everything to calm down, exhaustion taking over as Bambini finally ceased his rage. He was placed on his bed and left to sleep it off. It's amazing how things like that can affect people.

Such was the discipline, we would often sleep on the floor next to our bed-blocked beds to save time on the morning of a big inspection. Everything had to be perfect. For instance, the razor had to be laid out in bits, in order of assembly, on one of your army towels that was neatly folded in your locker. Accompanying the razor would be your toothbrush and soap. Hygiene was high on the army's list of priorities. At least once a week you would have to 'stand by your bed' in your sleeping gear and show your hands and feet to the orderly officer, who would inspect them for cleanliness etc.

Time flew. I couldn't believe it, but we'd been there for five weeks now, and the following weekend would be half-term. When you joined the junior army, back in the Seventies anyway, you were allowed, if you didn't think it was for you, to leave without penalty in the first week. A few of my platoon chose that option. I couldn't: I was there for nine years! The feeling of homesickness had gone now; we were kept so busy we barely had time to think about it anyway.

The following Saturday we would have our first leave – Saturday until Tuesday. Not a lot, I know, some of the Scots and Irish lads would stay as the journey home would take so long, they'd only have time for a cup of tea before they'd have to start the journey back. The Saturday came all too slowly. Those going home were lined up outside the spiders, proudly wearing their brand new, tailored two-dress khaki uniform. As we marched to our designated three-and-a-half-tonners, army-issue suitcase in hand, the atmosphere was one of excitement. With me, it was the prospect of seeing Pam for the first time in six weeks. I was reunited with the guys I'd shared our first truck journey with back in January. We were all in different squads, so rarely saw each other around camp. Steve Hooper and I were both travelling to Bristol Temple Meads, so we went together. It turned out he didn't live far from me. Standing on Reading station, we were obviously attracting the occasional inquisitive look. Two young soldiers – boys really – on their way home.

'What are you doing tonight?' Steve suddenly asked.

'Dunno yet, depends on what my girlfriend wants to do. How about you?'

'Same really. I'll probably go round her parents' place.'

The train was suddenly flooded with sunlight again as it exited the long tunnel and began slowing down. As we passed through the deep cutting, the area opened up around us to reveal a multitude of tracks all criss-crossing each other. The carriage rolled and creaked as it crossed the tracks. Looking at my watch, it was nearly eleven o'clock. After negotiating the endless stairs and tunnels of the 1840s station, we eventually exited the large wooden doors that fronted the building. I was a little puzzled that I hadn't seen my dad yet. Steve's parents were waiting for him in the ticket area, but as for me – nothing! Putting down my suitcase, I looked down the slight hill that rose from the main road, which formed an elongated 'U' with car parking in the middle.

'Simon', I suddenly heard a voice say. Looking around to see where the voice had come from, I noticed Dave, a mechanic who rented part of one of the barns at Baugh Farm from dad, from where he ran his small business.

'Your dad's busy so he asked me to pick you up.'

'Okay, thanks.' Too busy to collect his youngest son from the station on his first leave! To say I was disappointed was an understatement. The journey to Baugh Farm was a quiet one. As I climbed the stone stairs that led to the back door, nothing was as I'd imagined. I'd pictured in my mind a grand welcoming party, but there was nothing. As I walked into the kitchen, my mum was the only one there to greet me. This seemed all very strange. I didn't know just what I'd expected, but it wasn't this. I was starving, so a sandwich and a cup of coffee went down well. My brother, Mark, turned up from work not long after I'd finished. I shouldn't have eaten while wearing my army kit, but I wanted to keep it on until Pam came down. We had arranged on our last call that she would come at one o'clock. Eventually, about forty-five minutes after I'd arrived home, my father walked in. I stood up as he came through the door, and a slight look of pride crossed his face.

'How are you?' he asked as he stood in front of me, checking me over.

'Fine thanks,' I nearly said 'sir', such was the discipline where I'd just come from, but at that time I didn't think he deserved it!

'Sorry I couldn't meet you from the station, but I was called into work.'

'I'll take my case upstairs,' I said as I made my way to the hidden staircase in the corner of the kitchen.

As I reached the top of the old wooden staircase, I suddenly felt quite alone. You're never alone in the spiders; there's always someone somewhere. Even sitting on the toilet you could strike up a conversation with the guy next door! In fact if it did go quiet, you'd worry there might be a few of them outside your cubicle preparing to throw a bucket of water over you. It happens – frequently. You've just got to be ready for it, see the funny side, fit in without allowing yourself to be bullied.

I was sitting on my bed in my bedroom; a funny-shaped room that had a feeling it had been sort of thrown together many years before. Originally it must have been one big room, but someone had divided it into the bedroom with a bathroom opposite. I stood at the half-window it shared with the bathroom next door. Lighting a cigarette, I could see traffic on the newly built M4 just beyond the bottom of our garden. This is not how I imagined my homecoming was going to be, I thought, as I blew smoke out of the slightly opened window. I knew I shouldn't smoke in here, but I wasn't in the mood to worry about it right now.

I could hear the dog playing up downstairs. It must be Pam, I thought, as I flicked the remainder of my cigarette out of the window while making a mental note to pick it up later before anyone noticed. I buttoned up my uniform and checked myself in the mirror before descending the steep staircase. I should explain, the secret staircase at Baugh Farm was built into a massive thick wall. If you were in the kitchen, all you would see was a big oak panelled door with an old latch on it. Open the door and you would find a steep oak spiral staircase. There were two staircases, one to the first landing and the second, right above it, continuing to the third, attic, floor. I was unreasonably nervous as I lifted the latch and pushed the door open. I couldn't see Pam at first – she was still by the kitchen door, out of my sight line. Dad was sat in his usual place at the head of the table; Mark sat eating a sandwich to his right. Shit, this is embarrassing, I thought, as I took the last steps down into the kitchen. I could see Pam now, the first time I'd seen her in six weeks, and we had three pairs of eyes watching every move. No one officially knew we were a couple. It was meant to be a secret.

'Hi, you alright?' was all I could think of saying.

'I'm fine. You look very smart,' she replied, looking equally uncomfortable.

'Are you on the way to see Shane [her pony]?'

'In a minute. Do you want to come? I've got dad's car.'

'Yeah, that would be great. Give me a minute, I'll go and change.'

Before I went back upstairs, Pam gave me a pullover she'd knitted for me. That was embarrassing as well, but it was nice and I was grateful. I quickly changed into civvies, which felt strange as it was the first time I'd worn them in six weeks. I didn't really give much thought to what my parents might think. We hadn't talked at all really since I got home. Oh well, I'll make it up later, I thought as I made my way back to the kitchen. Truth is, I couldn't wait to get out of there.

Climbing into Pam's dad's Mini Traveller, I was aware that we were probably still being watched. All I wanted to do was to give her a hug and a kiss, but somehow I held back, for a little while anyway! After spending a couple of hours at the yard at Griffin Farm, Pam dropped me off at the top of our lane. I walked the hundred or so metres towards the farm. We'd arranged that she would come back later and we'd go to the local pub. I wasn't old enough to drink alcohol – and certainly didn't look it – but Pam was, so she'd go in and get the drinks and we would sit in the car and drink them in there. We spent a lot of time in that car. It was great. When we got back to the farm, mum had gone to bed and dad was dozing in his chair, the remainder of his glass of whisky in front of him.

'Ah,' he said, his eyes half open, 'been to the pub, have you?'

'Yes, well not in the pub, just sat in the car for a while.'

'Do you both want a drink? Help yourselves, it's in the cupboard.'

After getting us a drink, I sat at the opposite end of the table, with Pam sitting to my left. Luckily, both mum and dad liked Pam – why wouldn't they? Pam had told me once how frightened she and the other girls were of my dad when they had to go and pay their rent to him when we lived at Griffin Farm. He wasn't that bad really, but he did have this innate ability to make you feel, well, shall we say uneasy? I'd recounted my time so far at the Guards Depot with them over supper earlier, so the conversation tonight was more general. I asked how my elder brother, Tony, was doing. He was a captain in the 2nd Royal Tank Regiment; a tough act to follow! He had joined as a junior soldier a few years before me. He was a Life Guard as well until he had the opportunity to get a commission and become an officer.

'Look at the time, it's one o'clock,' Pam suddenly said. 'Time I was off.'

'Okay, I'll walk you to your car.'

When I returned to the kitchen, dad was making his way up the staircase to bed. As I sat back down, I remembered that I'd been up since five-thirty that morning. It had been a long day, and – in the end – a good one. It felt strange being back in my old bed. The room was quiet, with no snoring etc. going on around me, no distant cracks of gunfire on the ranges.

The weekend went all too fast, and before I knew it, it was Tuesday and I was back at Temple Meads Station waiting for the train. I felt like I had the first time, six weeks ago, except this time I knew what was coming. Consoling myself with the thought of my next leave and of moving on to our platoons in the new part of the depot, my musings were suddenly interrupted.

'Alright, Wol!' a cheerful voice rang out. It was Steve. 'Did you have a good weekend?'

'Yeah – you?'

'Yes, great. Is that our train?'

Looking down the track, I could see the dirty yellow front of a train slowly coming around the slight bend towards the long platform. The rectangular black and white sign on the front said 'London Paddington'. London, I thought, that's where we will be stationed if we get through all this. I'd only been there once before. Mum and dad had taken Mark and I on a day trip when we were young. The Trooping of the Colour, ironically. We stood on The Mall. Pushed to the front by my father, we watched the parade go past.

The mood was solemn as I walked into our barrack room. Most of the guys were back, busying themselves sorting kit out etc.

'Are you going for scoff?' Quiff shouted as he stood in the open doorway.

'Yeah, why not. Did you have a good weekend?'

'Yeah, great. You?'

I recounted the last couple of days as we walked/marched to the cookhouse. It was late February, and our next leave was mid-April. If we got through the next six weeks, we would be moving to our allocated platoons, which were at the other end of the camp, the newer end. Nothing had changed as we made our way along the queue, tray in hand, our knife, fork, spoon and mug that we carried with us now placed on the tray. White-coated chefs lined the other side of the long hotplate, each brandishing some sort of 'weapon', mostly ladles. They were the Army Catering Corps, or 'slop jockeys' as they were affectionately known in the military.

'We've got a march and shoot tomorrow,' I casually mentioned to Quiff as we finished off our – still oversweet – mugs of tea.

'I think we all have. Dreading it.'

'It will be alright. Don't worry about it.'

Back at the spiders, most people were back now. The atmosphere was quiet and subdued. As I stood in front of my locker, neatly arranging the new toiletries that Pam had bought for me, my thoughts went back to her. It had been great to be with her, even if it wasn't for that long.

'Coming down the NAFFI?' Bryce, the guy in the next bed, asked.

'Might as well. No hobbies or anything tonight is there?'

As I mentioned earlier, they kept us busy here, especially in the recruit squad. The junior army in those days must have been well funded. Two or three evenings a week we had hobbies. You could do whatever was on the list, and the list was long. Quiff and I went down to the stables every Wednesday. On Thursdays, for some strange reason, we chose marquetry. We spent hours cutting thin slithers of wood into shapes, as directed by the kit we were provided with. On Tuesdays we could go up to the gym. Someone asked if we could get a trampoline, then the next week there were two brand-new ones installed and ready.

Six o'clock came around too quickly, and sadness filled my body as I lay curled up in a ball under the blankets. It's amazing how quickly you forget the shock of the early-morning call when you've been at home for a few days in your own bed. Sitting on the edge of my newly bed-blocked bed, I pulled on my DMS boots. They felt strange, stiff; the soles felt like they had no give in them. Looking around me, I could see the other guys doing the same. 'Don't worry,' our trained soldier shouted, 'they're always like that after leave.'

I think we all felt the same as we were marched to the cookhouse for breakfast. Assembled in ranks of three, we had our combat kit on, mug and cutlery held in our left hands behind our backs. After breakfast, back at the spiders, Sergeant Ward was waiting for us.

'Right, you lot,' he started, 'just as a special treat, we're going on a march and shoot. First we'll go to the armoury and draw out your weapons, then a 10-mile march followed by the assault course, and finally we'll finish on the ranges. Understood?.'

'Yes, Sergeant!'

'I can't hear you: do you understand?' he roared.

'Yes, Sergeant!' we all screamed back.

It was a cold mid-February morning as we queued outside the armoury, waiting for our turn to enter the bunker-type building to collect our SLRs. Our combat kit, complete with heavy webbing, made it difficult to walk, let alone run. As you enter the large block-built building, you're confronted with a counter set in a weldmesh cage, and the armourer is behind the cage.

'Name!' he shouted, without looking up from his clipboard that sat on the counter.

'Wallington, Sergeant,' I dutifully replied as I tried to shift a bit of camo-cloth from my 'tin pot' helmet that was obscuring my view.

Handing me the rifle, I knew exactly what to do. Turning away from both Sergeant Ward and the armourer, I drew back the weapon's cocking mechanism to make sure the rifle wasn't loaded. After Sergeant Ward had also checked, I was dismissed outside to join the rest.

Before too long, Sergeant Ward joined us, carrying the GPMG (general purpose machine gun) for one of us to carry. We would all take turns with it as we ran – it weighed10.9 kilos-plus. We also carried two brown metal ammunition cases, which again were shared amongst us. Two PTIs had joined us now; one at the front to set the pace and one at the back to 'encourage' the stragglers.

After the command 'double march!', we were off. I think we all had the same thought as we jogged along in ranks of three – 'not the sand hill, please, not the sand hill'. Of course, our prayers weren't answered and before we knew it, we were approaching the base of the hill. The funny thing is, it doesn't look too bad from the bottom; it looked steep, but not too high. Despite the PTIs' protests, the neat group soon broke up into a struggling melee, with some crawling and some stopping for breath. Myself and a few others managed to make it to the top without stopping. Standing at the top, sweat literally dropping off the end of my nose, my lungs were on fire. Bambini, unsurprisingly, was at the back, Sergeant Ward and a PTI screaming in each ear as he struggled to the top.

At the top, we were again formed into three ranks. I was at the front now; on my right was a large lad from Northumbria, a 'sheep shagger' who called everyone 'mara'. His friendly smiley face was red now. It was my turn to take the gimpy (GPMG), so he carried my rifle while I did my stint. The ground at the summit of the sand hill was relatively flat. Unlike the cross-country run we had when we first got here, we were running as a squad now, so there was no way of avoiding the puddles – we had to run straight through them. It was a joint effort. We all had to finish. Behind me, I could hear the PTI shouting/encouraging the ones at the back to keep up. The gimpy was getting heavier with every stride I took, and my tin pot helmet felt as though it would fall off my head at any moment. Heavy breathing and red faces surrounded me as Sergeant Ward ordered us to change gimpy duty. I handed it back to the guy behind me and tried to shake my hand and arm back into action before taking my rifle back from my 'mara'. All our feet were wet now, and our sweat-sodden combat kit weighed a ton! It was a brief relief when one of the PTIs ordered us to mark time, 'run on the spot', while we waited for everyone to catch up and get the squad looking something of a collective again. Forty minutes later, we were descending the plateau towards the dreaded assault course. I say 'dreaded'; it wasn't for me, I quite enjoyed it. It was challenging, I admit, but it didn't pose any problems for me. I was physically fit. I'd spent my youth running around playing in the barn at the stables opposite my home, climbing on the hay and jumping from beam to beam.

A cloud of steam slowly rose into the tall pine trees that surrounded us as we waited for the stragglers to arrive. Some wanted to collapse in a heap on the ground, but we all knew that would only end up with more abuse from the PTIs. Then the last one finally stumbled into the back of the group.

'Ok!' the PTI barked. 'In threes, I want you to complete the assault course, and when you're finished, wait at the other end for the rest of the squad. Understood?'

'Yes, Sergeant,' we all blurted between desperate attempts to regain our breath before the next challenge.

We set off in threes, as ordered, probably about thirty seconds apart. The first obstacle to confront us was a red brick wall. It was about 8ft tall; I was 5ft 7in. Mara was first up – he was over 6ft, so he made it look easy. Straddling the top of the wall like he was sat on a horse, he waited to help. As I leapt and tried to grip the top of the slippery wall, I felt his massive hand grab the back of my webbing. I think we were both too enthusiastic because, before I knew it, I'd been thrown over the top and was heading towards the pine needle-covered ground below. As I groaned at the shock of it, I glanced back at mara, still astride the wall above me, a big red-faced grin spread across his face as he nodded towards the next obstacle. Struggling to my feet and rubbing my hip where I'd landed, I looked towards the next obstacle. It was the monkey bars This is easy, I thought, as I made my way towards it. The monkey bars consisted of what only can be described as three long metal ladders suspended above a large rectangular concrete box full of dirty brown water. The idea was to jump up onto the first rung and then, one by one, swing like a monkey from bar to bar without falling into the water below. Because I was light and quite agile, this didn't hold any fears for me. As I swung from bar to bar, I could hear the PTIs screaming orders as splashes from people falling in hit my face. The technique, I had discovered from previous runs on the assault course, was to keep moving. Don't stop; if you do, it's an early bath! It's easy to lose focus on what's going on around you when going around the obstacles. You've got to remember it's a team effort; everyone's got a part to play. Sometimes, it's an opportunity to catch your breath. My turn came at the top of the scramble net, a large net slung over a bar about 20ft up, near the tree canopy. Now I was sat astride the top of the net, encouraging and holding others as they swung themselves over the top. Groans of effort mixed with the smell of wet camo gear as rifles tried to free themselves from their owners whilst they took the plunge over the top for the descent down the other side. Somehow, with much screaming of encouragement, we all got round. Now it was just a short run onto the ranges.

'Right!' Sergeant Ward shouted. 'From the prone position [lying down], five rounds into the targets in front of you.'

As I lay there on the cold damp ground, legs spread apart, my elbows were positioned so you could twist your wrist to grip the rifle and hold it steady. Targets a hundred metres ahead of us looked like they were running towards us in attack mode. Don't breathe, I told myself. Every time you breathe in and out, the tip of your rifle moves up and down. Still breathing heavily from earlier efforts, I desperately tried to calm my breaths and focus on the target. Shots rang out around me as I tried to focus; the 'crack' sounds filled my head as sweat trickled down my forehead towards my right eye. Five shots done, I laid with my rifle on the sandy ground while waiting for the next order. In the distance, I could see the targets disappearing downwards into 'the butts', where they would be pasted up and put back on the range. The butts were a concrete-lined area underneath the range where the targets were lowered on a metal and rope frame contraption which the targets were attached to, with small, inch-square pieces of paper then pasted onto the bullet holes to repair them after the grouping of your efforts were recorded.

'OK lads,' Sergeant Ward continued, 'get yourselves into the kneeling position.'

Feeling a bit stiff now from the earlier run and assault course, I struggled to my knees. 'Don't stand up, you're under fire. Keep your weapons pointing down the range,' I heard one of the NCOs (non-commissioned officers) shout as I settled into the kneeling position. The cracking of bullets whistling down the range started again as we all deposited our rounds; the hot brass bullet cases were collecting around my right knee now as I waited for the next order.

'Standing position!' The next order rang out as the targets again began to disappear on the horizon.

Suddenly all hell was let loose. Looking to my right, I could see Bambini was holding his arm up to indicate he had a blockage in his weapon. Trouble was, he had instinctively turned to face the assembled instructors with the weapon still loaded and now pointing at them! Some ran towards him, while others tried to take cover wherever they could. One even dived into a makeshift trench for protection. The first instructor to get to him grabbed the rifle while at the same time driving his shoulder into him, knocking him to the floor.

The instructor who had dived for cover in the trench slowly appeared to check the coast was clear. To say Bambini got a bollocking would be an understatement. I can remember that his very existence on this earth was questioned, as well as his right to be here or even be in the Guards.

It must have been ten minutes before order and calm were restored. One of the instructors was frantically turning the small handle on the field telephone, which was his communication with the butts, as the targets slowly reappeared. Five rounds later, and after clearing my rifle ready for inspection, I made my way to the side of the range, where a steaming hot tea urn was waiting. Pulling my black plastic mug from its pouch in my webbing, I tried to blow the muck out of it before filling it with a much-deserved drink. I noticed Quiff making his way up from the butts as I took my first sip.

'You haven't had your march and shoot, have you?' I asked.

'No, tomorrow. What was it like?'

'Pretty tough, but you'll be alright,' I reassured him.

'You'll be in the butts then,' he replied with a grin as we lit a cigarette. As I took a drag, I coughed and sputtered. My lungs must have been thoroughly cleaned out by the run.

Back at the spiders, after sitting out on the grassed area cleaning my weapon and returning it to the armoury, I took a well-deserved shower before making my way to the cookhouse for some scoff. It was getting to the end of February and the nights were beginning to draw out. It would be April soon, meaning Easter leave, and I allowed myself that little bit of excitement as I made my way past the 'Kinema' – I thought surely they meant Cinema, but I found out many years later that it's the British spelling of cinema!

* * *

The remainder of our first term at the Junior Guardsman's Wing went by quickly. There were many hours cleaning; cleaning everything, it seemed – boots, rooms, weapons, roads and washrooms, to name but a few. It was the second week in April when we were lined up outside our spider to find out what platoon we would be moving to after Easter leave. There was an air of anticipation as we waited for Sergeant Ward to call our names.

'Wallington,' Sergeant Ward eventually called out.

'Yes, Sergeant,' I replied as I sprung to attention.

'Inkerman Platoon,' he said, without looking up from his clipboard.

I'd already heard that Quiff was going to Inkerman. He was lined up in the next squad up from ours. That's good, I thought, as I returned to the 'at ease' position.

One more challenge faced us before Easter leave: outward bound. We were off to North Wales, to Towyn in fact. About fifty of us travelled on the train to a small camp at the base of the mountains of North Wales. Some went on coaches, others in army vehicles. I just remember seeing the half-moon-shaped huts all neatly lined up on large areas of neatly mown grass. Every hut had bunk beds lined up on either side. The mattresses weighed a ton; I don't know what they were filled with, but they were hard, light blue and white, with two rows of buttons stitched through them at regular intervals. In the middle of the hut stood a large potbelly stove with a metal chimney that disappeared through the corrugated roof above it. I quickly bagged a top bunk near the fire by throwing my heavy kit bag on it. The camp sat in the base of a valley, with a big white-water river running alongside it. It was half past four when the door banged open. Sergeant Ward stood there in his denim green trousers and tracksuit top.

'Right, my lovely lot!' he shouted out in his familiar Scottish accent. 'Scoff is ready at the cookhouse,' he announced, pointing towards another corrugated-clad building at the far end of the camp. 'When you've had that, I want you in PT kit for six o'clock. We're going swimming tonight.'

'Swimming?' I said to Quiff as we walked towards the cookhouse. 'Don't fancy that. Bit bloody cold, if you ask me.'

'They're not asking you, are they?' he retorted as he pulled open the big wooden door that led into the small dining room.

Later, I was sitting on my bunk bed, wearing overlarge dark blue shorts with a regulation red tee-shirt tucked into the waistband, all finished off with the white drawstring tied in a neat bow. Everything was too big, I was thinking, as I contemplated my over white-legs. They were not that thin, but with the baggy shorts they looked like a couple of pipe cleaners sticking out of them! At six o'clock precisely, I spotted our squad sergeant making his way towards our hut.

'Wardsy's coming,' someone called out as he approached.

I almost fell into attention as I slid off my bunkbed onto the wooden floor below. The door swung open, revealing his tall figure standing there. Behind him, I could see the light was fading, grey clouds covering the mountain tops.

'Fall in outside, and make sure you've got your towels with you!' he commanded, without coming in.

Outside, we did as ordered: three ranks, rolled towels under our right arms, with said arm held behind our backs. We had done a lot of drill by now, so marching came a lot easier. The Brigade of Guards are famous for their pace and swagger – they call it 'bolo'; a slight round curve of your swinging arm as it reaches shoulder height is one of the things to look for. In no time we arrived at a large building, again corrugated, which turned out to be the gymnasium and swimming pool. Canoes lined the side of the pool, alongside orange lifejackets. Several PTIs were waiting for us, with two bobbing about in the blue water of the pool.

'Listen in, listen in!' the PTI on the poolside shouted. 'When I give you the command, I want you to get yourself a lifejacket and put it on, then get yourself a canoe and put it in the water. Do you understand?'

'Yes, Corporal,' we all shouted as we hurriedly made our way to the lifejackets. Shit, it's wet, was my first thought as I tried to work out how it tied up. Then I got it: wrap the tape around your waist twice. Now for the canoe. I was talking it through in my head as I progressed towards the water's edge. I've never been the best swimmer – I'm not that fond of water, truth be known – but I liked the idea of this. It's a swimming pool, it's got be safe, I kept telling myself. The canoe was lighter than it looked. Inside the hole I guessed you sat in was an orange nylon thing.

'Put that on!' one of the instructors in the pool shouted as I studied it. By now, the other one had exited the water and grabbed all the kit required to demonstrate our fate. It looked quite easy. He pulled on what we soon discovered to be a 'spray skirt', then sat beside his canoe on the side of the pool, and with quite a bit of bum shuffling he slid into his vessel. Spray skirt safely fitted around the hole he was sat in, he then glanced around for his paddle. The instructor had made a mistake – surely he couldn't have – he had left his paddle further up the pool and couldn't reach it. A few giggles went round as he paddled, with his hands, along the side of pool to retrieve it.

'Okay, get into your canoes!' the one in the water shouted.

After a bit of a struggle – the spray skirt kept getting caught up in my baggy shorts – I was in, grabbing my paddle, which I'd made sure was handy. Then I was off. It was a bit wobbly at first, but I soon got the hang of it. Any thoughts of staying dry had gone now, as every time I took a stroke with the paddle, water ran down the bit that was in the air and straight down my arm. Some of the guys were already tipping over, and the instructors in the water were pulling them out of their confinement so that they popped up to the surface like a cork.

Eventually we were all upright in a row, awaiting our instructor's demonstration.

'Right, pay attention!' he barked. 'I'm going to demonstrate how to exit your canoe should it turn over. Firstly, don't panic.' Easy for you to say, I thought. 'When you're under the water, I want you to feel for the bottom of your canoe, which is above the water now, then, without panicking, slap the bottom of it three times. When you've done that, imagine performing a forward roll and you will be out and safe.' Sounds easy, I thought. 'Right, who wants to go first?'

Stuff it, I thought, as I held up my paddle to volunteer.

'Okay, Wallington, paddle out to a clear area. When I give the order, drop your paddle, lean forward and roll. Remember, tap the bottom on your canoe three times, then roll forward and come back to the surface to join us.'

Sod it I, thought – shit or bust. I took a deep breath and rolled. Shit, it's cold, was my initial reaction as my lifejacket tried to strangle me as it tried to escape over my head. I could see bubbles heading towards the light above me. Shock shot through my body as I tried to remember what to do. Hit it; hit it three times, I remembered. Bang bang bang, I thought I heard, as I leaned forward and shot towards the surface like a cork out of a bottle. As I surfaced, trying to catch my breath, through chlorine-soaked eyes I could just make out my fellow canoeists trying their best not to laugh.

'Well done,' I heard the instructor say. 'Now get your canoe and paddle, and swim to the side and get back in it.'

One by one, we learnt the art of getting out of one of these things; useful training for future adventures in the 'white water'. Our hut was freezing as we clambered back in, still soaking wet from our training session.

'As soon as you're changed, get up to the cookhouse before it closes for your supper, then I suggest you get your heads down. You've got a long day tomorrow,' Sergeant Ward said as he closed the door on us. Returning from supper, we managed to light the giant potbelly stove and warm the place up a bit to dry our sodden PT kit. The smell of damp clothes drying filled my nostrils as I desperately tried to get comfortable in my sleeping bag on what felt like a straw-filled mattress.

'Wakey wakey!' was the cry that woke me from my better-than-expected sleep. As I struggled to focus, I finally made out the figure who stood in the open doorway; it was one of our instructors, PTI Corporal Jones.

'You've got ten minutes to get you PT kit on and fall in outside. Don't worry about ablutions, you can do that when we get back.'

My still-damp kit hung on my shivering body as I lined up with the others outside. It was six-thirty, barely light. Looking around, I couldn't make out the hills that were in front of us. What a state, I thought, as I looked at the bedhead hair of the guy to my front. I desperately wanted to run my hand over what hair I had, but I knew if I moved, I'd get a bollocking.

'In three ranks, left turn!' was the command that rang out. 'By the left, double march.'

We were off. We didn't know where, but we were heading for the large gates that we had come through yesterday. Turning left, following the corporal, we headed down a slight hill. The horizon seemed to end in front of us, mist appearing to hang like the sheet I held over my head when I didn't want to wake up in the mornings. As we approached a sharp right-hand bend in the single-track road, we carried straight on, leaving the tarmac behind. The pebbles felt weird under my plimsole daps as we continued running. When we were ordered to halt, I could hear a crashing sound which I could just make out now as the sea. 'I hope we haven't got to go in there,' I whispered to Quiff, who was stood beside me. No sooner had I finished my covert observation, than the instructor bellowed as he paced up and down in front of us. The sound of the pebbles rolling under his boot, coupled with the waves crashing in, made him – even when shouting – difficult to be heard. For a moment, I thought he said, 'Remove your shirts and plimsoles – you're going for a swim.' Turning towards Quiff, he wasn't there. I suddenly realised I had heard the command correctly because he was crouched down, undoing the laces of his daps. I've never been a, shall we say, good swimmer. We had to pass a swimming test back at the depot; I sort of winged it and just scraped through. This, though, was a whole different ballgame. For a start, it looked freezing. Indeed, it was freezing, and even after our run I was still shivering as I stood in great trepidation by the crashing waves.

'In you go,' the instructor ordered. 'I want you to swim out until I tell you to come back. If you reach land, it will be Ireland and you'll have gone too far!'

His attempt at humour didn't impress me as I tiptoed into the freezing water. I could see a wave rolling in towards me. Bracing myself for the inevitable shock, it felt like every drop of air in my body came out as I screamed like a girl and jumped up and down on the spot while trying to avoid it. Others around me, including Quiff, were just going for it and diving in. I didn't want to, but knew I had to, so I took a big breath and dived in. The salty taste of the seawater assaulted my senses as I came to the surface. My thick cotton blue shorts felt heavy as I started to attempt to swim. I managed to get my stroke going, a combination of front crawl and doggy paddle. 'How far do we have to go?' I kept thinking. 'And how far is Ireland anyway?' Thankfully, it wasn't too long before the guys at the front began to turn and head back towards the shore.

'I fucking hate swimming,' I grumbled at Quiff as I desperately tried to pull my gym vest over my wet and shivering body. Water ran down my legs as, like my shirt, I tried to pull my daps on. Still wet, I was about to get wet again, but at least the showers were warm, and the water diluted the salty taste as it ran down my face. I was starving – I couldn't wait to get some scoff – and I wondered what the rest of the day would hold. My brain was bouncing from one thing to another as I stood under the comfort of the warm shower.

'Come on then,' Quiff shouted from the entrance to the toilet block.

The queue for breakfast was a long one. I noticed Sergeant Ward sat at one of the wooden trestle tables with some other NCOs – they hadn't had to go swimming. I wondered what torture they were concocting over there. Sitting on one of the long benches that accompanied the tables, I contemplated the food in front of me. Should I eat the bacon, sausage and egg first and let the porridge cool down, or should I tackle the porridge? Egg first, I decided; the porridge was so thick I was able to leave my spoon standing to attention in it. To be honest, I think we all would have eaten anything that was offered, such was our calorie burn.

'Watch out, Wardsy's coming over,' I informed Quiff, who was sat opposite me.

'Everyone happy?' the sergeant asked as he reached the head of the table.

'Yes, Sergeant,' everyone replied through mouthfuls of scoff.

'Good. You've got half an hour before you have to be outside your hut dressed in denims and tee-shirts.'

'What are we doing?' one of the guys dared to ask.

'Now, if I told you that it wouldn't be a surprise, would it? One thing I can tell you, though, is that you're going to get wet again.'

Great, I thought, as I scraped the last bit of porridge from the bowl with my rather inadequate spoon. Back at our hut, I changed out of my heavy-duty jumper and pulled my denim jacket from my kitbag. Denims, as they were called, weren't actually denim – like your jeans, I mean. They were green cotton combat trousers with something like a workman's work jacket; a chore jacket if you like. I pulled my gym shirt on from that morning; it was a little bit damp, but I had a feeling that nothing was going to stay dry or clean for long around here this week. Before too long, with denim jacket buttoned up to my neck, I grabbed the rope to haul myself into the back of the canvas-covered three-tonner ready for our magical mystery tour!

Sitting on the slatted wooden benches as the vehicle wound its way up and down the Welsh hills and mountains, I could barely feel my arse as it had gone so numb. I noticed Quiff's puttee was coming undone. I couldn't tell him as it was too noisy, so I stretched my leg out as far as I could and tapped his knee with my boot. He jumped with shock as his thoughts returned to the here and now. 'What?' he mouthed. I pointed down at the now fast-unravelling puttee. After mouthing a 'thanks', he bent forward to fix it. Unfortunately, just as he started to do so, the vehicle pulled off the tarmacked road onto a rough gravel track somewhere up in the range of hills and mountains. The next thing I saw was him flying towards me. 'Shit!' I thought as he hurtled in my direction, and I ducked to the left just as he crashed into the canvas behind me.

'You alright, mate?' I asked as he picked himself up off the bench.

'Yeah, I'm alright. Thanks for moving – not!' he grumbled as he struggled to get to his feet in the now 'rock and rolling' truck. Much laughter followed his journey back to his seat.

After what seemed like ages – you can only see where you've been, not where you're going, in the back of these trucks – we stopped on a large grassy area at what appeared to be the base of a mountain. 'I hope we're not going up that,' I thought as I jumped from the vehicle. When we were all out and lined up, our instructor did what I hoped he wouldn't do and peered up towards the slate-coloured peaks above us.

'Don't worry,' he announced with a sarcastic grin on his face, 'you're going under it. You're going into that cave over there, into the darkness and beyond.'

Whispered mumbling surrounded me as I looked towards the small black hole at the base of the mountain. I could see Sergeant Ward sat on a large lump of rock with a pile of battered helmets at his feet.

'Okay, fall out and go and get yourself a helmet and wait at the cave entrance.'

I was strangely excited as I jogged across the grass towards the cave. I'd never done anything like this before, and I knew they were looking for possible candidates for an up-and-coming cadre course to be made junior NCOs. I wanted to be on it, so I'd decided to try extra hard and – importantly – volunteer for everything.

As I held the battered fibreglass helmet in my hands, I couldn't quite work out how, what appeared to be a lamp, worked. Still pondering, I heard our instructor tell us to gather round. 'Okay,' he started, 'this is a carbide lamp. It will light your way in the darkness you're about to be immersed in. It's powered by calcium carbide and water. Now, I wasn't that good at school – much like you lot, I expect – but the calcium carbide reacts with water and burns with a clean white flame. Don't ask me how, it just does. I'll light mine and then you can all take it in turns to light yours off each other.'

'Holy shit, it works!' I said to one of our group, Stinchcombe – or Stinch, as we all called him – as the flame on my helmet came to life. It didn't look that bright, outside in the late April sun, but when we entered the dark cave it was surprising how much you could see from its flickering light. The first sensation I felt as I followed the instructor was the cold. The air was still, but the cold seemed to cut through me. The lightweight material of our denims offered little protection as we moved deeper into the darkness. Our DMS boots soon became soaked through as we waded through the first stretch of water. The freezing water was now just below my knees as we went ever deeper into the darkness. I'm not that tall, in fact I was probably the shortest there. It didn't bother me that much, and on this occasion it really worked in my favour. The tunnel we were wading through was getting smaller as we progressed, the sides slimy and wet to the touch. As i took my next step, my foot suddenly went deeper than I thought it would and the freezing water was up to my waist. Catching my breath, I just managed to supress a scream as my balls seemed to disappear up into my body. As I got a grip of my feelings, I noticed the narrow tunnel had opened out into a larger cave, and one of the other instructors was sat there waiting for us.

'Right, lads, take a seat on that rock over there,' our instructor ordered, his creepy-looking face flickering in the light. 'Next we are going deeper into the cave, what we call in the caving fraternity a sump.' I could hear teeth chattering behind me as we sat in the cold darkness. 'Now,' he continued, 'in this sump, you'll find it a bit of a squeeze, but as long as you don't panic you'll be alright. Okay, who's going first?' I immediately volunteered. Best to get it over with, I reasoned, although the other monkey on my shoulder was constantly calling me a twat for volunteering! 'Right, Wallington. I'll go first and wait for you on the other side. Corporal Jones here will send you through. Understood?'

'Understood, Corporal,' I replied, through my now-chattering teeth.

Once again I was in the freezing water, this time laying on my stomach. From the flickering light, all I could see was brown muddy water. I couldn't see where I was supposed to go, but I knew there must be an entrance because the instructor had just disappeared in there. I'd been told to take off my helmet and hold it in front of me as I went through. I was also told the light would go out under the sump and would be relit when – if –

I emerged on the other side. Suddenly, a hand grabbed the back of my sodden trousers and, at the same time, pushed me under and forwards. It's difficult to explain the confusion and fear that fills your brain at such times. Total darkness surrounded me as I panicked, trying to push through what felt like a very small space. Everything seemed to go into slow motion as I struggled towards the tiny light I could just make out in the distance. The next thing I remember is what felt like a massive hand grab the back of my collar and drag me into this large, tomb-like area. My panicked state went wild as I coughed and spluttered to get my breath. Scrambling to my feet, I could feel the muddy water running down my face and into my eyes. I didn't feel cold anymore; I suppose the adrenaline had kicked in.

'Well done,' I heard the instructor say. 'Give me your helmet. I'll relight your lamp.'

More muddy water ran down my face as I replaced the wet helmet and sat in the corner of this small area, waiting for the next victim to emerge. A sense of great satisfaction flowed through my body as, once again, the instructor's hand grabbed the next candidate. It was Stinch this time. His curly black hair was brown now, and a lump of mud stuck to his ear as he too fought to get his breath. One by one, everyone emerged from the darkness and joined me on my temporary perch. The last one through was the other instructor, Corporal Jones.

Looking around, I could see what looked like graffiti on the grey-brown walls that surrounded us. Stinch took off his helmet and moved it closer to the cave wall. As the flame flickered, a black line began to appear, and before we knew it all of us were making our mark on the sump cave wall.

'What the fuck?' Quiff suddenly called out. 'My dick's dropped off!'

'What do you mean, your dick's dropped off?' someone retorted.

'No, you're alright,' I said as I turned away to check mine out. It was true; the cold had shrunken 'the old man' nearly up into our bodies. My nuts were the size of marbles, and about the same consistency as well.

'Listen in,' a voice came from the other side of the cave. It was Corporal Jones. 'We'll move on to the next obstacle now. Another squeeze, I'm afraid, a dry one this time though. In the same order as last time, follow me.'

As I watched Corporal Jones' boots disappear into the about 12in fissure in the cave wall, I didn't have a clue what was ahead of me, except the corporal's boots that is. Helmet off, as instructed, I pushed it ahead of me as I scrambled into the gap. I could hear the instructor's boots ahead of me as I wriggled myself forward. 'People do this for fun,' I thought as I fought my way along. Water dripped from the roof and seemed to funnel down my collar and neck as my jacket dragged along the ceiling. At last I could just make out the end. I could only see forward. Once again, as I neared the end a hand grabbed the epaulette of my jacket to assist me out. The scrabbling and crawling carried on for about another half an hour as we entered a huge cave deep under the Welsh mountains. We still couldn't see much, but you could feel the size of the place by the echoes of our voices. I was wondering where the exit was; maybe there's a hidden door, I stupidly thought, until the corporal announced: 'Okay guys, same way back.'

Even through the darkness, you could sense shoulders dropping in disappointment. I felt drained, defeated; I just wanted to curl up in a ball and try to warm my aching body. That's the point, though, isn't it? They've got to push us to the limit. Having cleared my head, with my energy levels refreshed, I took my place behind our instructor for the trek back.

Funny isn't it, how the journey back always seems quicker than the journey there? It didn't seem that long before – wet, muddy and cold – we walked back towards the clear blue skies of North Wales. A pile of army woollen blankets were waiting for us, along with the familiar brown paper bags (haversack rations) containing our lunch. As we finished our food, an army Land Rover made its way slowly up the track. In the back was a piping-hot urn containing the sweet tea we'd all become accustomed to.

'Wonder what's next,' I casually asked Quiff as we sat by a large lump of rock, drinking our tea.

'Stinch said something about abseiling.'

Abseiling – what's that?'

'It's the controlled descent of a steep slope, such as a rock face, by moving down a rope,' came a voice from the other side of the boulder that we were sat against. Corporal Jones suddenly appeared, as if from nowhere, to let us in on the plan.

'When are we doing that, Corporal?' I tentatively inquired.

'Tomorrow. We'll go back to camp now and get cleaned up. You know, kit washed and dried and you lot washed and dried.'

'Okay, thanks, Corporal.'

'At least the water's hot,' I mentioned to anyone who was listening back at the camp as I poured far too much washing powder into the cast-iron bath that contained my kit. Grabbing the bass broom that I'd borrowed from our hut, I turned it upside down and started to swish and turn the now-dirty brown water. The water was still warm as I reached in to release the tap. Standing there watching the water disappear, my thoughts turned to Pam, wondering what she was doing then. I was sure she wasn't watching a bath full of dirty Welsh water disappear down a plughole!

'Come on, Wol,' I heard a familiar voice shout from the wash house door. It was Stinch, holding a pile of dirty kit. 'Won't be long, mate, just rinsing them now.'

The rest of the afternoon was spent erecting a temporary washing line and replenishing our coal supplies from a bunker on the other side of the camp. The remainder of the day was spent tidying our hut, although it wasn't to the same standards as the spiders – we were, after all, on camp. After scoff, some of us went to the small NAFFI, a wooden shed tucked away behind the cookhouse. A pint of Vimto and a Kit-Kat went down well before I sneaked off to the cream-coloured telephone box to phone Pam at the predetermined time, eight o'clock. As I listened to the ringing, ready with my ten pence piece, I could picture Pam shuffling along the sofa in the front room to answer the phone.

'Hello,' the voice on the other end announced.

'Hi, write this number down please, so when the pips go you can call me back.'

There was a lot to fit into the ten-minute conversation. I knew her parents would be sitting a few feet away, her dad checking his watch and impatiently waiting so he could turn the telly back up! It was always good to chat to Pam. I assured her that if I survived the rock climbing, canoeing and whatever else they threw at us, I would be home on Saturday for a week's leave. With a renewed spring in my step, I made my way back to our Nissen hut to get ready for the next challenge – rock climbing and abseiling. As I wriggled into my sleeping bag, I thought about the horrible possibility of the dreaded early morning swim.

'What the f…' was my first thought as I heard a ringing bell. I turned and looked out of the top of my cozy bed, and could see Sergeant Ward vigorously turning the fire bell that was located on the outside wall of the hut.

'Hands off cocks, on with socks!' was his now familiar morning greeting. 'Have I got a treat for you lot,' he continued. 'A run and a swim to wake you up, ready for another busy day.' I'm not designed to swim, I thought, as I struggled, shivering, out of the Irish Sea. It's not for me. I don't mind being on the water, but I'd made my mind up that I didn't like being in it. The ride in the three-tonner felt familiar now; the drone of the engine, the view out of the back, looking at where we'd been, not where we were going. After some forty minutes, we arrived at the base of yet another mountain. The view was unfamiliar. A smooth grey slab of rock towered above us, and red and blue nylon ropes dangled from behind what looked like a rocky chimney perched on top of the sheer rock face. A few small trees were clinging on for all they were worth to the otherwise smooth surface. I could just make out Corporal Jones poking his head around the corner of the chimney above us. On the ground, we had been joined by a new face, a thin, muscular man wearing an army Physical Training Corps navy blue tracksuit top with three stripes on his arm.

'Listen in. My name is Sergeant Williams. I'm going to be teaching you to climb up that lump of rock and abseil back down again,' he introduced himself and explained what we were doing in one sentence. 'You'll be helped; you'll be assisted by Corporals Jones and Evans, so you have no need to panic.'

I was excited. This was my thing – I loved climbing. When I was younger, I climbed all the time; I climbed trees, I climbed the beams in the barn at Griffin Farm. If it was there and it could be climbed, I climbed it.

'Right, who wants to go first?' the sergeant asked. I just about supressed a squeal as I held up my hand as far as I could possibly hold it. How I managed to stop myself from shouting 'me, me, me!' I'll never know. Pointing at me, Sergeant Williams asked my name.

'Wallington, sir; er, I mean Sergeant,' I replied, still with excitement in my voice.

'Right, you get fitted with your harness, then I'll demonstrate.'

The sergeant climbed the rock with the sort of gusto that it was as if he'd done it before! As he climbed, Corporal Evans explained what we had to do if anyone fell. He told us that two of us – one on each rope – would hold the end of the ropes that dangled from the top of the rock face, and if the climber fell, we would run, as quick as possible, in opposite directions. That, he explained, would act like a brake and stop him before he hit the deck. He also explained the climbing etiquette regarding communication. The climber would shout so all could hear, 'ready to climb'. Three voices would then acknowledge, 'ready to climb', and then the climber would shout, 'climbing now'. Then off you went. Simples, I thought. Sergeant Williams was nearing the top by now. He appeared to be getting into some strange positions. He was upside down while negotiating that chimney thing.

That looks weird, I thought; surely they won't make us beginners do that. Before we knew it, he was flying down the rock face, kicking himself off it as he went. Impressive, I thought; I want some of that.

Freshly washed denims buttoned to the neck, climbing harness perilously close to my nuts, I began climbing. DMS boots weren't the best for this job, I thought, as my foot slipped on the rock on my second step. I was surrounded by different coloured ropes as I climbed. It's harder than it looks, I realized, as I carefully looked for hand and foot holds. Some bits were relatively easy, others were really tricky. I seemed to be having non-stop encouragement and bollockings from Sergeant Williams below me. The tips of my fingers were numb as I reached the base of the chimney. I felt physically drained. As I rested on a thin ledge, Corporal Jones took over with the instructions.

'Right,' he said, 'the only way to the top is backwards, upside down.' I could see his head poking into the top of the stack of grey rock. Moss grew in abundance in the dampness of the formation. 'Lean your shoulder onto that ledge on your left, then sort of walk backwards up the other side.'

I didn't really understand what he was on about, but I persisted. Upside down now, all I could see was a bunch of apprehensive faces looking up at me. It was a long way down. My arms were shaking with the effort – and fear, I suspect – as I inched my way up the chimney. It seemed like forever, but eventually I popped out of the top to join the corporal on the grassy bank there.

'Well done, Wallington. You've climbed before, haven't you?'

'Only trees and things at home,' I breathlessly replied.

'Okay, stand up and face me. Now I want you to do exactly as I tell you. Understand?' I nodded, wondering what the hell he was on about. 'Put your hands in your pockets,' he ordered. I did as I was told. 'Now I want you to walk backwards down the mountain.' You're taking the piss, I thought, although I dared not say so. 'Walk backwards?' I protested, with a slightly girly voice. 'Yes, walk backwards. Now go.'

Even in the short time I'd been in the army, I'd learnt to obey orders. If you were told to jump, you wouldn't ask 'why?'; you would ask 'how high?'. I must admit, I was quietly shitting myself as my body started to become horizontal to the ground below. I just concentrated on taking it step by step. The sense of relief was palpable as I reached the bottom. A little ripple of applause came from some of my mates, and Sergeant Williams congratulated me as he helped extract me from my harness.

It was lunchtime, and I was exhausted. I hadn't realized climbing would be so hard. I grabbed a bag of haversack rations and sat on a nearby boulder. Still shaking from my efforts, I tucked into the food in the bag, watching as the next victim began his climb. It was Quiff. 'Good luck, mate,' I whispered as he started. I love haversack rations, I thought to myself, as I finished my Tiffin bar. Not compo rations, though; they aren't so good – there were some good things, like the tins of boiled sweets and chocolate, but not the hardtack biscuits, which were like trying to eat a manhole cover!

Most of the guys completed the climb. One or two couldn't manage the chimney, but overall I think we did alright. The weather in North Wales had been good so far. It had been dry every day, even though we had ended up soaking wet every day. First stop when we got back to camp was the kit store, just another Nissen hut used for storing all the activity paraphernalia. The hut was identical to all the others, about 40ft long and half-moon in shape, the corrugated roof that curved down to ground level painted army green and the breezeblock walls at each end painted white. One of the rules in the military – and especially the Guards – was 'if it moves, salute; it if it doesn't, paint it'. We got a big clue as to what we were doing the next day when Corporal Jones told us to leave the abseil ropes in the three-tonner ready for tomorrow. Most of us were knackered after the day's efforts, and all ate everything that we could get our hands on. After scoff, Quiff and I killed an hour playing splits on the grass outside our hut. 'What's splits?' I hear you ask. Well, firstly, I don't think you'd get away with it now. What you do is stand opposite each other, about 2ft apart, then – wait for it – you take the bayonet or knife you're holding and aim it into the grass parallel to one of your opponent's boots. He then has to place his foot against the blade of your weapon, causing him to have to open his legs, hence doing the splits. He then launches his bayonet away from your boot. I'm sure you've got the idea by now! The late April sun had dropped below the hills behind us as we finished our evening activity. After grabbing my heavy-duty jumper from my kit bag, I pulled it on as we took the short walk to the NAFFI for a cup of coffee.

Tomorrow was Thursday, we'd be going back to the depot on Friday, then Easter leave started on Saturday. I couldn't wait. I was excited about seeing Pam and the rest of my family. When we got back on Friday, we would have to move all our kit up to our respective platoons before going on leave.

'What are you thinking? You're miles away,' Quiff said as he finished his tea.

'Oh, just thinking about what I'm going to do on leave. What are you going to do?'

'Well, I'll go to my parents in Suffolk and just sleep I think.'

Lying on my top bunk, the hard mattress had moulded to my body shape a bit now. The sounds of various bodily functions surrounded me. You know, the usual things: snoring, farting, talking in your sleep. At least I won't have to put up with that next week, I thought, as I drifted off to sleep.

Thursday morning wasn't as bright and sunny as it had been on previous days. Grey-black clouds hung over the hills and mountains as we made our regular morning exercise run to the beach. We were going to the Pontcysyllte aqueduct, a large arched structure that carried the Llangollen Canal over the River Dee. It took over an hour to get there in the three-tonner. I'm not sure what to make about abseiling, I thought, as I tried to massage my arse back to life while waiting to exit the truck. What confronted us when were back on terra firma was spectacular. A massive arched bridge towered above us. We were in the base of this valley, where the river trundled past at quite a rate, with large boulders turning the water white as it rushed past. The noise of the river almost drowned out Sergeant Ward's loud voice.

'Right, we're going to carry out two types of abseil today. On the first, you'll come down that wall,' he said, pointing at one of the massive stone pillars that stood in front of us. 'Then you'll complete a free abseil – that means you'll be dropping from the middle of the arch.'

Looking up, it was so tall I had to crook my neck to be able to see what looked like the inadequate railing that ran along the top of the aqueduct. I could make out two instructors at the top, busily rigging the ropes. A mixture of fear and excitement flowed through my body as I prepared to volunteer first. Stick to your goals, I reminded myself, as I waited to throw my hand skywards.

'The first five make your way up that footpath over there to Corporals Jones and Evans at the top; the rest stay down here.' As we made our way up the steep track, my legs were burning with the effort. I had to get there first, I kept telling myself as the pace slowed. As we neared the summit, the path was getting more light from the sky. Both sides of the valley were a sea of green from the trees that surrounded it. Exhausted, we climbed the metal stile onto the narrow footpath. I was immediately struck by how narrow the canal was. I could see a narrow boat just entering the aqueduct as we jogged towards the two corporals, it barely fitted. It was impressive to see.

'Ah, Wallington, you can go first,' Corporal Jones announced as we stood in a group, still catching our breath. 'Get you harness on as per yesterday. Stinchcombe, you'll be going next so you can get ready as well.'

The harness was as dangerously close to my tackle as it was yesterday as I swung my leg over the railing and perched precariously on the thin ledge. I'm not bothered by heights, but the guys down on the valley bottom looked awfully small from where I was.

'Right, listen to me,' Corporal Jones started. 'Same as yesterday; well, not quite the same – this time you will control the descent. Don't worry, put these gloves on. I'll hold you.'

You could have given me the friggin' gloves before I got over this barrier, I thought, as I grabbed one with my teeth to pull it on. A strong smell of stale sweat shot up my nose as I pulled it tight.

'Okay, you're going to do the same as yesterday, but this you'll be in control. Understood?'

'Er, yes Corporal – er, what do mean, in control?'

'I mean you're controlling the rope, not me. Don't worry, though, we've got your brakemen down the bottom waiting for you to fuck up.'

It was then I made the mistake of looking over my shoulder at my two brakes way down below me. It was two of the slowest, weakest members of our squad. Holy shit, I thought, better not mess up.

'Right – are you ready? Hold the rope with your right hand across your chest – that's your brake. Move your arm out and your body weight will allow the rope out. To stop, bring your arm back to your chest.'

For some strange reason, my right leg was shaking uncontrollably as I gently started to let the rope out while stepping out onto the wall below. With much encouragement from all assembled at the top, I slowly let the rope out until I was parallel to the ground below. I didn't dare look down again; I just focused on the chisel-cut stone blocks in front of me. Slowly, the confidence built. Corporal Jones encouraged me to push myself away from the wall as I let the rope out. It was great going out, but coming in was a bit trickier. I soon learnt you had to keep your legs straight and braced as you came in towards the wall. If you didn't, you'd find yourself losing your footing and head-butting the wall! Hints of blue sky were appearing between the clouds as I looked between the trees above. I was loving it. It seemed like ages, but about thirty seconds later I slowly touched down on the grassy area below. Apart from my left testicle briefly being pinched in the harness, everything was good. To be honest, I couldn't wait to get back up there and have another go, but all I could do was watch as Stinch began his journey down.

We all had a stint on the brake ropes. At one point, a little bored waiting for one of them at the top to get going, I looked around me and quickly worked out that if we had to run apart to engage the brake from the ground, I would end up in the fast-flowing River Dee. I was going to mention this, but thought better of it! We all had two goes on the wall abseil before breaking off for our much-anticipated haversack rations.

'Is that it, do you think?' I asked Quiff as I wrestled with the little blue bag of salt that I'd extracted from my crisp packet.

'No, this afternoon we're doing a free abseil apparently.'

'What's that then?' I enquired, vigorously shaking my bag of crisps to disperse the salt.

'It means, well, see that keystone in the middle of the arch up there?'

'Yeah., No way – we go from there?'

'Yes way,' he smugly answered. 'You were up the top when Sergeant Ward told us.'

After lunch, once again I found myself stood on the path that crossed the viaduct, a few ramblers had gathered further up the path to watch what was going on.

'Back again, Wallington? Sucker for punishment, eh!' the corporal chuckled as I stepped into the harness for the third time.

'Looking forward to it, Corporal,' I enthusiastically replied, always keeping my keenness levels high.

'Okay, this time you're doing a free abseil, so when you reach the keystone and let your arm allow the rope to travel through your hand, you'll drop like a stone. When you return your arm to the brake position, i.e. across your chest, you'll find you'll keep falling. That's the stretch in the rope; it will stop, eventually. Just bear that in mind and don't brake too late!'

That's a lot to take in, I thought, as I once again pulled on the gloves I'd been given and began to climb over the railings. The people watching had moved closer now, and one of them wished me good luck before I started my descent. Once again, like an idiot, I couldn't resist a look down before I started. I noticed immediately that I was closer to the river now. How's the brakeman going to do his job if I mess up, I wondered.

'Ready,' the instructor quietly said in a reassuring tone.

I nodded my head with such vigour my helmet fell down over my eyes. After he had pulled my chinstrap tight, it was my neck being pinched this time. Then I was off. As I reached the large keystone, I couldn't help but wonder at its size. Rather than being frightened, I was wondering how whoever built this thing got it up here. Moving my right arm out towards the bridge, I heard the familiar whirring of the rope traveling through the D-shaped ring on the harness. Try the brake, I thought, as I moved my arm back to the brake position. The instructor was right – I just kept dropping. It felt like ages before the rope stopped stretching, and then, without warning, I was heading back up to where I'd started. For a few seconds I was bouncing up and down like a spider on a web. I love this, I thought, as I let the rope out again. I soon discovered that with slight arm movements you could really accurately control your landing.

'That's brilliant!' I exclaimed to my brakemen as I struggled out of my harness. After one more drop that afternoon, we loaded up the three-tonners and started the uncomfortable journey back. As the scenery passed by the rear of the canvas-covered truck, my thoughts went back to the week we'd had here in Wales. I didn't fancy that potholing lark, but the climbing and abseiling were great. As we turned into our temporary home, it was starting to rain. At least we were going back to the depot tomorrow, then it would be the big move to Inkerman Platoon for our next adventure.

Chapter 3

Inkermann Platoon

SITTING ON MY old metal bed as I stuffed kit into my kit bag, I reflected on my time here in the spiders. I reflected on how nervous I was the first time I walked into this room, how sick my stomach felt with the anticipation of what was ahead of me. I looked at the red tartan thermos flask that my dad had sent me when I mentioned it would be handy to have. I recalled how when I unscrewed the lid, I found it full of Quality Street sweets, how Pam and my secret relationship was working out, and how much I was looking forward to being with her tomorrow.

'Are you ready yet?' Quiff's familiar voice came from the open door. 'I've borrowed a trolley from Joe at the stables – he'll kill me if I have it for too long.'

'Okay mate, coming now,' I replied as I got up from my safe place one last time. Inkerman Platoon was, like all the other junior platoons, situated in the more modern part of the Guards Depot, the east end of the camp. Two brick-built buildings side by side, both on two storeys. When we arrived, we were greeted by the platoon Corporal of Horse, Corporal of Horses Mayor – or 'Donkey Mayor', as he was known. He was stout in build, with a friendly face. After being directed up to the second floor in the left-side building, we made our way there to sus it out. The first thing we noticed was how modern it was compared with the spiders. As you entered the room, it appeared that each corner was a sort of bed space containing four beds, with larger wooden lockers than we had down at the old place. As we walked in, we were greeted by a slightly rotund junior three-bar (Corporal of Horse) named Ian Steven. Little did I know it then, but he was to become one of my best friends, although sadly he's no longer with us. Not only was he an excellent horseman, but he was a good guy as well (to us fellow cavalry boys anyway). Although we were in the same room, Quiff and I were in different bed spaces. It didn't take long to settle in. Most of the guys seemed alright and the place seemed to have a little more relaxed attitude as the rooms appeared to be run, for the most part, by the junior

NCOs. Earlier that day we'd been paid, so everyone was feeling flush with money for a change. Both Quiff and I knew Ian Steven a bit from the stables on the camp, so there was an instant connection. As he was the senior NCO in the room, he lived in a bunk (single room) in the corner. That was a great privilege – a privilege I was determined to get.

'Coming up the NAFFI later?' Ian asked as we walked/marched to the cookhouse. This was all new to us. We were in amongst the Guards recruits.

'Yeah, okay. I've only been in there once before. We normally went to Sandies when we were down the spiders,' I replied as we entered the new – to us – canteen for scoff. The canteen in the new part of the depot was much busier than the one we'd been used too. The older recruits used it as well, not just the junior soldiers like down the spiders. You could tell that by the amount of new unshrunk berets that were about. Most of them looked like they'd nicked a dinner plate and hidden it in their still-stiff new headwear. We soon discovered the journey through the depot for the senior recruits was a tough one: we were here for two years, they were here for around six months! We used to chuckle watching them quick-marching everywhere, arms flailing about like a wind-up toy.

The NAFFI was busy. Everyone would be going on leave tomorrow, so everyone had money. The junior soldiers had their own NAFFI. It had a bar, but didn't sell alcohol. It also had a television room and a snooker table. Right at the back there was a WRVS (Women's Royal Voluntary Service) area. The WRVS lady was a rather large, friendly woman named Ena. When Ian took us to meet her, she was sat in the corner, surrounded by what looked like vulnerable young soldiers. She wore a military-looking bottle green skirt with a light green blouse with a red WRVS logo stitched above her more-than-adequate left breast! Like I said, she was a friendly lady who some of the junior soldiers rather depended on. I didn't realise at the time, but I would have to visit her and spend a bit of time with her when I became a junior NCO and was on Orderly NCO (orderly dog) duties in the future.

Even being in a new room in a different bed, and being excited about going on leave tomorrow, I slept well. It was a Saturday in late April, and a bright sunny morning welcomed us as we stepped out of our block onto the paved area between the two buildings. As we walked towards the parade square where our transport was, my army-issue suitcase felt quite light. I could have got away with my small civvy one, but I wanted to bring more civvy clothes back as we were now allowed to wear them in the evening. Most of the guys were lined up to get the Brookwood station transport, so luckily the North Camp transport wasn't too busy. I noticed the fella I travelled with last time, Steve, at the back of the short line of people waiting.

'Hiya, mate,' I said as I joined him at the back of the queue. 'What platoon are you in?'

'Hi – Waterloo,' he said, with that ever-excited look on his face that he always seemed to wear.

The journey to Bristol was pretty uneventful. Some old chap insisted on getting us a coffee as we were in uniform. Stepping out through the big double doors at Temple Meads station, I immediately spotted what I was looking for – a grey Mini Traveller waiting in the car park opposite. It looked a bit different to last time as I walked towards the car. I could see Pam getting out of it. She hadn't seen me in full two-dress before. Last time when we met at half-term, by the time she came to the farm I had taken my jacket off. I could see a broad smile on her face from under the peak of my blue and red forage cap. We greeted with a long hug and a kiss. It felt good to have her in my arms again. We talked – nonstop it seemed – as she drove out of Bristol towards Downend and the farm. I had a week's leave, and Pam had the week off as well – life felt good. While we were Junior Guardsmen, we were paid, if I remember correctly, four pounds fifty a week. Our food and accommodation was all in, and though the food wasn't the best, it gave us the sustenance needed. I was fortunate to come from a family where I didn't know what it was like to be hungry. We didn't have grand food or anything, and I was always envious of Pam because she had lemonade at home where we had to make do with water or juice. I had taken the option when I first joined to put two pounds a week into my mum's Post Office account, to help her if she needed it but also to save money for when I was on leave.

I had a secret plan for some of the money – I was going to buy Pam an eternity ring. We were definitely an item now, but no one officially knew. It was Wednesday when we drove into Broadmead in the centre of Bristol. I'd discussed it with Pam. I wasn't great with secrets; I just wanted to show my love for her. She did so much for me, sending a parcel most weeks, with cigarettes and stamps amongst their contents. I knew the other guys were a bit envious. I was lucky – I knew and appreciated it.

Like a sunny hour in a cloudy day, the week was soon over. I hated going back after leave. I remember walking through Alan Turner's field on my way home after meeting Pam at the stables. I felt as low as a snake's belly as I trudged – shoulders hunched, hands in pockets – across the field. I tried to console myself by thinking of my mates and the cadre course we would be starting the following week. Sunday night was tough. We sat in the Mini, drinking my last pint of lager I would have for a few weeks. Pam was at work the next day, so dad would drop me off at the station before he went back to work. We'd got on well this last week. I really thought he was beginning to get some trust and respect for how much I was achieving.

'How was your leave?' I asked Quiff as we marched – well, walked in step – towards the cookhouse. Suddenly, a low-flying rookie came speeding past. I could almost feel the backdraft as he marched past us at double-quick time.

'What the fuck!' Quiff said as he instinctively moved to one side. 'Leave was good, thanks. We've got riding lessons on Wednesday afternoons this term, haven't we?'

'Yep. Can't wait. I did a bit of riding while I was at home.'

'I bet you did,' he giggled as he nudged me sideways with his shoulder.

'What size waist?' the storeman asked, as Quiff, Stinch and I stood at the long counter.

'What, me? Oh, thirty, Corporal, sorry,' I blurted out on the sudden realization that he was talking to me. 'Thirty!' he shouted over his shoulder, and before I knew it a head popped around the corner of one of the long green metal racks that stretched to end of the storeroom and winged khaki-coloured riding breeches in my direction. This was repeated twice more, along with cavalry-length puttees, before we signed the paper on his clipboard and made our way back to the block. Stinch was in Mons Platoon, just a couple of blocks away from Inkerman. Cavalry breeches were unique. As I tried mine on, I could feel they were tight around the calf, then rapidly went on a journey outwards – I mean really outwards – before slowly making their way back into the waist. When I had said at the stores that I was a thirty, I meant waist, not chest! They came so high up, I thought for a moment they might strangle me. We were supposed to wear army-issue braces with them, but mine wouldn't shorten enough to fit. Like battledress, the breeches were a thick woollen material but had suede leather knee grips. My riding kit now consisted of DMS boots, breeches joined together with puttees, KF shirt and tie with battledress blouse – yes, that's what it was called – on top. For extra safety, we also wore our berets! In the Seventies, not much attention was paid to health and safety.

'Why aren't Stevo's [Junior Corporal of Horse Ian Steven's] breeches baggy like ours?' I asked Quiff as he fought to attach the back of his battledress blouse to the buttons on the back of his breeches.

'Because he got them tailored.'

'Who tailored them?'

You know what's coming, don't you? 'The tailor,' he sarcastically replied.

'Yeah, I know, but which tailor.'

'Don't know. Ask him.'

I did as suggested and asked Stevo. He told me about a Grenadier Guard – junior, like us, but one term ahead I think – who was going to be a tailor when he joined his regiment. Apparently he did a bit of tailoring in his spare time. I have to find him, I thought, before Quiff does!

The next day, after a bit of asking around, I found him. His name was Mick Good, a junior Staff Sergeant in Blenheim Platoon. As soon as I met him, I was taken aback at how naturally smart he looked; not too tall, with blonde hair and blue eyes. I don't know why, but we immediately hit it off. He agreed to take my breeches in if I brought them round to his bunk one evening. Mick was to become a good friend to both Quiff and I. When we passed out of the junior regiment, he was the junior RSM (Regimental Sergeant Major) who commanded the parade. Everybody knew he had a great career ahead of him. I recall now with great sadness standing on the parade square at Combermere Barracks, Windsor, when I was in the mounted regiment, Donkey Mayor – our former platoon three-bar at Inkerman – calling Quiff and I over as we walked back from the stables. With tears in his eyes, the big man informed us that on the day Mick was leaving the depot to join his regiment, he'd stepped out into the road outside the Guardroom and was hit by a car. Apparently, he died instantly. It shook Quiff and I terribly. Even now, fifty-two years later, I still occasionally think of him.

Once both Quiff and I – or should I say Mick – had sorted out our breeches and had successfully passed our cadre course, the two of us, junior lance corporals now, proudly marched along Adair Walk with our two stripes with a crown above them, backed in red to indicate we were junior soldiers, towards the stables. It was a Wednesday afternoon in early May, with the sun shining over the Surrey countryside. This would be our first lesson as junior troopers in the Household Cavalry. The riding instructor at the depot was a guy named Lance Corporal of Horse Mai – 'Mai as in hay', he used to insist! As the five of us lined up in the yard, I was probably the most relaxed there. I'd been riding on a regular basis since the age of 5 or 6, so this was nothing new to me. The military saddles were a bit different, but apart from that I could see no snags.

The horse I was given was named Trojan. We had met before – many times in fact – when we used to come down to help on Wednesday evenings. He was a 16-2 dark bay gelding; he wasn't a cavalry black, none of them in the depot stables were. I didn't know their history, but I knew they were used by some of the officers for hunting and hacking out. The saddle felt more slippery than I was used to as I shuffled myself into position after mounting. Behind the C-shaped yard was a menage, a riding arena 40 metres long by 20 metres wide. A black-stained post and rail fence surrounded the sand and gravel surface, and a bunch of brightly coloured show jumps sat neatly stored on the grass at the bottom of the arena. Corporal Mai opened the five-bar gate to let us in. Again, I felt completely calm. Corporal Mai had selected our mounts based on our individual experience. Quiff and Stinch hadn't really ridden before, so they were given what we call in the cavalry 'plugs' – bombproof, steady and all those other terms that are used to describe lazy horses. To be truthful, I was a bit bored. I understood that the others had a lot to learn and I was willing to help them, but after an hour of walking and trotting around the arena, all I wanted to do was take Trojan out of here, head up towards the sandhill and give him a good run out – or as they say in horsey language, 'let him have his head'. Despite all I've said about being bored, I still enjoyed it. Just being around horses and sitting on one was good enough for me.

* * *

Now we were in our second term, things were a bit different. We still had the dreaded room inspections and shining parades, but they weren't quite as intense as they were down at the spiders. We had three afternoons of sport a week and two of education. As I've mentioned before, I never excelled in the classroom; in fact I didn't go to school much at all. That's partly why I ended up here, I suppose. While I sat in one of the classrooms, looking out of the window and watching a squad of senior recruits being rifted (marched very fast) up and down Adare Walk, the penny suddenly dropped. What the civvy teacher was saying made sense. Why hadn't the teachers at Downend cowsheds (my old school) been like this? They always gave the impression, as far as I was concerned, that they didn't want to be there any more than I did. This teacher was interesting, keen, engaging, and the classes – including me – followed what he was saying to the word. We watched a lot of military training films as well. It was difficult sometimes to stay focused. Itchy battledress was the first problem. As soon as the lights were turned off, all you could see was constant fidgeting and the occasional head suddenly twitching back into life as they fought to stay awake. In short, I enjoyed being educated now, and over the next two terms in juniors I won prizes for education – books mostly, which I still have to this day.

Not long after getting settled into life in Inkerman, we were on the move again. This time we were going on battle camp on Salisbury Plain. The familiar half-moon-shaped Nissen huts came into view as the old army green coach struggled through the gate at our temporary new home. The MOD sign at the entrance told us we were at Knook Camp, but we might as well have been back at Towyn in North Wales – it looked exactly the same. The coach stopped outside the black and white painted Guardroom to let us out. The hard vinyl seats didn't give an inch as everybody stood up and stretched, the journey from Surrey to Wiltshire having taken about two-and-a-half hours. With empty haversack ration bags in hand, we slowly egressed onto the road outside. Being a junior NCO now, I had more responsibilities with helping the management of others. As a lance three-bar, you could be tasked with taking the squad on a run or marching them from A to B. We also knew much more of what was going on, what we were going to be doing. I knew, for instance, that we would only have one night at Knook Camp before we went camping on Salisbury Plain tomorrow. This information would fly down from the platoon commander to Donkey Mayor and then to us; this usually came via my mate Stevo.

Familiar scenes met us as I opened the door to our hut. The bunk beds, with those straw-filled mattresses, made the room smell a bit like mouldy hay, and the stove was the same as in Wales. I suggested to one of the guys who had made his way to the other end of the hut to open the windows, as I opened those at my end as well. It didn't take long for the smell to clear and some sort of order to be established. Being unfamiliar with the geography of Britain in my teenage years, I wondered how far away Bristol was as I threw my kit on the bottom bed of the bunk I'd selected – rank comes with some privileges, you know! When everyone was settled in, us junior NCOs had to attend a meeting in the mess hall at 1500hrs. As I walked along the tarmacked path towards the big building at the far end of the camp, I was joined by Quiff. I could see him looking in all directions before sprinting across the grass to join me. I knew what he was doing: at the depot, you never, ever walked on the grass, unless of course you were litter picking or maybe weapon cleaning and you had permission. It may seem strange, but even to this day, some fifty years later, I think carefully before I walk on a piece of grass without permission.

'Okay, listen in,' the second lieutenant said as he half-straddled one of the dining tables in the corner of the dining room. 'Tomorrow we will be going about 10 miles onto the Salisbury Plain battle area to set up camp for three days. We will be leaving at nine o'clock sharp. Is that right, Corporal?'

'Correct, sir.'

'So, we will have to load as much kit as we can on the three-tonners this afternoon.'

In those days, commissioned officers in the Brigade of Guards all – I really mean all – came from a lot posher backgrounds than we did. They'd all been to public schools and had double-barrelled surnames. This one – Lieutenant Hardcourt-Player or something like that – was the same. You really didn't see much of them, but when you did, they tried to justify their existence by having these somewhat pointless meetings. I couldn't help noticing Donkey Mayor rolling his eyes in wonderment at nearly every sentence he made.

When eventually he'd had his say, Donkey took over and the real work started.

'Right, lads,' he started, rubbing his hands together as if he'd just wrung the young officer's neck. 'I want six "volunteers" from each hut over at the stores hut when we've finished here to load what we can for tomorrow. When we've set up camp on the site of an old fort, we've got to then get to an artillery display somewhere else on the plain. All understood?'

'Yes, Corporal,' came the reply, and we were off. Not that difficult, is it!

As soon as I had gathered my six bods together, we made our way towards the stores. At least it's dry, I thought, as I marched the guys towards the building. My sense of smell must have been acute that day, because as I entered the smell of canvas was overwhelming. All the kit we would need had been neatly stacked near the entrance by the forward party, the guys who came down a day or two before to get everything ready. You need an advance party as much as you need a rear party.

I'd never been in the front of a three-tonner, but I was loving it as the driver negotiated the rough ground as we made our way to the top of the hill. The truck then suddenly dropped off to the right – I honestly thought it was tipping over as I grabbed whatever I could to stay in my seat. As it rolled, even above the engine noise I could hear shouting and jeering coming from behind us. Settling back into my seat, I looked up and noticed what looked like a manhole cover in the roof of the vehicle. I quickly sussed it was a gun turret hole. Cool, I thought, as I resumed my focus on the hill ahead.

As we approached the large grassed flat area at the top of this hill, I soon concluded that this was the fort and our camp for a night or two. I could see Lieutenant Hardcourt-Player sat on the bonnet of the Land Rover ahead of us. He looked like he should be sitting on his charger, conducting a battle. His brown beret had his cap badge of the Grenadier Guards embroidered into it, unlike the other ranks, who had the standard 'stay bright badge'. His overlong dark hair stuck out from beneath the beret over his ears.

Thank goodness, Donkey soon took command, and before too long the tents were up and ready. They were arranged in a 'C' shape that faced a small copse of trees. The view from our camp was spectacular, with vast areas of green only broken up by the brown and grey lines of what I was told were tank tracks. The advance party were once again doing their stuff. Piles of cardboard boxes nearly filled one of the larger tents they had erected earlier – Compo rations, I thought, as I grabbed a haversack bag. A couple of days eating them would have their own consequences down the line!

Back in my usual place in the back of a three-tonner, I was focused on Quiff trying to fight that compulsion you get to nod off with the motion of a vehicle. The sound of the tyres on the road was hypnotic, and a rope that hung from the roof swung like a pendulum. I was tempted to slide down on the bench and see if I could kick the knot on the end of the rope in his direction, when the truck suddenly took a right turn onto a large gravel car park. Eyes wide open now, like a rabbit caught in headlights, Quiff had that classic look on his face – 'where the hell am I, what am I doing here, can I go back to wherever I was ten seconds ago, it was better there!'

As I let the rope go as I swung down from the vehicle, I could see what looked like the massive stands you have around a stadium. There was already a good few people sitting in them: different regiments, different types of dress, some in combats like us but others in two-dress. As we were the senior regiments of the British Army, we did what the Guards do and immediately formed three ranks and awaited orders. I noticed Lieutenant Hardcourt-Player exiting the Land Rover that had pulled up beside us.

The traditional pleasantries were exchanged between Donkey and H-P as they saluted each other.

'Right, men!' Donkey shouted. 'Get yourself a lunch bag from the back of the Land Rover and then find a seat in those stands over there. Stay together, don't split up; then you can eat and enjoy the show.'

It was like being in a rugby scrum at the back of the 'Landy' as everyone tried to grab a brown paper bag and a box of drink at the same time. Sitting about halfway up the tiered benches, I found myself more interested in the fact that I didn't have a straw attached to my orange drink than the senior officer who had taken his place on a lectern in front of us. Everyone winced in pretend pain as the microphone he was tapping screeched into life. Quiff, who had just taken a drink from his box (he had a straw!), had a face like he was sucking a lemon as he tried to keep the drink in his mouth.

'Good afternoon, gentlemen,' Colonel Tiddly-Push began. 'Welcome to the artillery ranges here on Salisbury Plain.' I felt a bit embarrassed about crunching on my crisps, but everyone else seemed to be eating so I didn't see why I shouldn't. Standing behind the colonel was a warrant officer holding a clipboard, with notes for his commentary, it later turned out. He kept looking at his watch and then looking out onto the horizon behind us, then began tapping his right ear and moving his head about like he was an Indian waiter at a curry house! Eventually, Colonel Tiddly-Push finished and allowed the warrant officer to take the stand. He didn't look confident, I have to say, as he stumbled onto the lectern. He too couldn't resist tapping the microphone as if he didn't know whether it was working or not.

'Good afternoon,' he began. 'Shortly you'll hear a load bang.' BANG! It was so loud I nearly bit my finger off instead of my sandwich. The noise completely drowned out whatever else he was saying. Half of Quiff's crisps were on the floor between his legs now. He obviously wasn't paying attention as he tried to retrieve some from his crotch, because he didn't notice the commentator pointing in the direction of an old tank sitting on the horizon. I say 'old tank', but on closer examination I worked out it was a life-sized wooden target. It was that sandy brown and black pattern, the same design as we used on the ranges back in Pirbright.

BOOM! A great big flash and explosion sent the tank target into a million pieces. Quiff was visibly shaking now, clenching his knees together so as not to lose any more crisps. Quiff loves his scoff!

This went on for a further ten minutes or so. After destroying a few more wooden tanks, the noise calmed down and the warrant officer continued his commentary.

'Remember that loud bang at the start of this show?' he asked, as everyone seemed to realize and remember it hadn't landed, or if it had, we hadn't seen it. 'Well,' he continued, 'if you look straight ahead, you'll notice an old tank at twelve o'clock on the horizon.' Noted, I thought, while gazing in the direction of twelve o'clock. Then without warning, a bang and a flash – or was it a flash and a bang, I can't remember. Anyway, it was amazing – that shell had been up in the clouds somewhere all that time. Everyone in the stands had forgotten about it, I think, and then there it comes, out of nowhere, bang on target.

'I wouldn't mind getting me one of those things,' I told Quiff as we walked towards our three-tonner.

'One of those what?'

'One of those guns or whatever they were called.'

'You mean the Milan anti-tank missile system?'

'Shitty death, how did you know that?'

'Because I was listening, dipshit!'

It was my turn to fight the sleep on the journey back to camp. When we returned, there was a lovely hot tea urn waiting for us.

'Compo biscuits over there if you want some,' our slop jockey – er, I mean chef – announced.

'You're alright,' I said as I pulled the tap down to release the tea into my mug. I value my teeth too much, I thought, as I made my way to the edge of the flat area where we camped. As I sat there sipping my tea, I remembered I'd saved some proper biscuits from my lunch pack. I was searching around in one of the side pockets of my combat trousers when I suddenly also remembered the date; it was 17 May 1973, my birthday. I don't know what I was thinking as I sat there on Salisbury Plain, munching a custard cream. I was now 16, and I'd grown up a lot in the last five months. As the wind blew the long grass on the hill to one side, I wondered what Pam would be doing somewhere over there in the distance. It was a Thursday, so she'd probably be finishing work soon, then off to the yard to see to her pony, Shane. As for me, I'd be squeezed into a two-man bivvy with Quiff – what a birthday! Anyway, I decided to keep it to myself. I didn't need or want the bumps, thank you very much.

'Hey, Wallington, you twat!' I heard Quiff shouting as he made a hand signal like he was plonking a large spider onto his head. In military speak, that means 'come here'.

'What's up, dipshit?' I retaliated as I made my way over to him.

'Lieutenant How's your father wants us over there for some sort of team race before supper.'

'For fucks sake!' I remonstrated as we walked towards an assembling crowd of young soldiers.

'Right, gather round and listen in,' our driver/corporal was shouting. 'The officer wants to speak to you.'

'Okay, men,' he began, 'the corporal and I have devised this quick team challenge for you before we finish for the day. The corporal will explain.'

'Okay guys, you'll have noticed, I expect, the two bed frames over there.' He was right, we had noticed them; they were the spring bits, if you like, of an army bed, the bit that goes between the head end and the feet end. He continued: 'You might also have noticed the bowl of hard-boiled eggs on the table there.' There was indeed a bowl of hard-boiled eggs on the table. 'In two teams of fifteen, five on each lap, you have to take an egg and eat it, then with one of the five on the bed, the other four carry him to the first obstacle. When that's completed, you swap places until the next obstacle, etc. Understood?'

'Yes, corporal,' we all muttered as we got our teams together. I was clearly the smallest and lightest in my team. I was the junior NCO, so I led it and decided I'd do the first stint being carried, to encourage them along.

'Is everybody ready?' Lieutenant Hardcourt-Player asked. 'In that case, three, two, one – go!'

Eating a hard-boiled egg as fast as you can isn't the most dramatic or exciting way to start a race, I was thinking, as I chomped away on my egg. I didn't have to worry, though, as I was on the bed and didn't have to run. Bits of semi-chewed egg were flying everywhere as the teams tried to encourage each other to get the race started proper. It seemed ages before I was roughly hoisted into the air. My knuckles were white through gripping the diamond-shaped wires of the bed springs. I could see and feel the springiness of the bed frame bearing down on my team's shoulders beneath me as they ran. I was still spitting out egg as I attempted to encourage them to the next obstacle. As I was tipped off in order to get the bed frame under some makeshift netting, I took a look back to see how we were doing. This seemed a doddle, as the others hadn't really started yet. I could see a crowd of people bunched up near the start but couldn't work out what was going on, so I decided to go and have a look. After instructing my team to wait where they were, I started to walk towards the assembled crowd. I could see one of our opposition team lying on the ground, with Donkey Mayor giving him heart compressions, CPR. As I stood there watching with horror, I saw Donkey shaking his head in the officer's direction. The corporal had reversed the Land Rover over and they proceeded to put the young soldier onto a stretcher and into the back of the vehicle. I noticed Stinch, head down and clearly distressed, walking in my direction.

'What's going on, mate?' I asked.

'Jones – he choked on the egg,' he said as he wiped tears from his eyes.

'Jones – I don't really know him, do I?'

'No, he's in Waterloo Platoon. A gobby scouser, but he was alright.'

'Where've they taken him?'

'Hospital, I think. Doesn't look good though,' he concluded as he continued his walk back to his tent.

I stood for a while just looking at the trees, as the wind blew them into the same shape as the hill, the leaves making a creepy sound in the now quiet camp site. When I got back to our tent, Quiff looked very subdued, sat outside and stabbing the blade of his bayonet into the grass.

'That was one hell of a shit storm,' he mumbled as I approached.

'You're right there, mate,' I agreed as I sat beside him.

Looking down the grassy hill we were camped on, I could see the olive green Land Rover making its way back towards the camp. I half expected to see Jones sat in the passenger seat, but no, he wasn't there. I looked towards the cooking area as I finished my cigarette. Lieutenant Dickhead was talking to Donkey Mayor; he had been off somewhere in the other Land Rover. No one seemed happy; the whole mood around the camp was low. We noticed some of the lads who were sat outside their tents getting up and making their way towards the cookhouse tent. Better go and have a look, we thought, as we walked towards the assembled group.

'Right lads, form a big semi-circle and sit down on the grass please,' Donkey ordered as we arrived.

'Please! Did he say please? There must be something wrong,' I whispered as we took our place in the semi-circle.

'Okay,' Lieutenant Hardcourt-Player began, 'you may have noticed recruit Jones having a bit of bother at the start of the race. Well, it's with regret I have to inform you Jones died from choking during that incident. I've just been back to Knook Camp to telephone and inform his parents.'

You could cut the atmosphere with a knife. No one spoke or even looked at each other. A few minutes passed, then our driver/cook announced: 'Scoff will be ready in half an hour. Don't forget your mess tins. Fall out.'

'Is that it?' I said as we walked towards our tent. 'A bit of bother? Bit of fucking bother? He fucking choked to death.' A sense of wrong swept over me as we walked. I was 16 today, and I'd just witnessed my first death. It seemed so matter of fact to them. I couldn't get my head around it all. What I really wanted to do was to call Pam and spill out how I felt, but I knew that wasn't going to happen. I had to deal with this one with my mates.

No inquiry or investigation was ever carried out, at least I wasn't asked to contribute if there was one. That's what it was like being in the military in the Seventies, I guess.

As you can imagine, the atmosphere wasn't great as we tried to eat the shitty compo rations that were slopped into our mess tins. I felt like Oliver Twist lining up for his gruel, but I wasn't about to ask for more! The sausages that poked out of the instant mashed potatoes looked like something that would come out of the other end of you, I thought, as I pushed them from one end of the rectangular aluminium container to the other.

We were to travel back to Pirbright tomorrow. I couldn't wait to be able to phone Pam. The atmosphere on the coach journey back was still sombre. Not even the view of Stonehenge as we passed stirred any interest. Back in Inkerman, unpacking my kit, I did have one pleasant surprise – well two actually. Pam had sent me a parcel of goodies and a letter. Such goodies normally consisted of fags, sometimes money, writing paper, envelopes and stamps, and of course a letter. The other surprise was that Quiff and I had been promoted to junior lance corporal of horses; another step on that long ladder, I mused, as I returned my now clean boots to my locker. On the Friday evening, I made my way to the nearest telephone box. I don't think Pam could quite believe what I was telling her during our longer than usual conversation.

'How sad is that?' she sighed when I told her about recruit Jones. 'What's going to happen about it?'

'I don't know. I'll keep you updated. Anyway, there is some good news amongst all this shit.'

'What's that?' she asked, her voice sounding more upbeat now.

'Me and Quiff have been made up to junior three bars.'

'What's junior three bars?' she tentatively enquired.

'We're now junior lance corporal of horses,' I somewhat grumpily replied. 'It's an easier life, that's what it is. It means I lead, not follow.'

'Well done you,' she somewhat condescendingly replied.

The conversation ended quite quickly after that, so I made my way to the NAFFI for a well-deserved pint of Vimto!

* * *

As I'd got used to now, we were kept so busy that time seemed to fly by. We had a battle camp in Suffolk later in the summer, but before that I had been chosen to be part of the Junior Guardsman's Wing shooting team, which meant spending three afternoons a week on the ranges practicing. We fired the military's old .303 rifle that was replaced by the SLR in the 1950s, but the .303 was considered to be more accurate. To be fair, it was a lovely weapon to fire. The ranges at Pirbright were in constant use; day and night you could hear them. The ranges we used for training were what they called 50–400, designed for defensive engagement of targets from 400m, 300m and finally 50m. Monday, Tuesday and Friday afternoons were practice days, when we'd be up there all afternoon either firing or pasting up in the butts. I learnt to shoot by messing about with air rifles at Griffin Farm. My brother, Mark, and our mates Barry and Jimmy Lovell would have mini battles in and around the yard. One day I got caught, cornered in a horse box that was parked in the yard when Jimmy found me. He opened the back door to confront me. It was supposed to be pretend, but – typical for Jimmy – he'd forgotten his air rifle was loaded and shot me at point-blank range in my left shoulder. Luckily I had my combat jumper on, a thick knitted jumper that my Auntie Dorris had made me for Christmas, and the pellet lodged in it. However, it still hurt. We didn't let Jimmy loose with the air rifle again, except when target shooting. Jimmy and I met when we went to senior school, Downend Cowsheds. We were both in J4, the thickos' class. He joined the junior Navy at the same time as I joined the Depot, and because our leave time never matched, we lost touch. Many years later, I saw him in a pub in Bristol. I barely recognized him – he was drinking double-double whiskies like they were going out of fashion. He told me he worked at the local washing machine factory, was back living with his elderly mum and spent his lunch break topping up his whisky levels. I thought I'd messed up my life, but luckily I had Pam to keep me on the straight and narrow(ish).

Donkey used to brief the junior NCOs every morning on the day's activities; usual stuff like drill or combat training, assault course and things like that. One morning, something a little different came up: 'Tonight, after your evening meal, you've to report to the gym for boxing.' Boxing, I thought – that would be a tall order for me, being a short-arse! I wasn't unusually short: I was 5ft 7½in. Don't forget that half inch; it was very important to me, as officially you had to be 5ft 8in or above to join the cavalry. They thought I'd grow that extra half inch. At one time they even contemplated making me stand in the dung heap down at the stables for an hour a day to see if that would help me grow!

When I signed on in December 1971, there were three criteria for joining the Brigade of Guards. You had to be white, not wear glasses and be 5ft 8in or over. I know – bad, wasn't it? Different times.

* * *

The sun was setting in the west as Quiff and I marched a bunch of Inkerman Platoon lads towards the gym at the spiders' end of the camp.

'What do you recon to this boxing lark?' I asked Quiff as we walked behind the marching squad.

'Load of bollocks, mate. Not for me. I'm going to volunteer for the netball team!'

'Yeah, you'd be good at that. It's a height thing, you know!'

Walking through the large burgundy red and blue doors of the old gymnasium, we were confronted by three PTIs and Donkey Mayor. Four large gym mats had been arranged in a square in the middle of the floor. I was surprised to see a load of lads from Waterloo Platoon assembled on the other side of the mats.

'Okay,' the PTI Sergeant announced, 'you'll be paired up with someone of the same or similar weight. You will box for two minutes. The best, or should I say the ones with the most potential, will be offered a place in the Junior Guards boxing team. Does everyone understand?'

'Yes, Sergeant,' was the somewhat apprehensive answer that echoed around the gym.

Unlike normal, I didn't volunteer first for this one. Not my cup of tea, I'm afraid. But eventually I could avoid it no longer. I was still inwardly giggling at Quiff's efforts as one of the instructors pulled my gloves on; he had just finished, and it had looked like two girls fighting in the playground! My opponent was a tall, skinny lad with a far greater reach than mine, so I knew I would have to take a few punches just to get close enough to get in the mix. As all before us had done, we started too fast. His flailing arms caught me several time before I was close enough to retaliate, but once I got my head down, trying to look up as I moved in, I planted a good right to his stomach which slowed him down for a second or two. That was enough for me to have a go at my main target – his head. How long does two minutes last, I was wondering, as the blows again rained down on me. I didn't think I'd done very well. I'd rocked him a few times, but the number of punches I had to take to achieve that made me assume I had lost. I was surprised when the referee/PTI told me that I was a 'potential'. I boxed one more time to see if I was good enough for the team. When I got back to my room that evening, I lay on my bed, my head throbbing with the battering I'd taken. I decided if that's what was needed to become a boxer, they could keep it. I thus respectfully declined my invitation to become a member of the prestigious boxing team. Later in the year, we went to the Junior Army Boxing championship finals in Aldershot. It was the Junior Guards against the Junior Paras; needless to say, without my help, we won. Talking of invitations, not long after we were made up to junior corporal of horses, I was called to the Junior Guards Company's admin office on Adaire Walk. After avoiding the speeding senior recruits recklessly rifting themselves along the walk, I removed my beret while negotiating the door into the ground floor offices.

'Ah, Wallington, my old love,' Donkey announced as I appeared at his office door. 'Major Long-Sleeper wants to see you in his office. Hang on a minute and I'll take you in. Do you own a suit, by the way?'

'A suit? Not here, Corporal. I might have one at home.'

Upon entering the office, beret now back on, I saluted the Welsh Guards officer.

'Ah, corporal of horse Wallington. Do you own a suit?'

I did my very best not to be sarcastic about whether or not I owned a bloody suit, as I pretended to give it some thought.

'Not that I can think of, sir,' I limply replied. I didn't have the bottle to ask why.

'Good, maybe Corporal of Horse Mayor can sort that detail out later. I – we – would like you and another to represent the Junior Guardsman's Wing to a reception for the Queen and the Duke of Edinburgh's silver wedding at St James' Palace the week after next.'

'Yes, sir, I'd be honoured,' I said, still wondering – stupidly – why they were so fixated on whether or not I owned a suit.

'Good, well done. Corporal Mayor will fill you in on the details in due course.'

'Salute!', I heard from behind me, as I did as ordered and graciously exited the office.

'Telephone home this evening and try to find this elusive suit. If you haven't got one, we'll allow you to draw some money from your Post Office savings account and buy one.' That's nice, I thought, as I made my way out of the office. On the way out, I noticed Mick Good busily sorting the mail out in an adjoining office.

'Alright, Mick,' I said, as I poked my head around the door. 'Anything for me – a suit maybe?'

'Piss off, Wol,' he said with a smile. 'If you need one altered, though, you know where to come.'

'Thanks, mate. I might have to take you up on that. So you're orderly dog this week then?'

'Yeh, for my sins. Now jog on and leave me alone; I've got loads to do here. I'll see you at the NAFFI later.'

As I made my way back to the block, I was trying to recall my wardrobe back at Baugh Farm. It wouldn't be any good asking my mum. She wouldn't have a clue. I'd ask Pam, instead. She'd know. That evening, before we went to the NAFFI, I called Pam. She confirmed what I thought: I did have a suit, a grey pinstripe, and it was in my wardrobe in my bedroom. After more than a little verbal schmoozing, she agreed to go and get it from the farm. She even agreed to bring it up on Sunday. As we now had most Sundays off, Pam had built the confidence to drive the Mini Traveller up to Pirbright so we could spend half a day together. It was great. The occasional distraction from this place was always welcome, especially with her. I could tell Quiff was getting bored waiting for me to finish on the phone. He had stopped making stupid faces and was now threatening to drop his trousers and moon in my direction. I'm not having that, I thought, as I quickly finished the call and joined him to continue our walk to the NAFFI.

Senior juniors had to take their turn, usually once a term, to be 'orderly dog', or as it is officially titled, Orderly NCO. One of the jobs was to visit Ena, the WRVS lady who based herself at the back of the NAFFI most evenings. The downside of the week was that you had to wear uniform while doing your rounds. After getting a drink, Quiff and I decided to go and see if Mick Good was there, as I'd told Quiff earlier about seeing him when I was at the company offices. As we suspected, there he was, immaculate as ever, sat beside Ena. From where I stood, Ena looked quite regal. Her chair was like one of those you have by your bed in hospital. It was even that same green colour. Mick was sitting beside her. His chair was a more standard NAFFI one, so it made him look smaller. Surrounding both of them were, shall we say, the more insecure recruits – those missing their mums maybe. Some sat at her feet, staring at her reverently, while others played board games and the like.

'Did you find your suit, Wol?' Mick enquired.

'Yep. Apparently I've got one. Pam's bringing it up on Sunday.'

'What's this for, young Simon?' Ena asked.

'I'm going to London, St James' Palace, to present the Queen and Prince Phillip with a painting from the Junior Guardsman's Wing.'

'Ohh, that's posh. Aren't you lucky, going to meet the Queen? How lucky.'

It was exciting, I thought, as I sipped my drink while trying to watch some random television programme on the large – for those days – NAFFI television. I wondered why they'd picked me? And where was St James' Palace? I'd seen Buckingham Palace when I was a kid, but apart from that I'd never been to London.

'Riding school tomorrow,' I mentioned to Quiff as we walked back to Inkerman. When we got there, he went left as I went right. When I got promoted, Donkey Mayor moved me up to the top floor of the other block. The room was okay, apart from one problem child – you always have at least one. His name was Allison, a sheep shagger (Coldstream Guard) from the north-east who spoke with a lisp. He wasn't a bad lad, he just didn't know how to – or couldn't be bothered to – look after himself. It goes without saying that he didn't look after his kit. He was what we called in the military a 'grot'. We also had a trained soldier living in a bunk (single room). He worked in the sports store, which was handy really.

The eight of us that attended riding school on Wednesday afternoons were coming on well. COH Mai was alright, although sometimes he was a bit up his own arse. As I mentioned earlier, I'd been riding for many years, so none of this presented any problems to me. But apart from one other, the rest had never sat on a horse before getting to the depot. This one afternoon a week would give them one hell of a leg up (pardon the pun!) before going into riding school when we got to 'uptown' Hyde Park Barracks.

Before getting the horses ready, Corporal Mai asked us to move some of the showjumping equipment into the menage. Great, we're going to do some jumping, I thought. Quiff didn't seem so keen, but I reassured him that he would be alright. Firstly, we built a standard 3ft show jump in the middle of the arena. Corporal Mai was going to demonstrate the correct way to approach and clear a show jump.

'Cooper, come out here and dismount,' he ordered Steve Cooper, my mate from Bristol, with whom I travelled home when we went on leave.

After what seemed forever, our instructor managed to mount his charger. His mount then proceeded to walk on before he'd got his boots in the stirrups or gathered up his reins. When all this was in place and he was happy, he stopped in front of the ride. Corporal Mai always looked smart. He wore nicely tailored breeches, black leather long boots with the obligatory spurs (an indication that you'd successfully passed the army riding course, the hardest individual training course in the British Army, we were repeatedly reminded), and his heavy-duty jumper was held neatly together with his red and blue Life Guards stable belt. Appearing from the neck of his jumper was a well-pressed and faded shirt, with a well-knotted tie that looked like it was trying to escape! We didn't wear head protection in those days; a beret would suffice as far as the army was concerned. Having said that, I never, apart from hunting or gymkhanas, wore head protection in civvy street. Corporal Mai wore his red and blue forage cap; the peak was neatly slashed and sported two brass bands that indicated he was a lance corporal of horse.

'Okay,' he started, 'I'm going to demonstrate jumping. I'll approach in canter from the right; a nice gentle pace, not too fast, is all that is required. Watch and learn.'

I think his mount, like ours, had got so bored he'd decided to take a nap. Mine, Landfall, had decided to rest his off-hind leg, which in turn sent me, on top, leaning to the right towards Quiff. After a couple of encouraging taps from Corporal Mai's spurs, he was off. As he reached the corner, he broke into a canter. His horse, as we say in equestrian circles, was a bit full of himself, a bit lively – defiant, if you like. He approached the other end of the school, then turned in towards the jump. All looked good so far. I could almost hear him counting the strides as he made his final adjustments before taking the relatively easy obstacle that was rapidly coming closer to him. This bit is no reflection on Corporal Mai at all; we've all been there. If you've ridden these (most of the time) wonderful animals, you will know what I'm describing. Danny, the iron-grey hunter type he was riding, suddenly, without warning, decided he wasn't going to do what he was asking. He dug his toes in just as the corporal was expecting him to take off skywards. He stopped. Of course, you can't defy the laws of gravity, so Corporal Mai continued skywards on his own. His forage cap went higher than he did as it flew off to one side, and the corporal, being heavier than his cap, was soon crashing down on the red and white wooden poles of the jump. I don't know, dear reader, whether you've ever fallen over and been more concerned about whether someone had seen you rather than if you were hurt. Well, it was a bit like that. He was up like a shot. Trouble was, eight sets of eyes had been ordered to 'watch and learn'. I tried to purse my lips as if I was kissing a frog in order not to laugh, while Quiff just fixed his stare on the pommel of his saddle. I'm sure I could hear a slight squeaking from somewhere in his direction. I found if I kept stretching my neck, it stopped my shoulders doing what they wanted to, which was to shake uncontrollably with laughter. Looking a bit like Captain Mainwaring from Dad's Army, Corporal Mai dusted himself down and replaced his somewhat battered forage cap. His tie had escaped from the neck of his jumper, and I noticed one of the brass bands of his cap had removed itself and was now sticking out of the sandy surface of the riding school. Steve had caught Danny and was dutifully standing patiently, waiting for our instructor to remount.

Everything now back in place, he remounted Danny and positioned himself back in front of us. 'Who's ridden horses before, or should I say, who thinks they could jump that jump?' he asked.

'Wallington has; he'll do it' Quiff kindly volunteered on my behalf.

'Well what do think, Corporal Wallington? Are you up for it?'

'I'll give it a go, Corporal,' I loudly answered, while trying to temper the feelings in my stomach that had suddenly manifested themselves.

As I attempted to bring Landfall back to life, or at least to stand back on the four legs that God had given him, I think he suddenly sussed that he was now the centre of attention. I noticed Steve moving Danny out of the way. He was a skinny, tall lad; his breeches were so baggy that his puttied lower legs looked like a matchstick man as he trudged through the sandy school.

To be fair, Landfall was a game horse. His transition from trot to canter was controlled and smooth, and as I turned into our approach, all the apprehension had gone. I was doing what I'd been doing since I was a boy. For a second, time stood still; I was back on the pony I used to look after, Phanton, back at Griffin Farm jumping the dry stone walls as I acted out the Pony Express in my mind. The next thing I remember was landing safely on the other side of the jump. Instinct must have taken over; all I could hear was the clapping of my mates on the other side of the arena. Corporal Mai had remounted now and soon successfully followed me over the jump, although this time I noticed he sat back more on his approach to avoid going out of the front door again.

The rest of the lesson continued with the corporal constructing a cavaletti-sized jumping lane and introducing the novice riders to the beginning of learning to jump.

'Thanks for that, twat!' I mentioned to Quiff as we made our way to scoff.

'No, you were brilliant,' Stinch said as we began to get in step as we passed the Guards Depot Regimental Sergeant Major's office. It was at the bottom end of the parade ground. The windows were so clean that they looked like mirrors as you approached, but the bungalow-sized brick building was a place you didn't want to be called to.

* * *

Wednesday, 23 May 1973 found me putting my civvies on, the infamous suit that everyone in authority round here had seemed so interested in. Posh invitation in hand, I made my way as instructed to the Guardroom at the main entrance to the depot. As I approached, I could see a white minibus parked outside. with a few guys discreetly having a smoke on the blindside of the vehicle.

'You look like you're going to the Palace,' one of them said as I joined them. 'If you want a smoke, have one now. We won't have many opportunities later.'

As I clambered in through the side door of the bus, I noticed the other junior soldier sat at the back. After joining him, the van pulled away. We were on our way; on our way to London. I was more excited than apprehensive, not knowing what to expect really. I don't think any of us did actually. As I settled into my seat, I felt a bit weird in the suit. We all wore the same red and blue regimental ties, so it looked and felt like we were going to church parade, which we had to attend once a month, only then we wore grey flannel trousers, regimental tie and regimental blazer. I asked my companion his name as we made our way towards the A3. He told me it was Bill – Bill Taylor from Blenheim Platoon.

'How come you got this gig, then?' I asked Bill over the noise inside the minibus.

64

'Dunno,' he replied. 'I was asked, no told I'd be going when I was orderly dog a couple of weeks ago.'

'Plus, that you owned a suit helped.'

'Yep, that's the one. It's a day out anyway, isn't it?'

Time passed relatively quickly. The green of the countryside soon turned into the grey of the suburbs. I couldn't get over how much traffic was around. As we got more into central London, the landscape changed again; it was a lot more grand now and everyone looked as though they were in a rush, with a massive river on our right which one of the senior guys helpfully informed us was the Thames. We didn't have a clue where we were, and he became our temporary tour guide. He pointed out the Houses of Parliament on our right as we headed towards Whitehall. There were statues everywhere we looked, then an oasis of green sat on our right side as we made our way down Birdcage Walk, as it turned right to Buckingham Palace. Then we came to what is known in the mob (the army) as 'The Birthday Cake'; it's actually the Queen Victoria Monument. As we travelled around it like a roundabout, ahead stretched a long red-coloured road. 'This is The Mall,' our guide continued, and before we knew it we turned left towards what looked like a small castle set amongst loads of trees. Two red-brick towers stood either side of a sandstone arch, and a big clock sat at the top of the building between the towers – it was eleven thirty. It was a lot to take in, but I remember going up a wide stone staircase. It had a red carpet, carefully fitted, which seemed to the eye to narrow as I looked up towards the grand black and gold doors at the top. Inside, we had to climb another, even grander staircase – the carpet again was red, really royal red; even the banister rail was covered in red velvet. I nearly fell up the stairs as I craned my neck in all directions to take it all in. At the entrance to a large hall, we were greeted by one of the footmen, again dressed in red livery – there was a lot of red about. He pointed towards the ornate gold easel that had been placed in the corner of the room. Sitting on it was what the Junior Guardsman's Wing were presenting. It was an oil painting. Not that big, about 16in by 20in, I reckoned. I can't for the life of me remember the subject matter, but I do recall that, as you might imagine, it was a military scene. Bill and I were placed either side of the painting, while the other two senior guys stood either side of their gift – another painting. After a while, a different footman came over, holding a massive silver tray. I'd never seen a tray that big. It was full of glasses; thin, flute-type glasses containing what looked like a fizzy sample you might give to the doctor.

'Just the one,' the senior Guards corporal reminded us. 'And don't drink it all at once. Remember, you've got to toast their Majesties.'

After a while standing there admiring the glistening chandeliers, the muted conversation in the room ceased as a small – smaller than I'd imagined – lady appeared in the large doorway. She wore a long white gown with what looked, from where I stood, like a bright light in her dark brown hair. I soon corrected my thoughts; it's not a light, you idiot, they're diamonds – loads of them, sucking every ounce of light available to shine like, well, diamonds! Following a lot of bowing and general sucking up, Her Majesty and her entourage headed in our direction. A lot of senior officers surrounded her; red tunics, covered in gold braid, seemed to be everywhere. Her husband, the Duke of Edinburgh – or Philip, as I like to think of him – appeared to be joking around with all he met. It certainly seemed to lighten the atmosphere. When our turn came around, I can remember I was starving. I hoped my tummy wouldn't start rumbling as I tried to control the now shaking glass in my left hand. If there was somewhere to put it, I would have, but I couldn't see anywhere so I had to stick with it.

When the Queen finally stood in front of us, she reminded me of my mum; about the same height, under 5ft I reckoned. She studied the painting while listening to her aide explaining what it was and who it was from. I'd been advised that if the Queen talks to you, bow and address her as 'Mam', as in Pam. Well, I wasn't going to forget that, was I? I just concentrated on calling her Mam, not Pam.

'You're from the Junior Guardsman's Wing at The Guards Depot, are you?' she asked, as her husband stood behind, scrutinizing us.

'Yes, Mam,' we both replied at what seemed to be the same time.

'How are you enjoying it?' Prince Philip asked. Shit, I suddenly thought; they'd told us how to address the Queen, but not the Duke.

'Er yes, sir, very much,' I replied in a subservient manner, not knowing if I'd messed up or not.

'Very good,' he continued. 'What regiment?'

'The Life Guards, sir.' I figured I'd got away with the 'sir' thing once, so I might as well continue with it – a shit or bust situation, I guess!

'The painting's wonderful,' the Queen chipped in. 'Do you like it?' she continued.

'Yes, Mam. It's very nice.' What else could I say? I'd only just seen the painting and hadn't even studied it closely. What I had noticed, though, was it was surrounded by what seemed more grand paintings in the room that fair dwarfed this one. Maybe she'll hang it in the loo, I thought. That's what posh people do, isn't it? I gripped my half-empty glass with both hands now as I tried to get rid of an image of our Queen in her downstairs toilet, with a nail between her teeth and a hammer in one hand, the painting in the other, contemplating where she could hang it. The painting is not the only thing that will be hanging, I thought, if you don't get these crazy images out of your mind. I watched them move onto the next victims/guests before looking and feeling a bit more relaxed.

After toasting the anniversary couple before they left, some food was brought round. Not much – a few fancy sandwiches and strange sausage roll-type things that I later discovered were vol au vents.

'Don't worry, lads,' one of the senior guys said as we made our way back down the staircase. 'We'll stop and get some scoff at a garage on the way back.'

It was two o'clock in the afternoon when we pulled out onto The Mall and made our way towards Admiralty Arch – another piece of top information from our self-proclaimed guide. In a minute, he continued, if we looked to our right, we would see the Piccadilly Cowboys on guard at Whitehall. Sitting up in my seat at the back of the bus, I studied the view through the window as we slowly made our way down this grand road. The further we travelled, the grander they seemed to become. Then, on the right, there they were. I recognized instantly which guard was on; the combination of red, silver and the white plumes told me it was the Life Guards. The few seconds during which I saw them had convinced me that this was what I wanted. I was 16, that funny, cocky age; a bit arrogant, I fear, but the excitement that flowed through me was palpable. We did indeed stop at a garage on the way back to Pirbright. A can of Coke – opened with the can opener that was tied to a piece of string by the till – and a Mars bar saw me happy for the rest of the journey into deepest, darkest Surrey.

'Well, how did it go?' Quiff asked as I carefully hung my one and only suit in my locker. I'd get Pam to take it back the next time she came up.

'Yeah, it was alright. Saw our lot on guard as we drove back. It was really cool.'

'Don't forget, we've got hobbies tonight down at the education centre.'

'Remind me again, what have we signed up for this time?'

'Marquetry.'

Marquetry – what's marquetery when it's at home?'

'Marquetry is the art and craft of applying pieces of wood veneer to a structure to form decorative patterns or designs.'

'Bollocks! How did you know that?' I sighed, as I tied my DMS boots up before scoff.

On the way to the cookhouse, we both agreed it might be a laugh. There were so many hobbies offered in the wing; like I've said before, not much time to dwell on any troubles you might have.

As we walked/marched back to Inkerman block, we noticed Donkey Mayor on his way home to his married quarters.

'Just the boys I wanted to see. How did you get on today, young Wol?' he asked me.

'Great, Corporal. It was a real eye-opener.'

'Good. Right, next week I want you to do Orderly NCO, okay?'

'Er, okay, Corporal. When do I start?'

'Monday to Sunday. Come over to my office in the morning and I'll run you through it.'

'Understood. Thanks, Corporal. See you in the morning.'

'Wow, not so fast,' he continued. 'Do you know the stock car club I run? Do you want to join and help?'

'I don't mind. What about you, Quiff?' I asked.

'Yeah, I'm up for it. When is it?'

'Friday evenings to get the car ready, then racing on Saturday night – Aldershot stadium normally. The car's kept at the garages behind the MT building. Seven o'clock sharp.'

Marquetry was harder than it looked. We were all given brand-new kits by our civvy teacher and shown what to do. I couldn't help, as much as I tried, but to stick my tongue out as I cut around the pencil line I'd made on my first piece of veneer. I hunched over my work in the clear knowledge that my tongue wouldn't stop mimicking what my hands were doing.

'Put your tongue away, dickhead,' Quiff helpfully advised.

'I can't. I can't stop it; my dad's the same.'

What with being sat in the minibus most of the day and then having to concentrate so much on the marquetry thing, by the time I got back to my bed space I was knackered. I had just finished getting my kit ready for the morning when the big double doors swung open. It was Stevo – Ian Stevens. He looked different in some way as he made his way towards my bed space. His fat, rosy-cheeked face was filled with a big grin.

'Alright, mate. You look happy. What's going on?'

I hadn't noticed when he came in, but he was holding his right hand over his left wrist.

'What's up with your arm? Have you hurt it? Have you got sick leave or something?'

Before I'd finished my observations, he lifted his hand away and revealed a big brass and leather wristband with four inverted stripes topped with a crown, brass with a red felt background, indicating he had been promoted to SQMC (Squadron Quartermaster Corporal).

'Aw, well done mate. That's brilliant – I'm chuffed for you.'

'Not just me,' he whispered as he moved closer to my ear 'I've heard – no, been told – that you're being made up to full three-bar as well, but keep it to yourself and act surprised when you're told, alright?'

'Okay, will do.' I glanced at my open locker door and noticed the three chevrons and cloth crown that was stitched onto my two-dress arm. If Stevo was correct, I'd soon be replacing the cloth crown with a red-backed brass one, the main thing that distinguished a lance three-bar from a full three-bar. It had been one hell of a day, I thought, as I crawled in between the crisp white sheets and soon drifted off to sleep.

'Here's your office for next week.' Donkey was showing me a small room in the Junior Guardsman's Wing admin block, from where I would be working as Orderly NCO next week. Orderly dogs, as it was known, had many tasks, so many in fact you were taken off all other duties for the seven days you were on it. The main one, I suppose, was dealing with the mail. Most junior soldiers – well most soldiers – depended on it. I say 'most', but there were some who never had any mail; nothing at all for term after term. Heaven knows what their home life was like!

It was explained to me what I had to do, but I didn't really need Donkey to tell me because I'd already gone through it all with Mick Good a couple of days earlier.

'So you start at eight o'clock on Monday,' Donkey said as we finished our tour. 'Oh, and by the way, you've been promoted to full three-bar. You can move into the bunk on your floor; the sports storeman's moving to the empty bunk on the ground floor. All understood then?'

'Yes, Corporal. Er, thanks.' it was a lot to take in. My head was all over the place as I made my way back to the block. My ambition when I joined, even though I started this journey not wanting to be here, was to embrace it and try to emulate my elder brother, Tony, who had joined the Junior Leaders Regiment. He had passed out as Junior RSM (Regimental Sergeant

Major) at Bovington, where he went on to get his commission to become an officer in the Royal Tank Regiment. It is quite a story, one that I'll come back to later in the book.

Sitting on my bed, I glanced across the highly polished red lino floor of what was now 'my barrack room' to be quite honest, I was feeling pretty pleased with myself. I wouldn't make Junior RSM – I knew that I'd need another term to achieve that. Tony had an extra term on me because he joined younger than I did.

'What's up?' Quiff asked as he bounced into the room. 'NAFFI break. Are you coming?'

Quiff's reaction was better than I expected when I told him on our way to the NAFFI. I was officially in charge of that block now. Ian Stevens was the senior NCO of Inkerman Platoon and looked after the other block. I was his second in command, if you like.

'Can you move downstairs and run that room?' I asked/told Quiff as we sat down with our drinks. 'The bunk's been taken, I'm afraid, but I'm sure you'll sort everything out.'

'Yeah, no problem. If you clear it with Donkey we could do it this afternoon.'

We managed to get Donkey Mayor to let us off PT that afternoon and I began my move into the bunk. The bunk was a small room, about 8ft by 12ft, in the corner of the barrack rooms. As you opened the door, you had a pretty good view of the room. To the left was the cleaning room and toilets. As you went in the room, there was a window on the left, a locker against the wall beside you and a bed against the right-hand wall, with a bedside cabinet beside it. As I looked around, I could see the magnolia walls were a bit taggy. You could see where former occupants had stuck posters to the walls with Sellotape. I'll soon sort that out, I thought, as turned the mattress over before making my bed up. Rank comes with privileges: I didn't need to have a bed block in here, and when we had room inspections – every day by me and every week by the platoon commander – my door stayed shut. Pushing the heavy wooden door into what was now Quiff's domain, he was busy rearranging his new bed space area to how he wanted it. After a bit of a struggle, we managed to shift one of the lockers to form a sort of screen from the others in the room.

'Scoff?' I suggested as I checked my watch. It was four-thirty. The lads would be back from PT in a minute, so we get ahead of the queue.

As I studied myself in the full-length mirror in the foyer of our block, I was happy with my turnout: two-dress trousers, army-issue shoes (highly polished) and two-dress shirt, highly scrubbed collar attached. I wondered for a moment why it was so tight – the front collar stud felt like someone was trying to perform a tracheotomy on me with a blunt pencil. How do I know what a tracheotomy is, I hear you ask. Well, one of the racehorses Pam and I used to look after at Griffin Farm had one. I remember having to clean it out, and if I ever took him hunting, you had to remember to take the plug with you in case you encountered deep water.

By contorting and stretching my neck for a few seconds, everything seemed to settle into place. My tie looked good, as did my heavy-duty jumper. Finally, with one last check of my red and blue stable belt, I was off. Sitting at my desk made me feel quite important. I was studying the laminated card that I was met with as I sat down. First job, it said, was to sort and record the mail. I'd noticed the two canvas mail sacks when I'd arrived. Okay, let's have a look, I thought, as I grappled with the string knot that held the first one shut. This one only contained letters, so wasn't so big. I suppose seventy letters fell out onto the floor as I shook it to within an inch of its life. After I'd collected them into neat piles on the desk, I opened the thick blue ledger that sat on a shelf beside me. It was easy to work out what needed to be done: all I had to do was continue what the last OD had done. The columns were for date, name, number, platoon and whether it was a parcel or both. Taking Mick Good's advice, I first divided the item into platoons, then names and so on, recording them as I went. I was surprised with myself at how well I did. I was sacked from a paper round when I was at school for getting it wrong. I could never understand why, as they were all the same paper, the *Evening Post*.

By mid-morning, the post job was completed. Next on my list it simply said 'daily orders to be delivered'. These said what the Junior Guardsman's Wing were going to doing the following day. In the depot, every wing or company issued daily orders. It allowed the authorities to know who was doing what and when. One of the first destinations where I had to deliver these A4 sheets of paper was the RSM's office, that place of fear I mentioned earlier in this chapter that we had to pass on our way back from the stables. Firstly, I had to go back to my block and change into drill boots (highly spit-and-polished hobnailed boots) and red and blue forage cap. At eleven o'clock precisely, NAFFI break time, I had to knock on the RSM's office door. Inside, I soon discovered, sat three – yes three – of the senior

NCOs in the whole Guards Depot. They were gods; they ruled the place. Even their seniors, commissioned officers, were wary of them. The most senior NCO, the Regimental Sergeant Major, sat at his desk in front of you as you marched in, and to his left sat two Company Sergeant Majors.

Deep breath, I thought, as I faced the door that read 'Regimental Sergeant Major'. As I had come in the front door of the building, I'd made a note of how slippery the highly polished floor was. I obviously didn't take enough notice, though, because after being ordered in and attempting to halt in front of the assembled ensemble, the next thing I knew I was on my back, making haste sliding towards the base of the RSM's desk. My forage cap was somewhere behind me, but I managed to keep hold of my clipboard. Looking up to my right, I could just see the top of one of the CSM's short-cropped hair and his Coldstream forage cap sitting on the desk.

'Are you tired? Do you need to have a rest?' I heard as I desperately tried to gain some purchase on the lino and get to my feet. After what seemed ages, I was standing to attention in front of him, God that is. From the corner of my eye, I noticed the other two desperately supressing a laugh.

'No, sir. Sorry, sir,' I weakly replied as I stood there, not daring to move. The heat my red face was generating could have warmed a small room, I reckoned, as I fought the desire to straighten my dishevelled jumper and belt.

'Well?' the RSM eventually asked.

'Standing orders, sir,' I croaked.

'Where?'

'Where what, sir? I dumbly replied.

'The fucking standing orders, junior corporal of horse, the standing orders!' I could sense that the joke was wearing thin now and it was time for me to leave, so with a still-shaking hand I gave him the sheet of paper, about turned, and as gracefully as I could, retrieved my cap from the floor and departed. Standing outside the office door, trying to sort myself out, I could hear the roars of laughter still coming from within. You twat; you fucking twat, I thought to myself, as I made my way back down Adaire Walk towards my office.

Apart from going arse over tit in the most frightening place in the depot, the day went well. As part of my week, I had to go and check the NAFFI at various times during the evening. I'd read in orders that short-sleeve order would start next week, so when I was doing my rounds I took the opportunity to sweet talk Mick Good and see if he would alter my KF shirt. The longer we served, the more kit we seemed to accumulate. I had managed to blag a couple of spare shirts amongst other things so I could have two tailored in summer order and leave two with long sleeves for winter order. My first trip to the NAFFI was at about seven in the evening. Being a Monday evening, the place was fairly quiet, the usual suspects sitting around Ena as she chatted and did her knitting.

'How did your trip to London go?' she asked as I took a seat beside her, still in two-dress, as were the rules. She gently tapped the brass crown on my arm band. 'Been promoted as well, I see. Well done.'

'Thanks, Ena. The trip was amazing, thanks.'

Because it was such a nice evening, I decided to walk down to the spiders and check out the Sandes Soldiers' Home, or 'Sandies' as we called it. On the way, I could pop in the stables and pat a horse or two's neck. Sandies was a grey corrugated metal-roofed building on Brunswick Road. The spiders' NAFFI, I suppose you could call it. The white railing on the front of the building could do with a coat of paint, I thought, as I climbed the three steps to the rickety entrance doors. Like the NAFFI, it was quiet. Looking at my watch, I concluded that the recruits in the spiders would still be on 'shining parade'. As I walked back through the spiders, it brought back good and bad memories. The mental trauma of being homesick and the fear of what we faced rapidly flooded my senses. Apart from the occasional shouted order escaping from the open windows, all was quiet. It was hard to believe that only a matter of weeks ago, I would be sat in there, legs astride my bed, kit lined up in front of me, cleaning whatever needed cleaning in complete silence, apart from answering questions on regimental history when ordered. Now look at me, I thought. Eight weeks ago, if you'd told me I'd be here, a junior three-bar running my own block, I think I'd have told you to do one!

'Alright. Enjoy your trip this morning?' Quiff greeted me as I stepped into Inkerman's B block.

'Who the fuck told you?' I remonstrated, standing at the bottom of the staircase that led to my room.

'Donkey Mayor. He thought it was brilliant. I think the RSM told him, and it must be all over the camp by now.'

That's just great, I thought, as I sat on my bed. After the day's efforts, I felt knackered, but I still had two more NAFFI patrols to do. I know this next bit will sound bad to most of you, but things were different back in 1973. In the army, for instance, who would have thought in just three years' time that I and seventeen others would be kicked out for no good reason.

Anyway, back then, the army was definitely run on a system of hierarchy. For instance, junior NCOs would have what was referred to as 'a fast black', a servant if you like, a Junior Guardsman who would do those annoying little jobs like making your bed or cleaning your boots. My fast black was a Scots Guard named Stewart. I wouldn't know his first name; we didn't use first names. Anyway, Stewart was a good guy who originated from the Scottish border region. I remember he had a slight hair lip and spoke with a strong Borders accent. I chose him, I'm almost ashamed to say, because his slight disfigurement made him vulnerable, and I was now in a position to stop anything like that from happening. I noticed Stewart had changed my bedding and tidied my bunk up. I heard through the open window the door of block A closing below. A quick look out of the window told me it was Stevo, Ian Stevens. Probably coming up here to take the piss, I thought, as I waited for the inevitable. Before too long, after a bit of commotion outside, my door swung open.

'Still on your arse I see, Wol,' he said as he jumped on my bed and got me in a headlock.

'Fuck off and get off me! I'm not in the mood,' I retaliated, while trying desperately to escape from his ape-like grip.

'Hey, it happens to the best of us,' he continued, 'but not normally in the RSM's office!' Releasing his grip, he lay back on the bed, so his head lent against the wall.

Ian Stevens was a good mate to me. Even though he was a 'dink' (Blue and Royal), he always had my back, as they say. As I write this in 2025, we last spoke on the telephone about a year ago. Sadly, he's no longer with us. Rest in peace, mate.

Looking at the timetable that was stuck to the inside of my locker, I noticed we had company commanders room inspection on Friday. This was a big one on the room inspection scale of things. Before going on my next NAFFI visit, I decided to get my other junior NCOs together in the cleaning room to make our plans.

'Okay, this place has got to be gleaming on Friday morning. You all know I'm orderly dog this week, so a lot of this job will fall on your shoulders. One of you, make sure our problem children – Allison, Jones and Wiggins – are up to speed with their kit and lockers,' I explained as tried desperately to resist the temptation to touch the iron that sat on the bench beside me. Knowing my luck today, it was bound to be hot and I'd make myself look like a right tit for the second time in twenty-four hours.

The NAFFI will be quiet this week, I thought, as I walked towards it. Everyone will be getting ready for the inspection. Friday evening will be busy, unless some of them get re-inspected because their rooms were in shit order. If your room isn't up to standard, the officer will make the room 'show again' that evening. It's not a case of tidying up and having another go, though: the room would have been wrecked by the RSM as he followed the officer around. When you got back to your room, it would look like a bombsite.

By the time Friday came around, the rooms in B block looked good. I'd got my work as orderly dog done ASAP so I could oversee the final, finishing touches before the inspection began. My rounds with daily orders had been rescheduled until the afternoon. Quiff and I were just checking his room – something wasn't right, but neither of us could quite suss it out.

'There's definitely a smell coming from around here. Whose bed space is this?' I asked as I poked around with the bed stick I was carrying.

'Allison's,' Quiff informed me.

'Oh shit! There's something here, isn't there?'

'I reckon so, but where? If we can't find whatever it is, there's going to be one hell of a shit storm coming our way any minute now.'

I knew the inspection was in A block, so I was aware of the predicament we were in. Everyone else were on PT, so it was down to Quiff and I to fix it. I felt like Sherlock Holmes as I stuck my nose into the shelves that contained his neatly folded PT vests. I didn't want to touch anything; it was Allison's locker, after all. So, using my bed stick, I probed behind the pile of shirts. I must have disturbed it, because the smell seemed to explode.

'Fucking hell, mate. Whatever it is, it's behind his PT shirts. Lift them out a minute,' I said as I stood ready with my bed stick to hit anything alive that came to attack us! As Quiff slowly picked the shirts up, the tension was palpable. 'There it is!' I said as I saw a dark woollen-type 'thing' gently steaming in the back of the shelf. Quiff stood beside me, holding the stack of shirts like he was about to deliver them to a guest in a hotel as I managed to hook this 'thing' onto my trusty stick.

'Got it,' I said as I carefully extracted what we now identified as a sock from the locker. It was an army-issue green woollen sock that clearly hadn't been washed – ever probably. It actually had what looked like a sole attached to it, such was the state of it. 'Put the kit back and open the window,' I told Quiff as I gingerly made my way across the room. 'We're going to have to sort that grotty little shit, mate,' I added with a sense of anger and relief. I made my way back up to my room to await the entourage turning up.

Once again, for the last time while being orderly dog, I found myself standing outside the RSM's office door. I knew what to expect now. He would be at his desk, his Grenadiers forage cap on the table beside him, accompanied by his immaculately polished pace stick. Behind him, beyond the window, lay the parade ground, but it was Friday afternoon so it would be empty. To my horror, as I raised my hand to knock on the door, it opened, and in front of me stood the imposing figure of one of the Company Sergeant Majors. These characters had a particular repertoire of one-liners, shall we say. I'm sure they had a secret society where they would get together to compare insults. They came – normally but not exclusively – during drill. It could happen anywhere: you could be innocently walking back from church parade, when, from nowhere, you'd hear, 'If you don't start marching, I'll stick my boot so far up your arse you'll be able to see it every time you clean your teeth!' Other favourites included, 'If you don't swing your arm to the shoulder, I'll rip it off and hit you with the soggy end', 'Christ, my granny could do better than that and she's been dead for twenty fucking years' or 'I'm going to shit in a box and send it to your parents for sending me theirs!'

Anyway, there I was, the CSM looking at me like he'd just stood in something nasty, when he turned and announced to the room – which, incidentally, had more people in than normal because, it being Saturday tomorrow, they were planning the regular Saturday morning drill parade: 'Gentlemen, look who's turned up. It's our favourite junior orderly dog. I think he's come to entertain us again.'

Shit, I thought, as he moved his massive frame to one side to let me in. I could see the RSM behind his desk, unusually – very unusually – smiling.

'Don't be shy, Junior Corporal of Horse, come on in,' he said, as I stood there quietly shitting myself.

I took a deep breath and marched straight into the lion's den. I managed to stay on my feet this time, but now I couldn't remove the sheet of paper that contained tomorrow's daily orders from my clipboard. The first one ripped, and I couldn't imagine him pinning a taggy ripped piece of paper to his neatly arranged noticeboard. In my mind, minutes passed as I fumbled about for another one, fully aware of the many critical eyes that were watching me, but eventually I was able to hand one to him.

'Well done, son. You've had a tough week, but you've kept your composure under pressure. Well done,' he said as he took the paper from me. 'Now fuck off and bother someone else.'

I did so – willingly. I was off like a whippet down towards the spiders for my next delivery.

'So, inspection was okay,' I confirmed with Quiff as we sat on my bed. 'What are we going to do about Allison? He could have dropped us right in the shit.'

'I know,' Quiff agreed. 'The whole room is pissed off with him. Trouble is, I don't think he can help it. The lads in the room reckon he should have a regimental bath.'

A regimental bath, or 'reggie bath' as they were known, consisted of being dumped naked into a bath and then scrubbed with a broom or with whatever came to hand – washing powder normally – until clean. This unfortunately ended up with the victim being scrubbed red raw by the sharp bristles of the broom. If you couldn't get a broom, a floor scrubbing brush would suffice. As we descended the stairs to Quiff's room, we were joined by most of the lads in my room. News travels fast – everyone seemed to enjoy retribution. I felt a twinge of sorrow for Allison as I walked towards his bed.

'Allison, you're a grot,' I started 'If Corporal Friend and I hadn't found your minging sock this morning, you know what we'd be doing now, don't you?'

'Yeth, Sergeant,' came his lispy reply.

'I'm not a fucking sergeant! I'm Corporal of Horses to you, wanker!'

'Sorry, Corporal of Horth,' he quietly replied. He knew what was coming; there was no way of avoiding it.

'Reggie bath!' I shouted to the assembled crowd, as Allison disappeared towards the washroom and his fate.

* * *

I think everyone enjoyed their time at Inkerman. That part of the Junior Guardsman's Wing was great fun. I played rugby for the wing team, the Gladiators, on a weekly basis during the season, while Quiff, a few others and I got to go to Aldershot stadium most Saturdays to help Donkey Mayor with the stock car racing. Pam would drive up as many Saturdays as she could, or I could persuade her. We had learnt that a few of us would 'pass out' of the Junior Guardsman's Wing into the proper army on horseback. I would ride my regular mount, Landfall, along with Quiff, Stinch and Bamby Walton, to name but a few. We had six weeks left in the junior army. Our next challenge was battle camp at a place called Thetford in Quiff's home county of Suffolk.

It was a long journey, even in a coach. The sun streamed through the windows as we made our way across the flat countryside towards Thetford Forest. I couldn't quite believe how long we were travelling along the roads that cut through the forest, the darkness of the pine trees hiding whatever might be beyond. Eventually we were crawling up a gravel track towards an open area in the middle of the forest. To our left was a line of large green tents, some with their sides rolled up to reveal the makeshift cookhouse and eating area. Ahead was a big lake with a couple of army green boats pulled up on the bank beside it.

Stiff from the journey, I climbed down from the coach. It was five o'clock as I stretched my arms out and looked around. I could see Donkey Mayor dressed in combats standing by a tent about 50 metres away, holding his right hand above his head. From a distance, it looked like he was dropping a large spider onto the top of his beret, but everyone knew what he meant – it was the military signal for 'get your arses over here'. He pulled Stevo and I to one side and briefed us which tent we were in and where the cookhouse was, etc.

'Okay, listen-in B block,' I announced. 'Tent twelve is for my room and tent eleven is for Corporal Friend's room. Understood?'

A muffled 'Yes, Corporal' came back as everyone grabbed their kit and started to de-camp into their allocated tents. 'Scoff's in that tent over there in half an hour. Don't forget your mugs and KFS's [knife, fork and spoon].'

As I entered tent twelve, the smell of canvas hit me, reminding me of camping holidays at Beer in Devon when I was younger. We went every year; the last time we went it seemed to rain all week, and my mum rushed into the tent to avoid the weather and fell on her arse, sliding from one end of the tent to the other. We never went again– I often wondered why!

'Open the flaps at the end,' I ordered, as I kicked some 'neckie' Junior Guardsman off the best bed in the room. 'Stewart, you're in the bed beside me,' I shouted over to my 'little helper'. Where the hell's my scoff rods (knife, fork and spoon), I thought, as I delved into every corner of my backpack. Why are they always in the last place you look? Eventually finding them, I grabbed my mug and adjusted my beret before making my way to the cookhouse.

We were here for ten days. Unlike outward bound or camping on Salisbury Plain, this was battle camp. For three of the ten days, we would be dug in somewhere out there in that big dark forest. A chill ran down my spine just at the thought of it. I joined the army to sit on a horse in fancy kit in London, not to live in a hole in the ground somewhere in Suffolk. Scoff was as expected, some sort of concoction thrown together by the army slop jockey chef, who was tasked to make something nutriticus with the mountain of compo rations that were stacked in the tent next door.

'Your shit will be like bricks after ten days of this crap!' I helpfully mentioned to Quiff and Stevo as they began delving into their first course. If I hadn't been so hungry I would have given it a miss, but I had to eat something. The spotted dick, out of a tin, was about the best bit, so long as you didn't have the custard, that is – that looked like something cur dog, Bonzo, had bought up.

That evening we were tasked with getting the two boats we'd spotted earlier from one side of the lake to the other and back again; a sort of relay race, I suppose. The boats were oblong-shaped alloy or metal small landing craft. If I remember correctly, you could fit about fifteen men in them at a push. There wasn't a bow or a stern to speak of, and the only method of steering was with one of the oars at the back. They were olive green originally, but a lot of the paint had been scraped away, knocked off by years of wear. The front end ('bow') was slightly narrower than the back ('stern'), but both were effectively flat, which made them quite hard work to row. They didn't exactly cut through the water. Quiff's team of ten had made their way to the other side of the lake with their opposing team to await us somehow getting across there and then swapping over. My lifejacket was still damp, and it stunk as I fiddled around trying to tie a bow in the soggy cotton tape that went around the waist. They were so bulky it made manoeuvring the short oars difficult. As captain of my ship, I decided to take charge and steer. I wish I hadn't – it was harder than I thought. I had a plan which I'd discussed with my team before we set off.

'It's all about teamwork,' I explained. 'Four on each side and row like fuck!' was the best advice I could come up with. We were all dressed alike – blue gym shorts and red tee-shirts – the sun was slowly sinking in the west as Donkey dropped his hand to signal the off. After crashing into the other boat, and a few stray battles with each other's oars, we managed to break free. The boat didn't actually need much steering, so I decided to move to the front to retrieve a mooring rope that was dragging in the water and annoying me. It didn't feel the most stable thing as I slowly moved forward. The noise was deafening, both from the bank and from the boat, as we ploughed through the lake. If we weren't wet when we started, most of us were now. The whole thing had gone to shit; there was more splashing of our competitors than rowing.

'Row, row, B block!' I shouted as we got to about halfway. A day's worth of pent-up energy sat on a coach was all being channelled into this now.

'Row straight for the bank,' I ordered as we closed in on our awaiting team. The bank was more of a beach, with gravelly sand, and as we got there the boat kept going. I thought for a minute it wasn't going to stop. Quiff and his team ended up running backwards rather than forwards to avoid us. The trouble was, we now had to get the bloody thing back in the water. There was nothing for it but for my team to wade in to push it back out. I shouted to Quiff not to waste time trying to turn it around, but to go back over the lake backwards. I could see the other lot trying to turn around and it looked like a disaster. As my team squelched back to the start, we were well in the lead, Quiff standing in the middle of the boat like he riding a skateboard.

'Don't walk too fast, lads,' I reminded my team as we made our way around the lake. 'We'll only get roped into dragging it out if we get there too quick.'

By the time we were finished it was getting dark. One of the instructors was lighting a fire in a massive pit in the middle of the grassed area. Pulling on my heavy-duty jumper, I heard the firm 'clunk' of the tea urn being lifted onto one of the trestle tables. Just what I need, I thought, as I grabbed my mug and made my way over there.

'Have you seen the shitter?' Quiff asked as I joined him in the queue.

'No. Where is it?'

'In the woods over there. I won't explain it; just go and see before it gets too dark.'

I thus ventured from the dusky skies of the camping area into the forest. Unexpectedly, without much warning, my stomach started rumbling. It was dark – well, it was dark in there. The combination of dry mud and fallen leaves made my still damp daps squeak as I walked. Where's this famous shitter, I thought, as I wandered in the direction Quiff had given me. Suddenly, I saw a figure in front of me.

'Alright, Corporal Wol,' I heard a voice say. 'Looking for the shitter? It's over there – just follow the flies!'

'Oh thanks,' I weakly replied as I walked – bum cheeks clamped closely together – towards my destination. I thought these compo rations were designed to bung you up, not do the opposite. My destination was in sight now, and I could indeed see the flies. My eyes had now adjusted to the dark, but when I saw the shitter I wished they hadn't. Between two trees, about 5ft apart, someone had dug a trench about 2ft wide and 4ft deep. I say 4ft deep, but I couldn't see the bottom, although I could just make out some bog paper down there. That someone who had dug the trench presumably made the seating arrangements as well. I can only describe it thus: a branch of another tree had been tied/secured between the trees, creating what looked in the now-dark forest like a swing between the two trees. It was no good. However, I was desperate now. It was a shit or bust situation, I'm afraid! I'm not the tallest of blokes, and I'm sure the person who carefully measured this thing out didn't have me in mind. I kicked off my shorts and shreddies (army underwear) as I continued to jog on the spot in desperation. There's only one option, I thought, as I placed my naked arse on the branch. Holding tightly onto one of the support ropes – I couldn't reach the other one – I shuffled backwards so both 'exit points' were over the branch. Why do humans piss and shit at the same time? Dogs don't, horses don't. That was the only thing I could think as, with the tiniest of pushes, the world seemed to fall out of my bottom. A palpable sense of relief swept over me when I suddenly remembered I didn't have any toilet paper. I saw a half-used roll hanging on a piece of string at the other end of the branch. How am I going to get that, I thought, as I attempted to reach out for it. I wasn't prepared to let go of the rope I was clinging onto, but I couldn't reach the other one. Should I try to shuffle along the branch? What if I fell in and broke something like an arm? Imagine being wheeled into hospital with a broken arm, covered in shit. My head was spinning with these thoughts while I was suspended over a trench full of human excrement and couldn't get off the bloody branch that was holding me prisoner.

'There you are,' I heard a voice from the darkness. It was a familiar voice; that heavy Scots accent told me it was 'fast black', Stewart. 'Get that bog paper please, mate,' I sort of pleaded with him. He did as ordered; he always did. 'Now pass it to me and turn around while I sort myself out.' When I'd finished 'sorting myself out', I asked him the most embarrassing thing that I've ever asked anyone. I'm fully aware that as you get older, life can be cruel and your body becomes increasingly prone to embarrassing you. But I was only 17, a junior corporal of horse. I held a position of power and responsibility, and I was about to hold my hand out to one of my subordinates to ask him to help me off the makeshift shitter in the middle of a dark forest in Suffolk that I was stuck on!

For days afterwards, I still couldn't look Stewart in the eye. Needless to say, I didn't use that contraption again. Instead, I chose the old military method, which was to wander off into the forest with your spade and some paper, dig a hole, do your business and fill it in before returning to your duties.

Despite my unfortunate incident in the forest, our time at Thetford battle camp was going well. The next challenge was spending a couple of nights in the trenches. Yes, you read it correctly – in the trenches. The instructor staff briefed the senior NCOs on what we had to do, whether we were defenders of attackers. I and my squad ended up as defenders. I had a map reference showing the area we had to defend. There was an instructor with us, so we weren't totally on our own. It was Tuesday morning when we set off on the 5-mile march in full combat kit, carrying everything we needed for the next two days. It was the height of summer and our kit was heavy and cumbersome. We had been issued with a field radio. It was the same size as the bergens we were carrying with all our kit in. It was so big that I needed a good strong guy to carry it. Now who might that be, I hear you ask. Yes, you're right – Stewart was that man. As usual, he didn't let me down. A lot of the march was on the sandy tracks that ran through this huge forest. I could tell from studying the OS map we'd been issued with that we were actually zigzagging around the general vicinity, picking up reference tags off trees or gateposts as we went. I marched behind or beside my radio operator, Stewart, carefully avoiding the 4ft-long aerial that protruded from the top of the pack. If it caught a branch or something, it swished around, desperately trying to take yours or somebody else's eye out. About two hours later, sweating now in our full combat kit, we arrived at the edge of the forest. Our instructor informed us that we had to 'dig in' – dig trenches, that is – and defend the forest that surrounded us. Okay, I thought, I'm the senior junior soldier here, so I took charge. Looking out over the grassy area in front of us, I concluded that if – no, when – we were attacked, they would come from that direction. They wouldn't come from behind – through the forest. Although the trees offered better cover, the amount of dead branches and bushes on the forest floor would make their progress not only slow but noisy. I made my decision and radioed my position, as ordered, to Donkey Mayor back at camp. Although old, the radio worked well. It had a receiver like the telephone we had at home, but army green. It sounded like Donkey was just around the corner. I later found out that he actually was; we were only about half a mile from our camp, as it turned out.

Following a quick break, we – I mean they – set to digging the trenches. They had to be 12ft long, 3ft wide and 6ft deep, and one end had to be covered. 'So we – you – have got to find something to make that happen,' I kindly informed them. Sitting at the base of a tall pine tree, having a much-deserved cigarette, I noticed something grey in the brambles not too far away. With our temporary roof in mind, I went to investigate. It was two sheets of corrugated iron, which looked like they'd just been chucked in there. They'd been left there for a reason, to test our powers of observation and resourcefulness.

'Stewart!' I shouted, at the same time doing that spider thing to indicate for him to come to me. Red-faced, with his KF shirt showing signs of sweat, he doubled over to me. 'If we can get these sheets of corrugated iron over to the trenches, we can use them for the roofs on both trenches,' I explained as I began trying to flatten the brambles with my boots. It soon became obvious that all the ingredients we needed to defend this area were already here.

It was late afternoon by the time we were somewhere near being able to defend ourselves. 'Right, listen in,' I announced. 'We'll have some scoff now before we stand-to at dusk.' Dusk and dawn were the two most likely times we were going to be attacked, so that's when we would all be in our trenches, prepared. Talking of trenches, the lads had done well, all things considered, digging a hole 12 by 3 by 6 with a foldaway spade that was only 2ft long. As I descended the steps that had been cut out at one end of the trench, the first thing I noticed was a nice cosy sleeping area at the other end, where they had used the corrugated iron I'd found to form a roof. As I turned to scan the front ground we were to defend, I came across my first problem. The trench was 6ft deep as ordered, and I was 5ft 7½in – don't forget the half, it's important to me! When I attempted, even on tiptoe, to check my area of view, all I could see was pine needles and the blue-grey sky in the distance. Standing there contemplating my dilemma, a large clod of earth landed in the trench behind me.

'What the fuck?' I shouted as I turned so quick my tin pot helmet nearly fell off.

'Stand on that, Corp,' my old mate from the spiders, Mara, explained. 'Push it up against the front of the wall and stand on it.' I did as suggested, and to my surprise it worked – I could see all that I needed to see.

'Pass me my rifle,' I ordered Mara, who looked so tall from where I was standing that his blonde head seemed to be the same height as the pine trees that surrounded us.

I took my place on my newly acquired 'tump' and swept my rifle across the horizon. That's good, I thought, so long as I don't have to move anywhere during the heat of battle. Anyway, it would do for now. I was starving; we needed rations. There was quite a breeze blowing through the trees as I tried to light my portable cooker to heat my compo dinner. Compo stoves were a rectangular green metal tin thing, 6 or 7in long by about 4in wide. They fitted neatly in your mess tins, two rectangular alloy vessels slightly bigger than your cooker. Water was in short supply. I'd studied the map earlier to see if I could locate any streams or water sources in the vicinity, but nothing was obvious. As I opened the cooker, two rows of what looked like teeth appeared to reveal the block of white petrol-smelling stuff, like a large firelighter basically. My legs were already getting stiff through crouching over my mini cookhouse. Looking around, I spotted an old log. That will do, I thought, and went to get it. You know when you think you see something but you're not sure whether you did or not? Well I found myself in that position as I crouched to pick up the log. I was sure I'd seen something out there in amongst the mass of trees, I stayed crouched for a few seconds, scanning the scene around me. I could hear my lads behind me, busying themselves cooking their scoff. Then I saw it, but there was also another movement. Was it one of our instructors? They had said they'd be in the area. Or was it the enemy, coming from completely the wrong direction at completely the wrong time? Like a dog on high alert, my hackles were up. Forgetting the log, still crouched down, I backed away to the trenches.

'Stand-to,' I whispered, getting my squad's attention as quietly as I could. 'Stop what you're doing, get your weapons and get in your trench. Potential attack spotted moving from the west.'

The late afternoon sun breaking through the trees to the west was blinding. I tried to tip my helmet as forward as I could to shade my eyes, but all that did was to cause the hessian strips of camouflage attached to it to completely obscure my vision. All the soldiers in my trench were at the front of the trench; I was at the back, perched on my own personal tump.

'Right, potential enemy spotted at eleven o'clock, 500 metres away,' I informed my men as they scanned the area in front of them. All I could hear was the freshening breeze blowing through the trees. Time seemed to stand still; a minute felt like an hour. Then suddenly, from out of nowhere, I felt a tap on the top of my helmet. I don't mind admitting, I nearly shit myself!

'Alright, lads.'

'Behind you!' I managed to blurt out before I nearly fell off my tump, still not managing to turn myself. I was now confronted with seven SLRs pointing in my direction. Reading the room, as they say, I noticed there was no sense of alarm or fear on any of their faces as they all looked up out the trench behind me. Mara smiled and nodded in the direction of what was behind me. As I put my rifle down, I turned, dreading what I might be met with. Oh for fucks' sake, I thought, as I looked up at the large, imposing figure that stood above me. It was Donkey Mayor.

'What are you aiming that way for?' he sarcastically asked.

'Well,' I started, thinking I've got to get in here quickly if I'm to bluff my way out of this one. 'While I was recceing the forest to our west, I noticed movement in the distance, so I ordered my squad to stand-to in case of attack.'

'Why, then,' Donkey went on, 'didn't you cover the whole area? You've got sixteen men in two trenches – use them affectively.'

Good point, I reluctantly thought to myself, as I agreed with his observations. I was going to do a 'yeah but' sort of retort, but thought better of it.

'Anyway, you were correct. There was movement over there; it was me. Trouble is, you were so preoccupied with one thing, you forgot the others. Anyway, if two of you will accompany me to the Land Rover, I've bought you fresh water supplies.'

'Yes, Corporal. Thanks, Corporal,' I weakly replied, indicating to Mara and Stewart to go and help.

I felt a right twat as I sat on my new seating arrangement, my tin pot helmet! I scraped the gunge that was called 'corn beef hash' out of my compo tin into my now hot mess tin; I knew it was hot because I'd just burnt my hand when I touched the folding wire handle. As it dropped into the tin, it immediately started to steam as it made its way towards every corner. To be fair, it smelt alright as it heated up. My next course – or tin – was spotted dick. Contemplating the prospect of washing two mess tins rather than one, I decided to eat my dessert directly from the tin. We didn't have ring-pull cans in those days, but somewhere in your compo rations should be a small tin opener; the trick was to save a spare in your webbing somewhere, so you always had one to hand. Time was getting on now as I sipped my coffee and contemplated the long night that faced us. I would divide my trenches into stags (sentry duties) – two hours on and two hours off. We would all stand-to at dusk and dawn, as we'd been briefed, and would all wear full combats and webbing while on stag. We each had four magazines of 7.62mm blank rounds and I had placed one ammo box of spares in each trench.

It's a weird thing how the light at dusk plays tricks on your eyes. The sun had completely dropped now and a light mist was rising from the grassy area in front of us. This was stressful, I thought, as I stared intently into the distance. My thoughts drifted to what it must have been like during the war, with real bullets and real enemies for days –sometimes weeks – on end. It didn't bear thinking about. When it was fully dark, we stood down, leaving the sentries on stag to keep a lookout.

'Can we have a smoke now, Corporal?' two of my guys asked. To be honest, I wanted one myself, so before allowing them to sit in the bottom of the trench, I thought I'd tell the story of the 'third light' superstition that came from trench warfare in the First World War.

'Before you light your fags, has anybody heard about the third light theory?'

'No, Corporal,' came the slightly irritated reply.

'Well, during the First World War, three Tommies stood in their trench on a night stag. One of them handed the tabs around. All was quiet. The first one lit his cigarette, and a German sniper spotted the flash of light in the night sky. The second Tommy lit his, and the sniper took aim. Finally, the third soldier lit his and "bang", head blown off. The moral being don't give our, albeit pretend, enemy the opportunity to see us. Hence, sit in the bottom of the trench.' With that, I nicked a fag from Stewart's open packet, slid down into the bottom of our trench and sat on my tump.

I'd carefully worked out the stag rotation so everyone had equal time off. From eleven o'clock until four o'clock there would be two of us on stag, while the other curled up in the bottom of the trench in the covered area. A starry sky filled the horizon as I scanned the danger area. An owl hooted somewhere in the forest behind me, but apart from the occasional rustles in the trees, all was peaceful. It was two o'clock when I kicked and nudged the next two into life for their turn.

'Remember, wake us up at four,' I reminded Mara as I struggled into the still-warm sleeping bag. Whose idea was it to join the army, I thought, as I closed my eyes. Not mine, I reassured myself. If I'd had my way, I'd be a couple of hundred miles away in my comfortable bed. I'm sure that I'd just drifted off when a load bang woke me. I looked out of the top of my sleeping bag to the trench beyond; Mara was looking into the distance ahead of him, then across to where we were.

'What's happening?' I shouted.

'Attack – we're under a fucking attack!' I wondered how I could see the panicked look on his face, then quickly realized it was the flare that was illuminating the sky above us.

'Stand-to!' I shouted as I tried to free myself from the vice-like grip of my sleeping bag. To say it was chaos would be an understatement. All hell had let loose, with thunder flashes exploding everywhere. As I looked out from my position on my tump, I tried to make sense of it all: I couldn't see anyone advancing on us, but I knew they were somewhere. Like seventeen rabbits in the headlights, I ordered my guys to stay down and wait. For a second it went quiet. Dawn was breaking, and the more we scanned the horizon the more we thought we saw. A crack, followed by many more cracks, stung my ears, and I desperately tried to locate where they were coming from. Remember, I told myself, they're attacking us, we're not attacking them, so we must have the advantage – stay quiet and keep you heads down. After what seemed like an eternity, we could make out the shapes of our enemy in the distance. I reckoned they were about a hundred metres away and moving slowly forward. I was still convinced they hadn't yet located us, so much so I decided to climb out of my trench and crawl to the other trench to inform them of my plan. My second in command, Junior Lance Sergeant Warren, was surprised by my presence as I slid quietly into his trench.

'Keep quiet and keep you heads down until they're nearly on top of us, then let them have it,' I whispered. Adrenaline coursed through my body as I stood on the bottom step of the trench, surveying the enemy. 'If we start firing, you start as well,' I said as I began my crawl back to my trench. I'd turned our 'coms' off earlier; the whistling and screeching of them would give our position away in no time at all. The sun was beginning to rise to our front, which was a big advantage to us as it silhouetted our enemy as they crept forward. They've left it too late, I thought; it's too light now. We could pick them off at random if we wanted to, but still I waited. As I stood on my tump, considering the situation, Stewart tapped me on the shoulder – how I didn't scream like a girl I don't know.

'You twat!' I remonstrated. 'What do you want?'

'Why don't we take them from the side?' he suggested, pointing to his left. 'We could surround them.'

'Good thinking, but I've got a better idea. Go and get four from the other trench and then take cover in the trees behind us. I'll join you shortly.'

Our enemy had taken cover now. We knew where they were; I just had to put my plan into action. I would take another two from my trench and join the five behind us in the forest, taking up position in amongst the trees. When the opposition inevitably attacked the trenches, we would take them by surprise from our new position. Before mustering my two from my position, I grabbed four thunder flashes from the ammo box and distributed them amongst the other two. It was no good me throwing them – I was, and still am, useless at throwing anything like that. I played squash to quite a high standard and played rugby for the junior regiment, but give me a ball – a cricket ball or something – no chance!

I could see from my new position in amongst the trees that they'd sussed out our trenches and were taking up their positions. Whoever was leading them – Quiff probably, but I couldn't make faces out because of the cam cream we were all wearing – positioned his GPMG at twelve o'clock as I looked at it, behind a mound of reedy-type grass. The rest of them were crawling and sliding through the dewy grass like lambs to the slaughter. You're going to lose this one, Quiff, I thought as I gave the command for the thunder flashes to be thrown. Within a couple of seconds, all hell was let loose. I could see the machine gunner scrambling to his feet and trying to run away as a nearby thunder flash exploded. The oncoming soldiers were now disappearing into the smoke created by all the munitions being set off. We were winning, we were in control, I thought, as I rolled on my side to extract a full magazine from my webbing. I felt someone kick the bottom of my boot. Rolling further over, it was him again, Donkey Mayor; this time he was waving a red range flag and making a hand movement like he was trying to slit his own throat. As the noise slowly ceased, I got to my feet. I didn't know whether I was going to get a bollocking or not.

'Well done, Wallington's squad,' he announced. 'You've won that battle, but you haven't won the war yet. I want you all to gather round on the grass area for a debrief.'

Everyone looked knackered as we sat in a large circle listening to the ins and outs of our actions. The highlight was the tea urn that appeared out of the back of Donkey's Landy before the debrief. I felt a little smug as I sat on the grass, listening to one of our instructors explaining why we shouldn't have left our trenches. I felt like saying, 'We won didn't we? I thought we were supposed to use our initiative?' But I decided to keep my thoughts to myself; to be honest, I was too tired to care.

Our time in the trenches finished that night when we had to ambush a patrol on a narrow track than ran through the forest close by. After a recce that afternoon, I was pretty confident about where I would set my trap. After supper, as I tried in vain to eat my hard tack biscuit, I explained my plan. Clearing my throat and taking a gulp of water to try to get the biscuit on its way to my stomach, I assembled my fifteen men in a circle around me. Using a broken branch, I drew out our ambush point – it was on a bit of higher ground that surrounded the track, there was plenty of tree cover and we would have the advantage of attacking from above. There wasn't a lot of opportunity for them to take cover, and if they tried scrabbling up the bank, we'd be waiting for them. I explained that this was going to look completely different in the darkness of the night when we set up the ambush, so they should be quite clear about their role.

'Any questions?' I asked as, for some strange reason, I tucked the branch under my left arm as if was a pace stick or something. The junior NCOs had a briefing from Donkey and the instructors during the afternoon before the night exercises. One thing we had to do was to make our camp good before we moved to set up our ambush, which meant filling in our trenches and making the whole area look as if we hadn't ever been there. When the attack had been made, we would have to navigate our way back to the Thetford base, so night navigation would be a significant test as well as the remaining threat of attack. As the night moved in, I sat against my favourite tree and lit a cigarette. My thoughts turned to, amongst other things, how soon we would be passing out of the junior army and becoming, if we passed, proper soldiers? Life would definitely change. We'd just be troopers again, and for a while we would also be recruits again. Heaven knows why. We'd spent the last two years learning the skills needed to become a fully trained soldier – weapon skills, drill and discipline were all nailed down. So why on earth did we have to do it again? I suppose that's the military for you.

'All done,' I heard Mara say. 'All done, what?' I replied. 'All done, Corporal.' 'No, what have you "all done"?' 'Oh, sorry, Corporal – we're all done filling the trenches in.' We weren't getting far with this conversation, I thought, as I got to my feet. 'Okay, that looks great. Thanks, everyone. We move out at twenty-two hundred hours – make sure you're all ready and prepared.'

Following a bit of a fight with my bergen and my webbing, I eventually got it sitting how I liked it. The next ritual was to stamp my feet up and down so that the bottoms of my combat trousers sat neatly over my puttees. Looking around at my squad, I did a quick visual sweep of their kit. I'd checked the blank ammunition earlier, noting the green tips to denote their status. One at a time, I ordered them to jump up and down to check there was no loose kit that might rattle and give us away. Finally, I ordered them to 'cam up', applying the brown-green cream to each other's faces to help break up their features in the field. I checked that my map was in the right-hand large pocket on my combat trousers and my torch was safely attached to my combat jacket. We didn't have head torches in those days; I don't think they'd been invented. Army torches were about 8in long, like a stubby walking stick. The light didn't come out of the top, but out of the side, and on the opposite side of the light was a metal spring clip that attached to your kit. I decided to finish off our camouflage before we left – it would be dark when we got there, so it would be harder to locate the ferns and other foliage we attached to various bits of webbing and in the netting on our helmets. Stewart, my radio mule, was probably carrying the heaviest load. Most of our rations had been eaten, so the rest of us were travelling a bit lighter.

Everyone knew the route – we'd recced it earlier – so by 21.30hrs we were getting into our ambush positions. As with the trenches, I had placed half the squad on one side of the track and the other with me on the higher bank. We would all be engaging the enemy downwards, so I could justify half my squad being opposite me, should Donkey kick off.

It takes around twenty minutes for your eyes to fully adjust to the dark. We were taught that if we came across light – torches, for instance – you were to closed one eye so you'd have at least one good eye after it had gone. It was as black as your hat in that forest, hardly any residual light coming through the canopy above. Senses were on high alert as we waited for the inevitable. Every gust of wind or crack of a branch sent my heart racing. I found myself imagining figures coming up the track, an innocent bush became someone crouching down with a weapon, and a lump of rock I hadn't taken any notice of in the daylight became another sniper. I found myself flicking the tape on the thunder flash I was holding, having trusted myself to at least be able to throw the thing downhill.

Suddenly, I was sure I heard something. I spotted Junior Sergeant Walker opposite, signalling in the direction of the noise. I held my hand up to indicate to wait. Surely, they knew we would be around here somewhere; they would be on high alert as we were. I looked at Stewart beside me, the whites of his eyes seeming to stand out from the dark camo cream that surrounded them. A quick nod and I pulled the tape on the thunder flash – I had about ten seconds to get rid of it. I didn't want it dropping at their feet seconds before it exploded, so I hung onto it for as long as I dare.

'Engage!' I shouted, just before the thunder flash exploded feet from the lead man's feet. I could see the confusion of bodies trying to find cover as the volley of blank bullets rained down on them. More thunder flashes exploded, the forest lighting up below us. Donkey didn't sneak up on me this time – he appeared from the same direction we had come. This time he was waving a red torch from side to side, another indication to cease firing.

'Another good result, boys,' I told my guys as we stood round in a huddle having a smoke break. The camo cream that was under my chinstrap was peeling away, making it feel like the bottom of my face was falling off. 'All we've got to do now is get back to camp without getting ambushed. We need to travel with caution, on high alert.'

It was two o'clock when we started our journey back to Thetford battle camp. We weren't that far away according to my map. We didn't have to walk miles to collect tags this time, just move as fast and stealthily as possible without being ambushed.

'Why don't we go a different way?' Mara suggested.

'What do you mean, a different way? I've already decided the route,' I reminded him.

'I know, Corp.' He had a habit of calling me 'Corp' 'That's what the enemy will think as well, so if we go an unusual way, we'll fool them. They wait for hours and we're home and dry – simples.'

I felt a little bit like Captain Mainwaring off Dad's Army when I said: 'Well done, Mara; I was waiting for someone to suggest that!'

Torch on and a quick study of the map found an alternative route that might fool them.

'Okay, I'll lead. Don't sling your weapons – I want them ready for potential engagement. All understood? Good – let's go.'

Mara was right. Two hours later, we strolled into an empty camp to find that. someone had carried the army chef – bed and all – into the middle of the grassed area that our tents surrounded. That's strange, I thought, as we walked past his sleeping self to our tents. Following a couple of hours' kip, I sat in the dining tent eating the best bacon sandwich I think I've ever had. The sleeping slop jockey had woken and dragged his bed back into his tent. Sitting on the narrow wooden bench looking out over the burnt ash from the last fire, my thoughts turned to the next steps in our journey towards the real job – 'state duties' in London. I knew it was a long way away, and there were going to be tough challenges along the way, but I thought I was ready for them.

'What time did you get back?' Quiff asked as he sat of the bench on the other side of the table.

'About four o'clock. What about you?'

'Six – we spent an hour in a ditch waiting to attack you lot!'

'Well, you see, that's why I'm a full corporal of horse and you're a lance corporal of horse. Down here for dancing', I continued, pointing at my still minging DMS boots, 'up here for thinking', this time knowingly tapping my head. Of course, I didn't mention it was Mara's idea all along.

'Fuck off, dipshit!' he replied with a smile as he tucked into his sandwich.

This was our last day of battle camp in Thetford. Tomorrow we would travel back to Pirbright, and next week we would start preparing to pass out of the Junior Guardsman's Wing to become real soldiers. Most of the day was spent cleaning our kit and packing it away. Stewart, as ever, was on hand to do, well anything really. Donkey Mayor ordered Quiff and I to organize retrieving one of the boats that had been untied and set free from its moorings, and was now sitting in the middle of the lake. Probably done by the same jokers who left the cook in the field, I thought, as I assessed the situation.

'Shall me and you just go and get it?' I suggested to Quiff as we stood on the gravel beach at the water's edge.

'How do you propose we do that?'

'Well,' I said, while considering all options, 'we row this one out to that one, tie that one to this one and tow it back – simples.'

'Go on then. You'd better be right.'

We were both dressed in denim green trousers and KF shirts. Neither of us thought through a plan – we just jumped in the boat, untied it and began to row towards our target. Trouble was, we hadn't considered the various scenarios that might face us. There only being two of us – one on each side – the bloody thing wouldn't go in a straight line. Either I was paddling too fast, or Quiff was.

'Hang on, hang on!' I shouted. 'This isn't working. We've got to row at the same time, like marching but with paddles. I'll shout the steps – er, rows. You know what I mean.'

To be fair, it did work better than our former efforts. However, all our shouting was beginning to draw a crowd on the nearby bank. Our target was in sight; we just had to get the mooring rope and somehow attach it to our boat and tow it back. That sounded simple enough.

'The mooring rope's in the boat,' I informed Quiff as I tried to reach out and grab a hold of our target.

'You'll have to get in it and get it,' Quiff helpfully suggested.

'You come over this side and hold them together then.' As he moved to my side, our boat rocked in the direction of the other boat and pushed it away. My knuckles were turning white as I tried to hold on to the side of the boat, arms fully stretched now. I could feel my stable belt catching the side of our boat as I stretched further out' 'Grab it! Quick, grab it!' I pleaded, with that horrible feeling of knowing whatever I did at this point would only result in one thing – I was about to go for an unscheduled and unwanted dip. Luckily – if there was any luck in this whole debacle – I managed to hold onto the other boat as the rest of me slid into the murky green water. I heard a cheer ring out as I tried to catch my breath at the same time as scrambling into our target. I felt like a kitten trying to clamber out of a bath as I struggled to hoist myself in. Eventually I got myself over the side and fell into the bottom of the boat. To say I was pissed off would be an understatement. Laughter surrounded me as I got to my feet and took a look around. Quiff had drifted away by now – luckily for him, as it turned out. If I could have got hold of him I'd have killed him. Looking across in his direction, I knew he'd been laughing; the tears rolling down his face gave it away.

'Just catch this rope,' I shouted as I gathered the mooring rope from the bottom of the boat. Well, dear reader, remember how bad I said I was at throwing things? This little secret of mine was about to go public, as it seemed the whole camp was now watching and cheering. My first attempt didn't even go in the right direction. I think I let go of it at the wrong time because it landed in the water behind me. The heavy rope was wet now and much heavier. Water ran down my arms, disappearing under the neatly folded sleeves of my shirt as I tried to throw the bloody thing for the fourth time. Quiff had managed to get closer again now, so with a much-reduced distance to cover, I managed to throw it in his general direction.

'Tie it to something!' I shouted as I examined the state of my soaked trousers and boots. My shirt was hanging out, making me look like a scarecrow. Eventually, between us, we managed to get the two vessels close enough together for me to jump back in with Quiff.

'Right, let's row back in the same way as we came out. Keep in time!' I ordered as we took our places either side of the boat. Our audience had settled down now for the long haul. Most were sitting on the bank, smoking, while some were laying back to soak up the sun. I felt like shit and I looked like shit, but I was beginning to see the funny side of it all. Another cheer went out as I jumped down into the shallow water near the shore to help the assembled crowd pull it up the beach. Then, without comment or reaction, I tried to walk back to my tent with some sort of dignity to dry off!

* * *

Sat on the coach watching the golden fields of corn pass by, my thoughts turned to Pam and her coming up on Sunday. Just two days to go. A twinge of excitement swept through my body as I closed my eyes to try and catch up on some much-needed sleep. It was good to get some proper scoff in me. It was also good to have a proper toilet to get some of the compo rations out. They're designed to bung you up, we were told. Bung you up? It was like passing a house brick, in my opinion!

The following day, Quiff and I went down the stables to catch up on our up-and-coming passing out parade. *Joe Day* was in his usual place, sitting on a kit box in the tack room, surveying the scene in front of him.

'What do you little fuckers want?' he grumbled as we appeared in the yard.

'What's new, Sarge?' I asked as we made our way to where he sat.

'What's new? What's new? It's NAFFI break and I've run out of milk, that's what's new. Can one of you fuckers go to Sandies and get some? You can take my bike.'

Of course, like an idiot, I volunteered. It had been a while since I'd ridden a bike, especially one as crooked as this one; the handlebars weren't in alignment with the rest of the bike, and it felt like I was permanently going around a slight bend. I thought I'd lost it when I came across a squad of junior recruits being rifted around D lines (the accommodation blocks). The journey back was even worse, as I was lumbered with the milk (only glass bottles in those days). When I rode into the yard, I had to hand over the bottle while still on the move so I could safely dismount.

'Right,' Joe announced after Quiff had made the tea. I was having trouble understanding what he was saying as he attempted to eat a slice of cake at the same time, as Joe only had one tooth left in his head: 'that's all I fucking need', he used to say. I shuffled discreetly along the tack box I was sitting on to try to avoid what seemed like a constant spray of cake crumbs coming in my direction as he talked. I was sure he was talking about our forthcoming passing out parade and which horses we were riding. I was delighted when he looked in my direction and said I was riding Landfall. 'That will do for me.' I thought as I finished my tea and made my way to the tap to wash out my cup. As I turned the tap off, I looked across the yard at Landfall's head watching me over his stable door. He was light brown – or bay, as it's known – with black points (mane and tail). Standing at around 16-2, he was a good fit for me, and importantly we got on well together.

As usual, Quiff was keen to get back for some scoff. As we walked/marched up Adair Walk, we couldn't help but chuckle at a poor senior recruit being rifted up and down the tarmac and made to salute the lamp post every time he passed it.

'That will be us in a few weeks,' I mentioned to Quiff as the rookie came flying past on his way for another pass.

'I know; I'm dreading it. What are you doing this afternoon?'

'Egyptian PT, laying on my bed sleeping – why?'

'Oh, I thought we could go up the NAFFI and have a game of snooker.'

'Yeah, later maybe.'

Walking towards the Guardroom at the depot was always a daunting prospect. I could see Pam sitting in her grey Mini Traveller, waiting for me All I needed to do was show my pass and sign out for the afternoon. It was very much down to who was on guard as to the reception you got.

'Afternoon pass please, Sergeant,' I asked the forage-capped face the other side of the window.

'What for? Where are you going?'

I felt like telling him to mind his own business, but – wisely as it turned out – toed the line and answered politely.

'I'm meeting my girlfriend, Sergeant. I booked it yesterday.'

'So you did, Junior Corporal of Horse Wallington. So you did.'

The strip light in the Guardroom behind him suddenly became obscured by the bulk of the Scots Guard sergeant as he lifted himself from his chair and came outside to join me. The blue armband with the red letters 'RP' (Regimental Police) seemed to jump off his sleeve as he towered over me.

'Is that, by any chance, your girlfriend parked over there?'

'Yes, that's correct, Sergeant.'

'Does she visit you often?'

'Quite often, Sergeant.'

'Have you heard about the IRA threat that's happening on and around military bases in the UK?'

'Yes, Sergeant.'

'Well, next time she visits, can you ask her to park a little further down the road? If she had a car bomb, we would be blown to fucking bits. Enjoy your day!'

Without replying, I took my ID card and sheepishly crossed the road to join Pam.

'Everything alright?' she asked as I swiftly got into the passenger seat.

'Yeah, no problem. Just drive please. I'll tell you in a minute.'

When I told her, she thought it was funny. I didn't. I got what the RP (Regimental Police) sergeant was on about: there was a real threat going round, and ironically, sometime later in the book, you'll discover why!

* * *

Things were definitely slowing down at Inkerman. I could sense our time as junior soldiers was coming to an end. It was Monday morning, we were due to pass out on Friday, and after passing out we had the weekend off, following which we would be moving into one of the seniors blocks on Adaire Walk. Why the hell we had to do another month in that place, I just didn't understand.

'Why can't we go straight "up town"? It would be a lot easier,' I protested to Quiff as I polished Landfall's head kit in the stables tack room.

'How am I supposed to know?. Ask Donkey.'

'I will. There's no way I'm being rifted up and down Adaire Walk like some overwound toy soldier.'

'Stop moaning and get on with your kit. There's a competition, you know – "best turned out mounted" it's called and I'm going to win it.'

'Not a chance, dickhead. That plaque's already got my name on it.'

We were doing a lot of rehearsals. It was funny to be sat on a horse, watching the rest of the boys passing out marching around in front of us. Mick Good was Junior RSM, so was taking the parade. There were eight of us mounted, led by Corporal of Horse Mai. From where I sat, it looked good; it certainly felt good. This was a leap into the unknown for all of us. In a month's time, we would be fully qualified soldiers – Troopers in the senior regiment in the British Army, the Life Guards.

The day of the parade was bright and sunny. The stables were busy, with eight junior recruits rushing around, finishing our horses off before going to get changed. The parade started at eleven o'clock. My mum, dad and Pam were coming up; it was a big day for all concerned. Mum and dad had never been to the depot before, but Pam was familiar with the place so could direct them as required. We walked back to our block the back way across the sports field to avoid meeting any of them before the parade. The far side of the main depot parade ground was bathed in morning sunshine as we hurried along the far edge of it. We could see the bright colours of the families gathering in the temporary stands that had been erected for the parade.

As I opened the door to my bunk for what would be one of the last times, many memories flooded through my mind. I never thought I would feel emotional about moving on. After all, I didn't want to be here anyway when I turned up in January 1972. But now I got it. I was grateful for what the Junior Army had done for me. It had given me discipline, a sense of pride and confidence that I still carry to this day. It had given me mates that I also still have to this day. And despite the way I and seventeen others were ultimately treated, it gave me pride at having served in what I still consider to be the finest regiment in the British Army.

The whole room was organized chaos as everyone rushed to get ready. The whole of Inkerman were passing out today. No one was being 'back-squadded'. It was a great achievement by all the staff and the junior NCOs that everyone got through it. I did think about giving a speech, but that wasn't really my style. I'd stood in the middle of the room last night and told them that they should be proud of what they had achieved and enjoy the day, and that I'd see them all on the other side when we reassembled in C block on Adair Walk next week.

Landfall looked good as Joe walked him over to the mounting block, his clipped coat shining as much as his leather saddlery.

'Remember,' Joe reminded me as I swung my right leg over the saddle, 'don't fuck up.' A big one-toothed grin spread across his face as he went to get the next guy ready. That day I had the first experience of people-watching from the back of a horse. Little had I realized how much – whether it was on guard in Whitehall or when Trooping the Colour – you can see up there. In front of me were the backs of all the foot soldiers on parade, and in front of them were all our relatives and the senior officers taking the salute. I found that if you occupy your mind with such things, your horse also relaxes and doesn't start a fight with stablemates to his left or right. Before we knew it, the entourage who were inspecting the parade and taking the salute were making their way across the parade ground towards us, the mounted contingent. Running the stables at Pirbright was Corporal Major Wright. Yes, they had a senior NCO running a yard of twelve horses. Talk about jobs for the boys! Someone at regimental headquarters had decided that they could lose him down at the depot for the last couple of years before he retired. Anyway, he accompanied the inspecting officer, the commandant of the depot, and introduced us as we were inspected. 'Where are you being posted?' the colonel asked me as Landfill proceeded to try to eat his shiny row of medals. 'Knightsbridge, Colonel.' I nervously replied. 'Ah, you're going to be a "donkey walloper" are you?' 'Yes, Colonel,' I dutifully answered, while wondering what a donkey walloper was. The inspection and parade went well, with Mick doing a great job as Junior RSM. I was awarded 'best turned out mounted', which really pissed off Quiff, but hey ho, someone has too lose. After the parade, and after we'd seen to our horses, we could go to meet our parents. I could easily make out Pam's happy smile as we walked amongst the crowd. It was a bit embarrassing that she kept putting her arm through mine; no one was meant to know, remember. I learnt a few months later that everyone had sussed that one ages ago.

The weekend, as usual, flew past. I'd taken most of my civvy kit back home with me. I knew we would be shifting rooms and locations quite a bit in the next few months. On the Tuesday morning of the following week, I and the rest of Inkerman Platoon were walking away from the block for the last time.

Chapter 4

Goodbye to the Depot, Hello Knightsbridge

Via Summer Camp

NO RANK NOW, no privileges. Back where I'd begun, sharing a bed space with Quiff and a weird-looking Coldstream Guard who was a massive David Bowie fan.

'How the mighty have fallen,' I depressingly mentioned to Quiff as I sat on my bed-blocked bed

'Depends how you look at it. Think about it, this is the start of our next journey. They can throw as much shit as they can while we're here, but remember, we've done it all before. Bring it on, I say, bring it on.'

'I'm glad you've got that good attitude. You'll need it – march and shoot tomorrow, and log run on Thursday.'

He was right, of course. Nothing that they threw at us worked. We remained resilient and refused to march around everywhere like a demented moron. The whole four-storey block on Adaire Walk was full of ex-juniors. Unlike the new recruits, we didn't have stiff new kit and unshrunk berets. We were 'bolo' and proud of it. We were even back to having a trained soldier in our room; we hadn't had that since we were back in D lines, the spiders. Our trained soldier was a right tool. To start with, he was TA (Territorial Army), not a proper soldier. Allegedly he was in the SAS (Special Air Service) TA, but he didn't look like that to us. He looked and acted like a lazy twat!

One Sunday, Pam was coming up in the afternoon and this trained soldier decided to have a kit and locker inspection. He ordered us to empty our lockers and wash and press everything in them. I politely asked him why, as he knew I had the afternoon off.

'Unless it can be done in an hour, it's not being done because, as you know, I'm going out this afternoon,' I informed him in no uncertain terms.

'You'll do as I say!'

'Look, mate,' I retaliated, 'you're a trained soldier; we'll be trained soldiers too in a couple of weeks, so why don't you back off and take a chill pill.'

Seeing him marching across the room towards me, I just opened my locker door and pulled off my gym shirt. As he reached me, I turned – naked from the waist up, super fit – towards him.

'Problem?' I politely asked.

'Yes. If I tell you to do something, you do it.'

'Agreed, as long as it's a reasonable order, at a reasonable time; not some dick-swinging "I'm senior to you" order.'

'That's the trouble with you ex-junior soldiers. You think you're special,' he continued.

'Oh, we're getting somewhere now, aren't we? Listen, Mr SAS man, me and a few others in this block ran rooms just like this for longer than you're likely to. We didn't resort to petty bullying to vent any frustrations we had; we treated our guys with respect. I'll tell you what I'm going to do – I'm going to check the other rooms in the block and make sure this order hasn't come from a proper soldier, and if it hasn't, I will return and do what I intended to do anyway and go out for the afternoon.'

When I returned, relishing our next verbal confrontation, he was gone, probably to the NAFFI bar to show off his fake-looking SAS beret. I do remember we didn't get any trouble from him for the remainder of our time there. Having to do that really put me off the depot. All any of us wanted to do was to join our regiments and get on with our futures. Passing out of the Guards Depot proper was a low-key affair – no families invited, just a small parade on the drill square and a "good luck with your futures" sort of thing. In the case of us guys, who were joining the mounted regiment, we had a strange start to our senior journey. We were joining the mounted regiment on summer camp, which was only a couple of miles from the depot at a place called Stoney Castle. It was a Friday afternoon as the three-tonner we were travelling in pulled into the double-sized gateway into this massive field. To the left we could see rows of tents – large tents like the ones we had at Thetford. As the truck rolled its way towards the tented village, I noticed a makeshift arena had been pegged out on the open ground in front of the accommodation. Brightly painted show jumps were set out in what looked like a well-worn grass course between the obstacles. The horse lines were constructed from scaffolding, forming lines of black and occasionally grey horses. I have to admit, I was excited as I jumped down from the vehicle.

I didn't have a clue why, I just knew I was excited. Standing there on the sunburnt grass, the smell of horses and horse manure attacked my senses.

'Are you the depot lot?' I heard someone ask as I was suddenly bought back to reality.

'Yes, Corporal' Stinch said from his vantage point still on the back of the three-tonner.

'Okay, you've got to report to Polly – *Polly Perkins* – in the stores tent.'

'Where's that, Corporal?' I politely asked.

'Right there beside you, with the sign "Stores" written on it.'

Feeling a right twat, I finished off helping to unload our kit and stacked it neatly near the entrance to Polly's tent. I say tent; they were either very big tents or small marquees, depending on how you looked at it.

We stood for a while, trying to work out how we should approach this. You can't really knock on a tent door, can you? Well, it isn't even a door – it's a flap.

'You go in first,' Quiff said as he pushed me towards the heavy canvas entrance.

Prick, I thought, as my eyes tried to adjust to the darkness inside, a single light bulb shining dimly in the darkness above our heads. Quiff and Stinch had joined me, and we all stood in front of a trestle table neatly covered with an army blanket, forming a barrier between us and what lay beyond. Similar tables were stacked high with kit; all sorts of kit – piles of blankets, tin pot helmets, neatly stacked between two piles of white sheets. There were even a load of head collar ropes hanging from a hook on the canvas wall. All three of us were still gazing around like we had just discovered lost treasure when someone appeared from behind a blanket type door at the far end of the tent. He wore army green denim trousers – I noticed instantly they had neatly sewn creases in them – and his shirt reflected his trousers, with sewn-in creases down both short-sleeved arms and sewn-in darts on the back, making it all look immaculate. You quickly learn in the military that as soon as you talk to someone, you scan their arms and shoulders for signs of rank, so you know how they should be addressed. *Polly Perkins* wore a familiar leather wristband with four inverted chevrons and a crown attached to it, which told us he was a corporal major, or sir!

'What can I do for you?' he asked, in an accent I didn't recognize but which reminded me of my Uncle John from Northampton – a bit geezer-like.

'We've just arrived from the regiment, sir,' I dutifully answered.

'Oh, you lot. Eight, isn't there?'

'Yes, sir, that's correct.'

'Okay, your accommodation while you're here is in tent B, opposite. I don't want to see you until eight o'clock on Monday morning. If you want to go up town [cavalry speak for Hyde Park Barracks], there's a three-tonner leaving in half an hour. Check with the driver when he's coming back down on Sunday. You can sleep on the sixth floor – introduce yourselves to Henry in the cookhouse and he'll sort you out with some scoff. If you stay here, try not to get in the way and don't annoy anyone. The scoff house is behind this tent and the bar is the next tent down. Any questions?'

'No, Corporal Major. Thanks,' we mumbled as we quickly exited the tent into the afternoon sunshine. I say exit the tent, but there was that embarrassing moment that always seems to go on longer than you think when Stinch couldn't work out how the tent door actually worked. It felt like forever that I was at the back of the line of three, trying to nudge the two in front of me out. I briefly looked over my shoulder to see Polly standing there with that look that tells you: 'What the hell have we been sent here?'

'Let's go to London,' Quiff suggested as we moved our kit into tent B.

'What for?'

'I don't know, for a laugh I suppose. Come on, let's go.'

I managed to bag a bed in the far corner of our temporary home by chucking all my kit on it. Stinch was opposite me and Quiff was on my left. All eight of us were spread about fairly evenly. It already felt more relaxed than the depot. There weren't many people around – they all seemed to be at the horse lines, working. The grass felt strange under my feet as I changed my army socks for civvy ones and changed into my trousers. It's difficult to believe, but back in the Seventies in the Household Cavalry, if we left the barracks in Knightsbridge, we had to wear the appropriate civvy gear. We were briefed on this before leaving the depot: we had to either wear a suit or flannel trousers and a blazer, and always a shirt and tie. What the hell am I going for, I was thinking to myself, as I finished tying my tie and pulling on my blazer. I'm a country boy from the outskirts of Bristol, not the city type. All I really wanted to do was go and meet the horses and have a wander around the woods that I could see on the other side of the camp.

'Got your money?' Quiff asked as I climbed into the back of yet another three-tonner. A nod was the best I could come up with as the truck moved away. It was sort of familiar with the journey from when I went to St James' Palace for the Queen's wedding anniversary presentation, but once again we could only make out where we'd been. I felt like I had when I was first driven to the depot from North Camp railway station.

I could see lots of people walking and running in the late afternoon sun along a sandy track that ran alongside the road we were travelling down. On my left, the metal railing suddenly turned to red brick and concrete buildings. The windows that overlooked the park looked like mirrors. Then the buildings stopped and a large brick wall took over. I felt and heard the engine whine as it slowed down, then after a sharp right turn we were entering what felt and looked like a parade ground.

'This must be it,' Quiff excitedly shouted as the vehicle started to reverse towards a large, mostly concrete building with the same-looking windows as I'd just spotted on the way in. As I jumped down onto the concrete surface, I looked up at the buildings around us, struck by how they all seemed to sit on massive concrete pillars. Lots of darkened windows looked at us wherever we gazed. Our driver joined us and gave us a quick tour, or heads up, on where we could go and where we couldn't.

'The scoff house is up there on the first floor,' he instructed as he pointed upwards to the concrete box that loomed over us. 'It won't be open until seven in the morning. The NAFFI bar and shop is on the floor above, but that's shut as well. The stables are over there.' He pointed at two wide concrete ramps, one going down, the other up. 'Don't go there, not until you've got your passes. See that big concrete pillar with a big crest at the bottom over there?' We both nodded. 'Well that's where the lift to the accommodation is. You're on the sixth floor – riding school and mussies [musicians] live up there. Find an empty room on the right, looking over Knightsbridge; you can kip there tonight. I'm going back to Stoney Castle tomorrow at 1300hrs if you want a lift. Don't be late'

With that, he was off, heading towards the corner where both building met and disappearing into the shadows.

'Come on then, let's go and check it out,' Quiff suggested as we began to walk towards the imposing building ahead of us.

The whole place was the same construction. Between pillars and arches of concrete was red brick or large black and silver windows. As I looked up in wonder, I noticed the reflection of the trees opposite in the windows. I couldn't get how new and modern everything felt as we climbed the steps up to the first level. What we guessed were offices ran the length of the building, blue red blue being the colour of choice on every door and sign. A large glass-fronted office with a big glass door dominated as we made our way into the concrete pillar that contained the lift. I couldn't believe how quiet it was as we stood there, watching the red lights in the lift make their way to level three. As the lift doors opened, we were met by a similar scene to the one we'd just left, only we now stood on grey lino rather than concrete. The lino almost invited us to follow it into yet another corridor, which this time stretched both left and right. In front of us, the lino gave way to terracotta floor tiles that clearly indicated the wash rooms. They say, I once heard, that psychologically, when you're given two choices – like when you go into a shop or pub – you instinctively turn right. Well, Quiff turned left, the correct way as it turned out, as mussies lived to the right. After finding an empty room, we began to explore what was to become our home for the near future. The lockers were built in along both sides of the four-man room – they were bigger than we'd had before – and your bed sort of slid underneath or stowed away under said lockers, leaving the room looking bigger than it was. A gap was created by the design of the cupboards, allowing you to sit on the bed even when it was stowed away – quite clever really. The window that filled the front of the room had a long radiator sitting under it. Being six floors up, the view was impressive. Way below us was Knightsbridge. A busy road led my eye towards Kensington in one direction and Piccadilly in the other. To be honest, I didn't have a clue what I was looking at. I could have been in any big city, but I was here, in the capital city, London. I couldn't really believe it.

'So, what are we going to do now?' I asked Quiff as I took my tightly rolled-up sleeping bag from my holdall.

'We go out, I suppose. I need some scoff anyway. I don't know about you, but I'm starving.'

'Yeah, me too. But where shall we go?'

'Don't know. Let's just go and explore.'

Half an hour later found the two of us standing in front of the guardroom window, a bit taggy-looking having spent the last hour or so in the back of a three-tonner. The noise from the busy road outside made understanding the RP corporal behind the glass difficult. He was writing our temporary passes so we could move about the barracks more freely. Looking around, I noticed a coffee vending machine in the corner by the lift doors. On the wall above the buttons for the lift, a sign told me we were on level two. I was confused. I thought we were on the ground floor. This didn't make sense. Up the stairs one level was the parade square, so what was below us?

'Do your tie up properly. Use the mirror by the door,' the corporal barked through the heavy glass widow.

'Yes, Corporal.' The sudden order bought me back to reality.

With my tie knotted to the satisfaction of the RP, we were let out of the large black metal gates onto Knightsbridge. It felt a bit like being let out of a cage. A stiff breeze funnelled its way between the tall buildings as we followed the red brick wall towards the funny-looking junction ahead of us. As we walked, the smell of horses caught my senses. There must still be horses here, I thought, as I stopped to peer through one of the 4in breaks in the wall. I could see a pair of big black doors surrounded by the ever-present concrete pillars. The smell was clear now – that must be the stables. As I tracked the gap in the wall to its top, I saw a massive canopy above me. Walking backwards now, neck craned upwards, I couldn't believe what I saw: a horse looking over the canopy out over Knightsbridge.

'Quiff!' I shouted. 'Look up there; a fucking horse!'

'Alright, no need to shout, or swear for that matter. There are civvies about.'

'Sorry. But look, a horse.'

I still couldn't believe my eyes as we carried on walking towards the junction. Neither could I quite believe the sheer number of people who surrounded us. They all seemed to move in unison as the traffic lights changed, and we seemed to be swept along with them as they moved. I noticed the sign for the underground station, with the street sign above it telling me this was Sloane Street. Red buses were everywhere: number fifty-two for Crystal Palace, one said, while another was going to somewhere called Chelsea.

'Look, there's a Wimpy over there,' Quiff shouted amongst the chaos that shrouded us.

'What's a Wimpy?' I asked.

'Scoff. Come on, I'm starving.'

It was something of a relief to close the door on the busy streets outside. Looking around, all I could see was a row of tables and red benches bolted to floor. Large red tomatoes sat alongside other condiments on the white plastic-topped tables. Each table had a large illustrated menu standing proudly amongst other bits and pieces.

'This one will do,' Quiff said as he slid onto the bench.

By the time I'd undone my jacket and manoeuvred myself onto the bench opposite him, he was already studying the menu. I could see the back of the head of a lady on the next table along, a cloud of cigarette smoke hovering above her as she drank the last drops of her drink.

'What do you fancy? Have you ever had a Wimpy before?'

'No. I don't know,' I mumbled as I tried to answer two questions at the same time.

'Have the breakfast meal. It's good.'

'Is it? I'll take your word for it. What's a bendy sausage, anyway?'

'It's a sausage that, somehow, they cook bendy.'

From that day on, I became very fond of Wimpys. I particularly liked the thin chips and the frothy coffee served in a glass cup and saucer. The big tomato, I soon learnt, was the famous red condiment. I remember you had to check yours was full before sitting down. If it wasn't, a bit of sly swapping about was required. We used that Wimpy in Sloane Street quiet often during our time up town. Sometimes we would stick a match in the top of the large tomato, snap it off flush so it couldn't be seen, then put it on another table and watch as people struggled to squeeze the ketchup out. You know what they say – little things please little minds. Very true in this case!

The evening ended with somehow – I still don't really know how – us two 17-year-old fresh-faced kids being let into a strip club in Soho. We weren't officially old enough to drink alcohol, let alone go into one of those places.

* * *

I woke with a start. Someone, somewhere, was blowing a bloody trumpet. Where was I, I wondered, looking around the room. Everything was clean and white. A beam of sunlight broke through the narrow gap in the curtains and bounced back off the mirror that was above the sink at the other end of the room. I managed to extract my left arm from my army sleeping bag and looked at my watch. It was seven o'clock. I returned my arm into the sleeping bag and checked myself over while inwardly cringing at the thoughts that were flowing through my confused mind. Satisfied I was still in one piece, I struggled myself out of the sleeping bag and went over to attempt to kick Quiff into life.

'Come on dipshit – it's seven o'clock.'

'Oh shit. Where the hell are we?' he protested as he wriggled out of his sleeping bag like a caterpillar coming out of its chrysalis.

'We're in Knightsbridge, don't you remember?' I reminded him as I drew the curtains and lit a cigarette. 'If we get a move on, we might get some breakfast.'

'Alright, won't be long,' he agreed as he pinched my fag and took a drag.

The barracks still felt and looked like a ghost town as we climbed the concrete stairs to the canteen. All – I'd say six – sets of eyes looked at us as we peered around the door before gingerly entering. On our left, the hot plates were still steaming with the heat coming off them. A black guy stood behind them, wearing immaculately pressed chef's whites and one of those funny hats that they have.

'Who are you two?' he asked while scanning us up and down.

'We've just joined the regiment from Pirbright and we're at Stoney Castle now. Well not now, we're going back this afternoon.'

'Passes!' he demanded, the whites of his eyes standing out against his dark skin.

After showing our new passes, he allowed us to take one of the hot plates out of this contraption they were stacked in. It looked a bit like a broken jack-in-the-box as it slowly responded to some of the weight being taken off it. Scoff rods, plate and bowl neatly assembled on our trays, we gingerly moved forward, pushing our trays along the chrome rack beside the glass-fronted hotplates.

'Porridge?' our host asked as he reached over to take our bowls.

'Cheers, Henry,' one of the troopers shouted as he left the room.

Better not call him Henry yet, I thought. A bit of respect, you know?

'Thanks, Henry,' Quiff said as he took the porridge out of his hand.

'Er, thanks Henry,' I mirrored as I nearly dropped the bowl. It was hot and heavy.

The next stop on our journey along the hotplate was a joint effort. I used the tongs provided for bacon and or sausage, while Henry had control of eggs, tomatoes and beans. Quiff liked his food. Actually, I'd go further than that and say he was – and still is – obsessed with food. While I managed to grab two slices of bacon, Quiff was at the sausages. One sausage successfully on his plate, he went for a second.

'One sausage!' Henry suddenly shouted, as if the place would implode and we'd all die. Such was the panic and anger in his voice.

As quick as you like, Quiff ended his two-sausage mission and, with a cheeky grin, put the second one on my plate. Neither of us was surprised when telling the story later in the week to hear that this was why our server was known as 'one sausage Henry'.

As I climbed down from the three-tonner back at Stoney Castle, I was knackered. I couldn't remember what time we'd got to bed last night, and all I wanted to do was go and lay on my bed for an hour or two. The other guys looked well rested and fresh as we tumbled into the tent. Blankets, sheets and pillows had been thrown on my bed. Got to make that now, I thought: where's Stewart when you need him? He'd actually gone to join the 1st Battalion of the Scots Guards, somewhere in Germany I believe.

A sudden shaking of my shoulder brought me out of my slumber. As I slowly opened my eyes, I could see it was Stinch. I recognized the dark curly hair instantly.

'What's up?' I murmured as I contemplated rolling over and going back to sleep.

'Scoff. It's scoff time.'

'Oh shit, what time is it? How long have I been asleep?' My questions had him confused; all he was interested in was waking me so I didn't miss scoff.

'Come on, I'll show you where it is,' he continued as he tugged on my limp arm.

'Where's Quiff?' I asked as I steadied myself after standing too quickly.

'Oh, he's already gone. Come on, let's go,' he insisted as I was semi-rifted from the comfort of the tent. As we walked across the grass towards a bigger tent with the sides rolled up, I could see dozens of KF shirt-clad men sitting on foldaway benches eating off foldaway tables. I'm sure the chatter ceased for a while as we joined the back of the queue.

'What are they like?' I whispered to Stinch as we waited.

'What are who like?'

'This lot.' I wanted to say 'bigger boys', but didn't think that would be appropriate – 'the senior guys' was the best I could think of.

'Oh, they're alright really. A bit of piss taking, you know, banter, but on the whole, alright so far.'

We joined Quiff and our five other fellow recruits at a table outside the dining tent. After sarcastically thanking him for waking me – not – I found myself with nowhere to sit. Looking around, I could see a wooden folding chair at the end of one of the occupied tables. Shit, I thought, I'm going to have to go and ask if I can use/borrow it. I've never been that self-confident in such situations. Maybe I'll just eat standing, I thought – no, don't be a lightweight, my inner self told me, get over there and get it!

'Is this anyone's chair?' I nervously asked a youngish-looking chap who was sat at the table.

'Yes, it probably belongs to the MOD, but if you want to use it I'm sure they won't mind.'

I was struck by how polite he had been while still managing to take the piss out of me. I was still working it out in my mind as I carried the chair to our table and my rapidly cooling supper. I tried not to stare at him as I ate, but I couldn't help it. I was fascinated by the fact that he didn't seem that tall and he had a harmonica in the top pocket of his KF shirt.

'That guy I just borrowed the chair from – well, I didn't borrow it from him, it's the MOD's actually – but that guy over there, he had a mouth organ in his pocket. I wonder what he's got it for?'

'He might play it, dipshit,' Quiff helpfully replied.

When the laughter had died down, I made a mental note to think before I spoke in future. Trouble is, it never really works, does it?

The evening was warm as the sun began to drop towards the tree line to the right of me. As I finished my last drop of tea and stubbed out my cigarette, I decided I needed a crap. I'd earlier noticed a temporary sign that had an arrow drawn on it with the word 'toilets' on it. Trouble is, the 'toilets' bit had been overwritten with the word 'growlers'. When I arrived at the entrance of this tent-like affair, the first thing that struck me was how many people were having the same thoughts or needs as me. I was hoping that with it being early evening it might be quiet, but not a chance. As well as not being able to put this off, I had a feeling there was one of those horrible new experiences waiting for me in there. I was right, of course. As I stepped onto the duckboarded floor, the horror hit me – a long row of what can only be described as boxes with holes in the top of them, each one separated by thin hessian screens. To the front of me I could see crumpled trousers or cavalry breeches; some of the owners were leaning forward, chatting even, while others tried to preserve their dignity by sitting back and fixing their gaze at the temporary roof above them. One part of me told me to get out of there and go and crap in the nearby woods, while the other suggested I probably wouldn't make it to the woods and that we had another week here so get on with it. Pulling your trousers and pants down at exactly the same time as sitting down is a skill of its own. At least it was warm; someone else has just been here, I thought, as I tried to begin my first ablutions in the growlers.

There I was, my gaze fixed on one spot, when someone turned up to my left. 'Alright?' he said as, without fear or trepidation, he dropped his kit not a couple of feet from my face. I don't know about shitting, I thought as his white hairy arse hovered beside me, I think I'm going to throw up! He even had a paper tucked under his arm, which, when he'd settled, he proceeded to open and read. With everything sorted out, my thoughts turned to getting out of there while maintaining some of my ever-diminishing dignity. I couldn't – no, wouldn't – stand up bold as brass and wipe my arse. But I couldn't do it sitting down, as the box hole wasn't big enough. I did try, but no, the only thing for it was to lean forward so my head nearly touched my knees and hold that position until the job was done. As I began my somewhat undignified walk out of the growlers, I heard the guy reading his paper fart and then wish me a good day. I can't avoid the growlers, I thought as I washed my hands under the cold water, but maybe I could visit in the middle of the night when its quieter? Knowing my luck, though, it would probably end in an embarrassing disaster like at Thetford battle camp.

Walking back to our tent, two things were on my mind. One was that I hoped that lot playing football over there didn't kick it in my direction and force me to look a complete tool trying to kick it back; the second was whether anyone would mind if I visited the horse lines to see the horses. I quickly made the decision to go over. It looked quiet enough; all I could really see as I approached was black and white horse heads tossing as they ripped at their hay nets. I couldn't live in the same proximity as these fine animals without saying 'hello'.

'You're one of those new rookies, aren't you?' a voice asked from the front of one of the stalls.

'Yeah, I suppose I am,' I replied as this figure appeared from behind a cavalry black's arse, picking hay out of his heavy-duty jumper.

'What are you doing?' I bravely asked.

'I'm on night guard. You'll have to do this next year, I expect, if you pass riding school that is.'

'Yeah, I guess we'll be starting that when we get back to Knightsbridge.'

'Yep, six months of hell. It's the toughest course in the army, they reckon.'

We continued to talk as he introduced me to some of the blacks in the lines. They all looked well and contented as they munched and bickered with each other in the evening sun.

One of the reasons we stuck out like sore thumbs, I concluded as I walked towards the cookhouse, was that us rookies were the only ones wearing berets. Everyone else either wore forage caps or SD (service dress) caps. Service dress caps in their current form were introduced in the Second World War, but only the cavalry wore them now, so they were pretty exclusive to the mounted regiment. Discipline was starkly different to Pirbright, with no marching everywhere you went. You'd have to salute the officers whenever you saw them, but apart from that the job seemed to be wholly focussed on the horses and their welfare.

Most of our days were spent as *Polly Perkins*' fast blacks. A trailer of hay was delivered, so we were tasked to move it to the horse lines. One day – one of the worst days of my life, as it turned out – I was sent to the cookhouse to be the 'kitchen bitch' for the day. I can honestly say, forget the march and shoots and the gruelling assault courses, the nights in the trenches, the freezing pot holes we were submerged in, the nerve-racking abseiling or anything else for that matter – nothing compared to this kitchen duty. By mid-afternoon, my arms were so ingrained with grease that the water ran off them. The shitty apron I was given was black with thick grease, my back was killing me from constantly leaning over the big trough they called a sink, and every time you thought you might be on top of the job, some bloody slop jockey would bring another loaf in. It was six o'clock when I was released out of there. I must have spent half an hour in what was by then a lukewarm shower expending even more energy trying to clean myself up. I didn't want any food; I'd dealt with enough of that. All I wanted was a couple of pints and bed.

The next day, we were all attending a course – apart from Quiff, that is, who was in the cookhouse. I'd told him it was great, he'd get loads of scoff and it was a doddle. Stinch and a few others were going back to the depot to attend a motorcycle training course, while myself and a few others got to do a first aid course. Stinch came back with his motorcycle licence, despite having fallen off, and I spent the afternoon blowing into this weird doll-like thing's mouth. In short, Stinch had got a licence and a sore leg, and I'd got a certificate and a sore mouth and lips!

* * *

To start with, the bar at summer camp to start was an intimidating place. Firstly, we weren't old enough to drink alcohol, and secondly, when, as rookies, we walked in, the whole place fell silent – like a Wild West movie. The bar staff never checked our age. I found out later that the army's attitude was if you are old enough to serve, you are old enough to drink! In the bar, we tried to merge into the background by sitting quietly in the corner. Trouble was, I seemed to have sat right in the way of the two troopers playing pool, so every minute or so I had to give way to a pool cue being perilously moved back and forth beside my left ear. Sitting around the trestle table in the crowded, smoke-filled tent, we tried to work out who would be in riding school when we started our course the following week. There were eight of us in our tent, all Life Guards, and about the same number of dinks (Blues and Royals) in our neighbouring tent. The Blues and Royals were called dinks as in 'dinky do's', for Blues. For what it's worth, we Life Guards were called 'tins'.

Looking out through the entrance to the tent, I could see it was getting darker. Shit, I thought as I nursed my pint of lager, I was meant to walk down the road to phone Pam this evening. The last weekend of camp was coming up, so on Sunday it was open day, when family and friends could come and watch mounted games and the showjumping competitions.

One of the star attractions was 'tent pegging'. It was the finale, really. The arena would be cleared and the competitors would wait in the collecting ring for their turn to gallop diagonally across the arena, aiming their lance, a 12ft spear basically, at a wooden peg that had been driven into the ground. All these events required assistance, and that's where us rookies came in. The day was busy for us and I'd probably be working most of the time, but I knew Pam would enjoy. It turned out even busier than I expected.

The weather was behaving itself, and a bright sunny day greeted us as we walked to the dining tent for breakfast. Quiff and I's first job was blowing up and attaching balloons to the tops of a load of tin pot helmets. There were around six troopers on each team, and those with blue balloons were dinks and the ones with red balloons were – you guessed it – tins. The blue team assembled on their horses at one end of the arena, with the reds at the other. To make it more fun, no one had saddles; they were in blanket-ride order. Military saddlery all has a purpose, most of which I'll attempt to explain in later chapters, but the blanket that's placed under the saddle is actually just a regular blanket, folded in a particular way so if you throw it over your horse correctly, the four unfolded corners – loose corners, if you like – should be on the nearside back corner. When It's sitting correctly, you secure it with your leather surcingle and away you go. It's trickier than riding with a saddle, as you haven't got stirrups to assist you.

Back in the arena, we were assisting the Life Guards team. All competitors were armed with 2ft-long bamboo canes. The objective was to charge the opposing team and burst their balloons by hitting them about the head with your cane. I must remind you at this juncture, dear reader, that this was before much regard was given for anyone's health or safety. A beret or SD cap, in the military's opinion, was perfectly adequate protection if you fell off!

I have to say, it was great fun to watch. The rivalry was plain as they beat the shit out of each other. I don't know who devised these games – an officer, I expect. As well as the balloon thing, we had mounted tug of war, with five on each side, still in blanket order, with a long rope spread between the opposing teams. Like tug of war at ground level, the rope had a piece of white rag attached to the middle of it, and the first to pull it over the line was deemed to have won. The knack, I soon discovered from careful observation, was to keep your mounts together and sideways to the rope, and then – in unison – dress your horses left or right, depending on what team you were on. Inevitably it all went tits up. Some fell off, some were left dangling off the rope, and some were left fighting to survive in amongst the cavalry blacks' legs. The net result, as you might guess, was ten cavalry mounts charging, bucking and farting around the arena. It was chaos. And guess who had to catch them? Us poor rookies, that's who Other duties included returning knocked-down poles during the showjumping and knocking in the pegs during the tent pegging. The day went really well. I got to be with Pam on the sidelines during events, and although a few were injured, nobody – surprisingly – died.

The following morning, the move back up town began. Horseboxes of all sizes and colours turned up from I know not where and began transporting the blacks and greys back to London. It was mid-afternoon when we squeezed into the back of a three-tonner full of the contents of *Polly Perkins'* stores tent and made our way to our new home, Hyde Park Barracks. For Stinch, Jarvo and the others, it was their first time visiting up town, whereas Quiff and I were old sweats at the job, and annoyingly, wouldn't stop talking about it!

After we'd finished carrying the stacks of blankets and other kit down the narrow staircase to the stores, we were told we could go and find our rooms on the sixth floor and move our kit up there. We were ordered to assemble at eight o'clock the next morning to begin our training in Riding School.

Chapter 5

Riding School

TO US, THE other ranks' accommodation at Hyde Park Barracks was very modern and new. The geography of the barracks took some getting used to. At the bottom end of the parade ground, where the three-tonner had deposited all *Polly*'s stores kit, stood the forge. Two big black sliding doors hid the massive forges. During the day it was a hive of activity, muscular, vest-clad farriers with leather aprons working away on the horses that had been listed on the blackboard the day before. Our quickest route to the sixth floor was via a staircase at this end of the building. Four flights of stairs took us to the fourth floor, the Life Guards' floor – 'don't go on that floor', we'd been warned, 'you won't make it out in one piece!' Four more flights of stairs and you passed the Blues and Royals' floor; that one wasn't too bad, apparently. Finally, the sixth floor, as I explained earlier, was the home of the musicians at the far end and riding school at the end where we entered from the staircase. After rapidly ascending with as much kit as I could, my legs felt like they were about to explode as I stood outside the double swing doors that led into the long, grey lino corridor. The corridor – and the rooms' floors, for that matter – weren't as highly polished as the depot. There wasn't a bed block in sight. Quite the opposite, actually. It seemed very laid back and relaxed. The focus here, as we were soon to find out, was horses and kit. In short, turnout – turnout for the Queen's Life Guard, turnout for anything that involved wearing any sort of uniform outside these walls.

I was allocated room 6B. My bed was in the far corner on the left as you looked from the door. On the right was Jarvo's bed, then in front of him, first on the right, was Quiff. The fourth bed, the one by the sink, was unoccupied. No one wanted the bed by the sink; the sink was used as much as a urinal as a sink during the night, so you never knew what might happen when it was too dark to see anything and somebody was half-asleep. I was surprised that there were no showers. Every four rooms shared a toilet area, which had three toilet cubicles, sinks and a bathroom. The baths were deep enamel ones and took ages to fill; typically you'd set one running, leave it while you went back to your room, and by the time you returned someone else had nicked it.

At 4.30 pm, Quiff and I led the guided tour to scoff. Only about half the regiment had returned – the rest would be back tomorrow – but it was still busier than the last time we were up there. Most of the large round tables were taken by troopers in their green denims. Armed with brown plastic trays, we collected noshing rods from the grey cutlery tray – no carrying your own KFS to scoff up here. The boys who hadn't been up here before looked suitably impressed as they made along the hotplate. We all managed to squeeze around a table by the window that ran the whole length of the room overlooking the parade square below, with Hyde Park the other side of the perimeter wall. It was five in the afternoon and the park was busy. It was one of my favourite places, sitting there eating or drinking coffee and having a cigarette while watching the various people running or walking past. Down on the parade square, there was a royal blue articulated horse box busily unloading the remainder or the day's horses When they'd finished, the massive wooden gates swung open as he drove out onto the road and away to Newbury, I presumed, because that was written on the back ramp of the vehicle.

After scoff, we decided to go up another level and recce the NAFFL There was the shop containing the usual NAFFI stuff, like a mini-supermarket really, then next-door to there was the bar. It was closed, but looking through the narrow glass panels we could see quite a large room with built-in upholstered benches all the way around three sides, with tables and chairs surrounding them.

We could feel the barracks coming back to life as we walked towards the staircase and up to the sixth floor. Some of the windows were open, and laughing and the occasional shout broke the silence of this side of the block. If we opened our window which overlooked Knightsbridge, the traffic noise was something else. I must remember to phone Pam tonight, I thought, as I opened the door to our new room. The only phone box I knew of was down opposite the guardroom; all I had to do was to go down in the lift and I would be there. Trouble was, someone had warned one of us recruits not to travel in the lifts alone, especially at night, as you could end up a victim of the fourth floor. Sounds creepy, doesn't it? Well it was, as I later discovered!

'Shall we go and sus the NAFFI bar out tonight?' I suggested to other guys in the room as we tried to work out where everything went in our larger-than-we-were-used-to lockers.

'Yeah, I'm up for it,' Stinch agreed.

Even with the lights on, the NAFFI bar still appeared closed. I pushed the door, half expecting it not to open, and was surprised when it did. A young dark-haired girl sat on a bar stool. She looked bored at getting the Monday evening shift, or maybe it was always like this. One other person was sat in the corner of the room, a trooper in denims nursing a pint of bitter – Double Diamond, I guessed. I remember him staring at us a lot, which was a bit unnerving really. Every time I glanced in his direction, there he was, eyes fixed in an intense stare. I did contemplate giving him a friendly nod, but thought better of it. The evening was riveting, as you can imagine, but one good thing was that there was a public telephone on that floor so I didn't have to go down to the guardroom to phone Pam. The sixth floor was quiet for the most part. The occasional sounds of mussies practicing wafted down the corridor, but apart from that all was well.

* * *

At eight o'clock on a Tuesday morning in 1974, a total of fifteen of us – eight Life Guards and seven dinks – lined up on the stable bricked floor outside the forge. Two NCOs approached from the office area one level above us. They both wore one-dress – dark blue tunics fastened right up to the neck, and breeches that matched their tunics and disappeared into highly polished black long boots. Both had three gold braid chevrons with a crown above them, which told us they were corporal of horses. They also had a gold spur stitched to the arm of their uniform, which informed us they were remount riders or riding instructors. Finally, they both also carried – with much swagger, I thought – a yellow whip.

'Good morning, gentlemen,' the first one, Corporal Smith, announced. 'You lovely lot are about to start your six-month journey through riding school.'

'If you follow us, we'll take you to meet the riding master,' the second NCO, Corporal Jones, informed us, adjusting his red and blue forage cap.

The silence was palpable, as no one knew this officer's name. I knew he was a captain and that he was a Life Guard. His name, though, I just couldn't remember.

Junior recruits Easter term 1976, I'm on the back row forth from left.

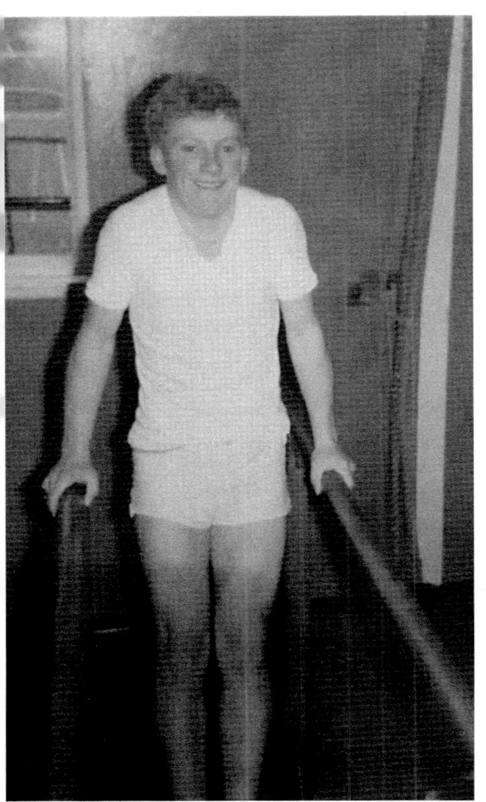

Above left: In the Gym, Junior Guardsman's Wing Pirbright.

Above right: Riding School at The Guards Depot stables, our happy place!

Major-General James Bowes-Lyon
Commanding The Household Division
request the pleasure of the company of

JUNIOR CORPORAL OF HORSE WALLINGTON

at a Reception to be held at St James's Palace
at 12 o'clock on Wednesday 23rd May 1973 on the occasion
of the Presentation of the Silver Wedding Present
from the Household Division to
Her Majesty The Queen
and
His Royal Highness Prince Philip, Duke of Edinburgh

Invitation to St James Palace to present the Queen and Prince Philip with an oil painting to celebrate their silver wedding anniversary.

Above left: Quiff and I outside Inkerman Platoon, I think the flash surprised me!

Above right: Military plaque Title (Passing out parade 1973, best turned out "mounted")

Above left: Cloaked up, Horse Guards riding Pan-Am.

Above right: (Box sentry on Pan Am, note no yellow keep out boxes painted on the ground and no warning signs, we dealt with situations ourselves)

Wedding day February 1975, note Jarvo on the left, Stinch and Terry are standing behind him and Quiff on the left, I had one of my front teeth knocked out by Pan Am so I was trying not to smile!

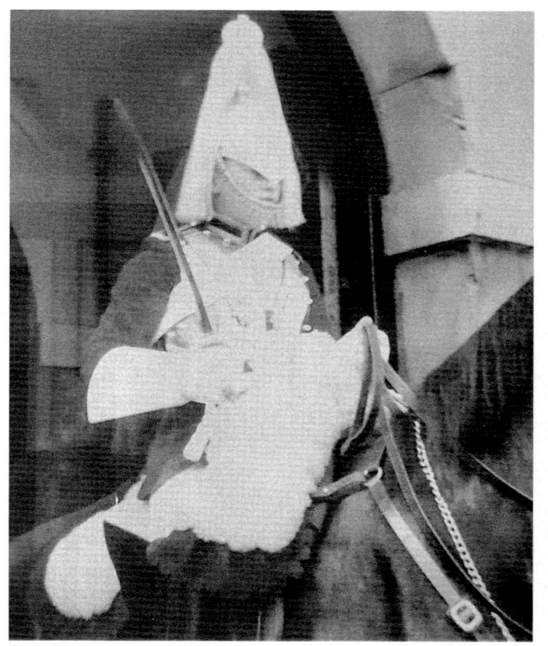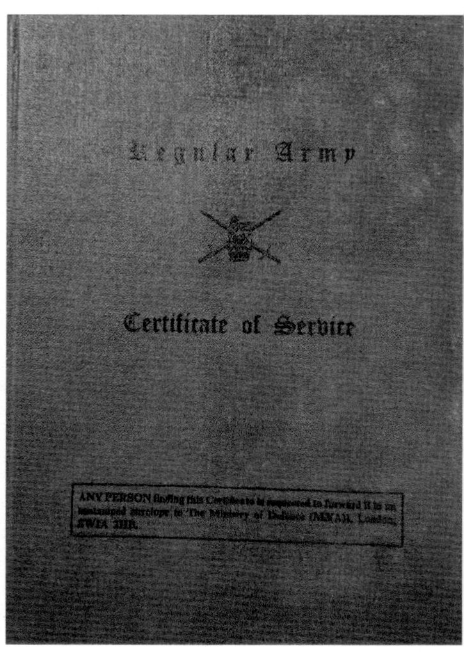

Above left: (one of my first box sentries, it was Saturday afternoon, Pam had travelled from our first married quarter in Penge and took the photograph)

Above right: My red book, the very book that was given to me when I was dismissed and subsequently taken back and amended.

Summer camp 1975, Pan Am on the left and Opel (I think) on the right.

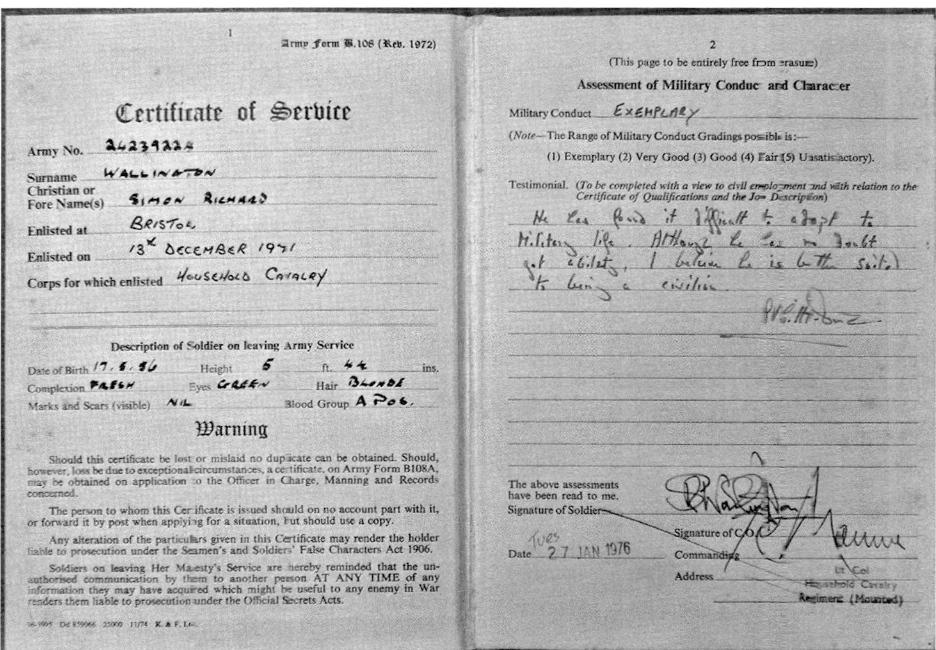

Top: Inside the red book, note the testimonial.

Above: Terry Quiff and I meeting with the late Lord Etherton (on the right) giving our statements in the Cabinet rooms in Whitehall.

Right: Back at summer camp 1975, that year Pan Am and I won the handy hunter competition with Jonny B and the junior nco's and troopers show jumping.

Above left: Terry Quiff and I in Hyde Park Barracks after attending the memorial of the IRA bombings of The Household Cavalry on the 20th of July 1982.

Above right: Terry looking pleased with himself in our room on the fourth floor, note the handy sword rack in the background!

One of the regular letters I received from Pam, we've still got them!

Above left: The sand hill at The Guards Depot, looks nothing dosn't it, trust me it's a killer!

Above right: Me in my study.

The Cenotaph
parade 2023.

Above left: The Life Guards cypher.

Above right: Ribbon that was given out as a "sorry" gesture after the Etherton enquiry.

Three troop in Brighton after riding there from Hickstead where we were staying for a week, I'm second from left.

'His name is Captain Jackson. Don't worry, you won't forget it once you've had the pleasure of meeting him. His office is in the riding school. Follow us.'

There was no 'form up in two ranks' or any of that nonsense that we'd become so used to in the depot. We just casually followed the NCOs across the parade ground towards yet another red brick and concrete building. Beyond the building we were heading for, a massive tower block loomed over everything. The sun, which was still rising behind us, made the windows look like mirrors. At the very top, it looked like someone had placed a lead-coloured hat on it. The whole place, I have to say, was impressive.

'Remind me,' Quiff asked as we followed our new leaders, 'what's the spur on their arms for?'

'Remount riders, you plonker. Don't you know anything?'

A quick dig in the ribs put paid to my piss-taking as we neared yet another concrete ramp. As we walked around this one, I spotted two massive wooden sliding doors on the side of the building. Just before them was another door, which we headed for. One of the three-bars opened it to reveal a staircase leading up to the next level. Intrigued now, we followed each other up the narrow stairs. At the top, we found ourselves in a large room with windows running all along one side. One of our instructors began to flick on a long row of light switches which slowly brought the area beyond the window to life. Open mouthed, I stared in wonder at something the like of I'd never seen before. It was an indoor riding school. Not some taggy post-and-railed arena in the corner of a field, this was amazing, state of the art. It had sloping tongue and groove wooden sides, large mirrors everywhere, and when the doors slid shut it was completely enclosed. The mass of strip lights flooded the area with light. I couldn't wait to get a horse and get in there. Without warning, one of our instructors brought the room to attention, and he saluted as an officer emerged from an adjacent room.

'Gentlemen, may I introduce you to the Household Cavalry's mounted regiments' riding master, Captain Jackson.'

What I thought was a quite elderly looking gentleman stood in front of us. His uniform sort of matched that of his instructors; it actually reminded me of a German SS officer that you'd see in war films. As it turned out, I wasn't far wrong!

'Good morning.' he said, desperately trying to crack a smile. 'All being well and with your hard work, you will spend six months here. At the end, you'll be skilled enough to turn out as a state dutyman. The next time you meet me will be in there' – he was pointing his leather officer's whip toward the window – 'where you'll be assessed on your ability and we can see what we're up against.'

He disappeared back into what turned out to be his office and shut the door. A wry smile spread across Corporal Smith's face as he tucked his whip under his left arm and indicated that we should follow him.

The next stop was familiar. We were back at the stores, and behind the counter stood a tall guy who walked with a slight stoop. He owned a large German Shepherd dog. How did I know this? Well, as we lined up at the counter, someone hadn't shut the little door under the counter. While waiting, I suddenly had this strange feeling that someone – or something – was touching my bollocks. There wasn't anyone the other side of the counter, so it wasn't from there, and Quiff was waiting in the doorway, some distance away. Then it happened again, a gentle nudge this time. It was enough to bring one of my hands from behind my back to the front to check I wasn't imagining this feeling. As I did so, I felt this spongy wet thing on my hand. Stepping back like I'd been pushed by a ghost, I saw that it was a lovely golden brown and black face that belonged to Sabre. I knew his name because from the back of the stores appeared a stooping man, telling his dog to get back in his basket. Stooping man turned out to be *Ruby Redfern*, a Life Guard corporal who worked in the stores for *Polly Perkins*.

Apart from our black long boots, the Junior Guardsman's Wing contingent of the recruits were issued with a second set of breeches and denims. The most important things we were issued with, though, were our SD caps. Wearing these, rather than a beret, made you less conspicuous amongst your peers, we found. All we needed now was to pass our khaki ride, which would entitle us to wear spurs and complete the trooper look.

Sitting on my bed during the NAFFI break, I found myself staring into my SD cap, trying to work out how the senior guys 'slashed' their peaks. Somehow, by doing some sort of magic, you transformed the peak from sticking outwards to lying flat on your forehead. Asking someone how it was done was a non-starter, as that would mean venturing onto the fourth floor – don't go down there, never go down there, it's not safe, we'd been told. When I put it on, the oversized peak did what it was supposed to do, I guess, that is protect you from the sun or rain. So why did everyone slash them? If I'm honest, apart from tradition, I still don't know.

After NAFFI break, the corporal took us recruits down the even longer ramp to the Life Guards stables. This was the first time we'd been allowed down there. The ramp had what looked like chevrons cut out of the concrete all the way down to the bottom; they even tracked around the slight bend at the bottom. Our corporal solved the mystery by explaining that they helped with grip, and that in cold weather they were heating elements to stop the ramp freezing over. At the bottom, Corporal Smith gathered us all together. We stood in a fairly big yard that appeared to be surrounded by offices on two sides, with a big wooden door in another corner.

Corporal Smith told us: 'Okay, this is the vet's yard. You bring your horses here if they need to see the vet colonel or the farriers for treatment. These windows surrounding it contain the saddler's shop and the tailor's shop. There's a door under the ramp in the corner that will lead you to all those facilities. Behind the wooden door is the forage barn. There are a couple of loose boxes in there as well, for the colonel's and the riding master's horses. There to your front,' he continued as he pointed his whip towards this long slightly dark tunnel, 'is the Life Guards stables. Four Troop rooms are on the right, while their tack rooms are opposite them on the left. All understood? Good. Follow me.'

The tunnel had a bit of a cold feeling to it as we followed Corporal Smith over the stable-bricked floor towards the daylight at the end of the building. Our curiosity got the better of us, and we quickly looked into each troop stable as we passed. The red-blue-red signs were attached to the wall of each troop, the first being 1 Troop and so on up until 4 Troop. Three troops of Life Guards and three troops of Blues and Royals made up the Household Cavalry mounted regiment. Above us, on the upper floor, was where the Blues stables were. The fourth troop stables were where we were – recruit troop or riding school troop, but mostly known as rookie troop.

As we reached the end of the corridor, a large opening with black iron grid-like affair protecting it ended the building. Beyond it was yet another ramp, which appeared to make its way up to the Blues floor above. As I gazed out of the void, I could make out a large white Georgian-type house rising towards a sky that was somewhat obscured by everything that surrounded me.

'Four troop,' the Corporal announced with some pride, as he threw his arms open like he was doing that 'ta-dah' thing. But rather than a 'ta-dah' moment, it was more of a 'dull thud' moment. Apart from three chestnut horses at the far end of the room, the place was empty. Where are the blacks, I thought, as we continued our tour.

'All four rooms are identical,' our guide went on. 'Sixteen stalls on the left and fifteen on the right, with two loose boxes at the end. On the right between the last stall and the loose box is the dung shoot. Follow me, I'll show you.'

This really is impressive, I thought, as I followed everyone towards the big wooden doors at the end of this massive space. Amongst the concrete beams above us snaked ventilation pipes, looking like they'd just come off the set of *Doctor Who*.

'Okay, this is the dung shoot,' Corporal Smith continued. The more he used his riding crop as a pointer, the more I wanted one. 'When using it, always make sure there's a bin in place below. If you don't and there isn't one, guess who will be going down there to clear it up?'

As we peered down the dung shoot, we could just make out, in the darkness, a large galvanized bin. I was sure I could make out shadows in the darkness. 'Is there anybody down there?' I asked our guide.

'Probably. There's a civvy that works down there swopping the bins around ready for them to be taken away. He's known as the "dung rat". And by the way, always check that he's not working down there before you tip a load of shit down.'

At that moment, a rumbling sound came from the dung shoot in front of us. It was coming from above. The alloy box in front of our manhole rattled as the shit, quite literally, fell from above. All the horses at that time were bedded on shavings, another innovative thing with which I wasn't familiar. The bedding of choice in those days was still straw, so this was all new to me. Our next stop on the tour was the feed room, on the left as you passed between the stable room and the corridor beyond. Large galvanized feed bins filled most of the fairly small room. The corporal lifted the first lid to reveal bran, the next contained crushed oats and finally there were horse nuts. Opposite the feed store was the cleaning room. A long wooden saddle horse stood in the middle of the room, with hooks hanging from the ceiling and the walls, which gave it the impression of a torture chamber.

'Now, pay attention, this is important,' our guide announced as we stood beside a large blackboard. 'This is where you'll find what horse you're riding on what day and what time your lessons are. Don't forget to study this daily. Understood?'

'Yes, Corporal of Horse,' eight slightly bored-sounding voices rang out as we followed him to our next destination. 'Hope this won't take long. I'm starving,' Quiff whispered as we crossed the corridor towards the double wooden doors opposite the troop stables.

This final port of call was the tack room. It was lined with saddle racks attached to the wall, but most were empty. There were only two civvy saddles and bridles in there.

'Don't worry, we will be moving your horses and their kit in this afternoon,' the corporal said. 'You can dismiss now and go and get some scoff. Be back here in an hour and a half.'

'Do you know who the black guy is?' I asked Jarvo (*Derek Jarvis*) as we stood in the lunch queue.

'No, haven't got a clue.'

'That's Henry – "one sausage Henry", as he's known. He's got a thing about sausages apparently,' I knowingly informed him as I tapped my nose in that dodgy way some people do.

Scoff in Hyde Park Barracks wasn't bad, to be fair, with three square meals a day. So long as you stuck to the rules, you had less chance of being assaulted with a ladle, or even – if you really pushed your luck – a knife. Army chefs – slop jockeys – were gobby fuckers when they were standing behind their hotplate brandishing some piece of kitchen equipment as a weapon. But off duty, they somehow disappeared. You never seemed to see them around the barracks. A bit like the mussies, they didn't associate themselves with us lot.

At 1.30 pm back in 4 Troop, it was quiet time in the troop rooms for the horses. The troopers who weren't on guard or were getting ready for guard were either up on the fourth floor cleaning their kit or in the cleaning room down here, cleaning head kits (bridles) and suchlike. Evening stables started at 3.30 pm, when the horses would get their final mucking out, feed and hay net for the day. We all gathered around the blackboard to see which horses we'd been allocated for riding school for the next six months. I was desperately hoping I wouldn't get a plug (a slow, usually lazy horse who tended to spend their career either in riding school or as a musician's mount). Next to my name I saw 'Windrush', followed by 3 Troop – just next-door, I thought, as I studied some of the other horses on the list. Quiff's allocation was named 'Warlord'. Stinch had 'Sausage' – what a shit name, I thought, as we waited for further orders from the three-bar.

It had been explained to us at summer camp how the horses were named in the cavalry. They all had their military number branded into the near fore hoof and 'LG' branded into their off fore hoof. My eventual guard horse,

Panam, had the number LG52. Their names were chosen from a list that troopers and NCOs contributed to from the letter of the alphabet for that year, like car registrations really. If I remember correctly, in 1974 we were at the end of the alphabet and the letter was Y, so the remounts (young horses) coming in that year would have a name beginning with that letter.

'Wallington!' I heard our corporal shout. 'You can go to 3 Troop and get Windrush and put him in the second stall on the right, then go and collect his tack and put it in the tack room.'

I was grateful most of the troopers weren't there as I pensively walked into the entrance to the troop room. A sea of horses' heads and arses greeted me as they contentedly munched their hay. Apart from the occasional tail swishing, it was a very peaceful scene.

'Can I help, young man?' I heard a voice say.

'Er, yes, I've come to collect a horse,' I replied, desperately trying to work out where the voice came from.

Suddenly, I heard one of the loose box doors being slid open, and who should appear but 'harmonica man' from summer camp. Now I'd met him standing up, I definitely knew I wasn't the shortest cavalryman here. He was well turned out, his tailored KF shirt being neatly pressed, as were his denim trousers.

'What horse are you looking for?' he asked.

'Oh, Windrush, please.'

'Windrush, Windrush, Windrush,' he kept repeating as we walked back towards the blackboard at the front of the troop room. Above every stall there was a nameplate with the occupant's name on it. We passed names like Rockingham, Panorama and Noddy, but no Windrush. The horses looked well; a bit wooled up after being at summer camp for three weeks, but that would soon groom out, I thought.

'He should be on your right, just about where you are now,' harmonica man shouted from his place looking at the blackboard.

'Yep, here he is,' I shouted back, as I gently patted the horse on the bum as I edged my way along the side of the stall to his head. I was undoing his head collar rope by the time harmonica man returned.

'Riding school, 4 Troop, is that correct?' he asked as he waited while I backed Windrush out of his stall.

'Yeah, that's right. I'll come back in a minute for his kit, if that's alright.'

Three Troop felt warmer than 4 Troop. I guessed it was because it was pretty full of warm horses. Windrush dutifully followed me the short distance to his new home. He seemed good-tempered and willing, which I thought was a good sign. On my way back to 3 Troop, I kept telling myself not to forget his name plate. I needn't have worried, as when I got back to the now empty stall, harmonica man was precariously balanced on the feed trough and water trough, carefully removing the nameplate from its holder.

In no time at all, I was carrying the last of Windrush's tack out of one tack room to the other. The saddles and head kit were the same as we used at Pirbright. The saddles were British Army UP (universal pattern) style: a metal arch formed the pommel which was screwed onto a wooden frame which became the tree of the saddle. The leather seat and sides were then attached and you ended up with a saddle weighing around 30lb. This would be the saddle Windrush would use on state duties, it would just be rigged differently, but more of that when and if I make the 'kit ride'.

The recruit – or should I say riding school – troop room looked a little fuller now. We had ten horses in there now, we'd hung all the saddlery in the tack room and marked up the horses' names on the narrow blackboards above their respective saddle racks. Last job for me was to somehow get Windrush's nameplate into the holder above his stall. I didn't know Windrush well enough yet to start climbing in his stall, so I asked Quiff to hold him out in the centre of the room while I accessed the holder.

'What do you need to do that for?' Quiff asked as he took the nameplate from my hand and proceeded to reach up and slot it into place. Bollocks, I thought, as I nodded and went to fill his hay net – the horse's, that is, not Quiff's, even though he ate like a horse.

It had been a good afternoon's effort, Corporal Smith told us, before we were given the order to feed away. The horses were fed three times a day up town: breakfast was after morning exercise (watering order), then there was lunch time, and finally, upon completion of evening stables at 4.30 pm, all the individual feed bins were lined up, in military fashion, two side by side down the centre of the room. The troopers would stand at ease in front of the pillar that divided the stalls, which was a dodgy place to be as the horses got exited knowing they were about to be fed. The odd kick would lash out, and the wooden ball-type things that were attached to the ends of their head collar rope banged against their feed bins. Being the last troop room in the building didn't help, as the orderly officer for that day would inspect the troops before 'feed away', starting with 1 Troop. As he came in the room, we were brought to attention while he walked down both sides of the room, pretending he knew what he was looking at. Once Lieutenant

Who-Jimmyflip, or whatever his name was, had gone, we were ordered to 'feed away', when at last we would take our feed bin into the stall and feed our horse.

* * *

Cavalry blacks are unique members of the equine world. Ask anyone who's had the pleasure of working with them. They are all bred at the same stud in Ireland, they are mostly Irish draught or draught-crosses who are chosen for their strength, athleticism and temperament. Along with the blacks, they have the trumpeters' greys and officers' chargers. When you study or groom a black horse, you soon notice they're not actually black, they're a very deep brown. In similar fashion, what looks like a white horse is still classed a grey.

Once you've successfully got in and then out of the stall, avoiding teeth, hooves and being crushed deliberately by your horse, you can wash your horse's feed bowl out and finish – 'rug up', as it is referred to. Then, and only then, can you go and get your scoff.

'First day in the school tomorrow. It's alright for you, you've been riding for years,' Quiff observed as we climbed the stairs to the other ranks mess.

'You'll be alright, you've done plenty of riding at the depot. Remember, a lot of our ride have never even sat on a horse before.'

The following morning, the corridor connecting the troop rooms was busy. The Life Guards were on Queen's today (Queen's Life Guard at Whitehall), so most of that day's guard horses were tied up outside their troop stables, either being groomed or chalked up – more of that later. I was explaining to Quiff as we made our way to 4 Troop about the bits we were using. They were the standard 6½in reversible military bit. When you're on ceremonial, the horses wear what is known as black kit, a double bridle (two bits and four reins); the main bit is a Banbury bit or state bit, all very complicated I know, but more of that later too.

The day in Hyde Park Barracks started at a quarter to six in the morning. The horses that weren't on guard that day and were not on stable rest went on morning exercise (watering order), as it was known, when groups of horses about twenty strong would clatter around the streets of London, waking everyone as they went. Troopers would ride one horse and lead another, all led by an officer at the front of each ride. Us in riding school weren't qualified yet to take part, but our horses would get plenty of exercise being in the indoor school twice a day. The men that were left in the stables while watering order was out would muck out the stables and get everything ready for their return.

Us riding school monkeys were on a totally different timetable. All of us would carry out morning stables, mucking out, filling hay nets and sweeping up We seemed to spend a good part of the hours we were in the stables sweeping up. The whole area, including our part of the corridor, would be swept morning, noon and evening. In wide areas, we would form a line and sweep in unison, so you'd start at the top of the troop room and, side by side, with strict dressing kept, we would work our way down to the shit shoot. It was a thing of beauty to observe. After feed away, it was up to breakfast, remembering to avoid a rap on the knuckles from 'one sausage Henry', then back down to the troop to groom and get your horse ready for your first lesson at 10.00 am.

Sitting on my bed, I was trying desperately to pull my long boots on. Doing so much riding as a kid gave me over-large calf muscles. They weren't freakishly large, just large enough to make normal boots painful to wear. I clearly wasn't on my own because I'd noticed several guys around the barracks with boots that had clearly been altered by the saddler. All I could do was to force some bigger boot trees into mine and try to stretch them a bit. We were still in summer order, so our dress code was KF shirt with sleeves neatly rolled and pressed, khaki beeches with stable belt, long boots and, just for maximum safety, SD cap!

You never rode in the corridor. Horses were walked up onto the square, where there stood concrete mounting blocks. They weren't for us, though, they were for dutymen in state kit and officers. We carried on walking across the parade ground, down the ramp and into the riding school. Everything was drill – cavalry drill – be it on foot or mounted. The first order when you were correctly lined up would be 'stand to your horses', which meant standing in front of your horse, facing it, then holding each ring of the bit, one in each hand, and with your elbows up at shoulder height you wait for the next order or to be inspected. Your lovely horse, however, has direct access to you head, chest and face. Horses breathe through their noses, and they also like to clear their nose when they feel the need, so it's not unusual to be sprayed directly in the face by snot and whatever they've just eaten! After inspection – to make sure both you and your horse are correctly turned out, and your horse's kit is correctly fitted and secure – the next command will be 'prepare to mount', so you move to the near (left) side of your mount and place your left hand on the pommel of the saddle (the highest bit at the front) and your right hand on the highest bit of the back of the saddle and prepare, when the order 'mount' comes, to act like a jack-in-the-box and spring upwards. When you've achieved this, you must wait, with straight arms like you're on some piece of gymnastic equipment, until the whole ride is in the same position. When it is – and believe me, this can take some time – a nod from your instructor means you can throw your right leg over the saddle and try to get some of the feeling back into your arms.

Riding school in the Seventies was in two parts. The first fourteen weeks was khaki ride, which did what it said on the tin really, as we learnt all the cavalry drills whilst at the same time, for some, they learnt to ride. After you'd successfully completed khaki, you would progress onto kit ride, with six weeks of learning to ride in state kit – a completely different kettle of fish, I can assure you. To be honest, some of us could have skipped most of the khaki ride. We'd learnt the drills in the school in the Junior Guardsman's Wing at Pirbright, but just being there and watching was somewhat amusing. We had one officer on our ride. Of course he had a groom to get his mount to the school every lesson, but that didn't mean he got away with any of the riding challenges. Second Lieutenant Hardcourt-Player, or whatever his name was, appeared on our ride on day one. He was a dink officer who, unusually, couldn't ride. Most – no all – cavalry officers in those days came from extremely privileged backgrounds, so were almost born in the saddle.

Captain *Alex Jackson*, who had his made his way up through the ranks, seemed to delight in giving these chinless wonders a hard time. I remember we were working in the jumping lane one afternoon. For those who don't know, a jumping lane is four jumps with a stride (12ft) of distance between them, set alongside the side wall of the school and enclosed with spare jumping poles so as to form this enclosed lane. The idea was that you didn't need to hold onto or steer your horse through it, so the instructors could get up to all sorts of fun and games.

This particular afternoon, about ten weeks into khaki ride, we built the jumping lane and the ride lined up in the middle of the school. We were in winter order now, so heavy-duty jumpers were the order of the day. It's a lot harder to explain in words than it actually is to do. You start, in a trot, at the gallery end of the school, the end where *Jacko*'s office was. You approach the lane in trot, drop your rein and allow your horse to make its way to the other end, jumping the jumps as they go. At the far end was a massive mirror attached to the wall above the wooden sloping walls of the school, the theory being that if you keep your head up and look in the fast-approaching mirror, your upper body will stay in the correct position, which will improve balance and stability. Still having the affliction of volunteering, I had first go. I did a fair bit of jumping before joining up, so this was nothing new to me. Windrush was keen as mustard as he turned into the lane, and the trot almost immediately became a canter as he popped over the fences. As soon as he'd landed after the fourth fence, I gathered up the reins to slow him before we reached the mirrored wall and the sharp left turn. All went well, so well in fact the instructor kindly ordered me to cross my stirrups over the saddle in front of me and do it again. Not having stirrups is a whole different thing. For a start, army saddles are highly polished, and couple that with thick woollen breeches and your arse feels like a duster sliding across a highly polished table. Doing as ordered, I began my second approach. Windrush had refreshed his memory by now of the many times he'd done this, and how many riding school monkeys he'd dropped on his way down this lane. Before I'd even got into the lane, he was off. I gripped on with my legs so hard, he probably thought I was kicking him on. I don't remember the jumping bit – I definitely wasn't checking my position in the mirror, just hovering my hands above the loose rein, ready to pull them taut as soon as I could get away with it. By the time we'd reached the wall, I had slid so far forward I wondered whether I'd ever be able to have children! Still struggling to stay aboard and desperately trying to gather up the reins, we rounded the corner. I did the only thing I could think of, what you do when you're riding bareback, and leant backwards. Somehow we made it around the corner and I managed to recover control. As I restored some dignity, I glanced up at *Jacko*'s window, and I'm sure I saw a ghostly figure towards the back of his dark office, laughing.

A great deal of carnage followed that afternoon. Like me, most were okay with stirrups, except of course Will. Will Freedman had come direct from the depot. He wasn't an ex-Junior like most of us, and was a tall, thin, gangly bloke. I don't ever recall having met someone so thin. To be fair, he wasn't the sharpest tool in the box either. We used to call him 'the scull'. In equine parlance, he couldn't ride one side of a horse – he hit the deck more times than a drunk staggering home on a Saturday night. Even with stirrups, his horse buried him in the last corner of the jumping lane. It took him ten minutes to catch his mount as it ran around the school, bucking and farting. You let it go, you catch it, was our instructor's philosophy. Cavalry blacks are unique characters. They tend to do exactly the opposite of what you're expecting. With Sausage, for instance, a greedier, lazier beast you wouldn't want to meet. He was so broad, that when you sat astride him it was actually painful for my short legs to spread that wide. Fortunately, I didn't ride him much, but when I did, I must have looked like I was performing some sort of yoga move on his back. Remember the 'Thelwell' cartoons of little girls riding fat little ponies? Well that's how I felt.

When they're 'broken in' or trained to accept someone sitting on their back, horses work on three natural indicators, or aids as they are known. First off, there are voice commands, which can be strange clicking sounds you somehow make with your mouth. Tone and speed are important – an elongated 'wooooe' in a calm voice is better than screaming 'woe, woe!' as you take off around the school. Then there are leg aids. A gentle squeeze of your legs should act as a command for your mount to go forward or backwards. They even can be used to ask him to move in various directions. The final aid is your hands. The idea is to put all three aids together, using the combination of them to make your horse do as it is asked. All three can be further enforced by mechanical aids. Spurs, whips and bits are mechanical aids, as are the saddle and what type of bridle you employ. You could also add martingales and nosebands to the list. As a mounted dutyman, some of these aids are immediately removed from your arsenal of tools. If you are on state duties, for instance, you're not allowed to use voice commands, at least you weren't in the Seventies when I served. Part of the state kit were very severe swan-necked spurs, which had to be worn by everyone as part of the kit. If you had a charger that was willing and keen to go forward – the clue is in the description, 'charger' – one little tickle from a spur of that severity was like a racing driver launching his car off from a green light. Imagine, if you can, riding in formation – a state escort, for instance. You are constantly being pushed into, and at the same you're pushing into someone else. This leads inevitably to your spur being dug into your horse's belly by someone else. Couple that with having to hold four reins (double bridle) in your left gauntlet-gloved hand and a sabre in the other, and your charger is now prancing around like a demented ballet dancer wondering what to do next. Just for good measure, pop a metal helmet on your head with a peak that's determined to slice your nose off and a plume that's constantly falling into your field of vision. That's what it's like. There will be plenty more on this subject in later chapters.

Eventually, Will got his shit together and remounted his horse. His SD cap had made its way onto the back of his head, making him look like a character in a comedy movie. We'd been waiting in the middle of the school so long now that Windrush had decided to take a little nap. All he needed was a little squeeze to wake him up, whereas Sausage, who was next to us, required a lot of kicking in his fat belly to bring him back in the room. Corporal Smith had waited patiently as all this went on, slapping his whip against his boot and checking his watch.

'Okay,' he finally announced, 'because of Freedman's efforts and incompetence, we've run out of time, so prepare to dismount – dismount! – and walk your horses back to the troop.' Although it was funny at the time, I think everyone felt sorry for Will. We all knew this was a tough course, but I personally just wanted to get on with it. I didn't want Will holding the ride back.

This was a big day, a Friday afternoon. Pam was coming up for the weekend, and we were being issued with our state kit. The kit ride was still a few weeks away, but it would give us time to put it on – a knack in itself – and also to clean it. As we lined up along the narrow underground corridor, waiting our turn to enter *Polly Perkins'* store, Quiff was in there getting his kit. When he gave his hat size, seven and a half or something – large anyway – and he'd tried a few on, I suddenly heard *Polly* shout down the store, 'For fucks' sake, *Ruby*, see if there's a coal scuttle down there!'

We didn't have much time to try kit on, and there was so much of it that two trips were required. Eventually, the pile of red, silver and leather – some white, some black – surrounded my locker. The lockers were supposedly, designed to secure all your state kit, hence they were quite large. The kit included helmet and plume – the plume in its plume bag, away from the helmet – and two Life Guards red tunics – one for cuirasses and one for best (cuirasses, or breastplates, made black marks on the front upper chest of your tunic). Cuirasses were attached by shoulder straps known as scales and a white buckskin cuirass belt. There was also a white cartouche belt with black cartouche pouch (handy place to keep your fags), white buckskin breeches, jackboots with spurs, state sword and white buckskin gauntlets. There were many more bits and pieces to the kit when you started taking it apart; I'll explain more later when I write about cleaning it.

* * *

It was nearly 7.00 pm when I made my way down Brompton Road to meet Pam. She'd booked a room in one of the many small hotels along that road. As always, I was pleased to see her waiting outside the salubrious-looking building which was to be our accommodation for the next couple of nights. After dropping off my bag, we walked back up the road towards what had become our temporary local, The Gloucester, in Sloane Street. Us riding school rookies had decided to keep a low profile, at least while we were still in riding school. The two main cavalry pubs were The Paxton's Head, which was just across the road from the barracks, and The Baker and Oven, which was in a back street opposite Harrods – the bigger boys drank there, and we didn't think it was a good idea to mix alcohol-afflicted troopers with new recruits. The Gloucester was busy, but I soon spotted Stinch at the bar. Quiff wasn't there yet; he was always late. 'Doing his hair I expect, the tart,' I whispered to Pam as we waited for our drinks. A couple of pints went down well before we left and went for some food.

'Fancy a Wimpey?' I asked Pam as we left the pub.

'A Wimpey? Is that the one that you and Quiff went to when you first came up here?'

'Yep, that's the one. Come on, you'll love it.'

It wasn't too late when we got back to the hotel. I had to get back for morning stables at 6.00 am Saturday was half a day in riding school, morning stables, breakfast, then a blanket ride in the school to stretch the horses' legs, then a bit of grooming after NAFFI break, and finish-off stables before feeding away at lunchtime and then you could get off. Two of us took it in turns – or were on a rota, I should say – to be on stable duty over the weekends. Sunday was bran mash day, so the horses didn't have any exercise. A rest day with a warm bran mash cleared out their system, or so we were told by the powers that be. I stood at the guardroom window, having my civvy dress checked. The growing threat by the IRA had made some bright spark officer change our civvy walking-out dress, with the regimental blazer and regimental tie ditched for standard blazer and normal tie, whatever that was. All that happened was we unpicked the badge off our blazers and bought the cheapest tie there was in the NAFFI shop, and there you were, completely transformed – no one would ever know, would they? I bet we easily blended into the background amongst the denim-clad folk wandering around the West End in the Seventies! I could see Pam waiting across the road opposite. She was wearing blue jeans and a brown chequered wraparound jacket, tied in the middle with a matching belt. Here we go, I thought as the RP handed back my ID card, let's go and blend in. No one will notice this fresh-faced kid wearing formal trousers, shirt, tie and blazer, with a lovely looking denim-clad girl on his arm! When I was eventually released into the big bad world, Pam and I spent the afternoon sightseeing. We walked the mile to Horse Guards, passing Buckingham Palace on the way. I pointed out St James' Palace, where I'd visited as a junior to present the Queen and the Duke of Edinburgh with their silver wedding anniversary present. Luckily – I say luckily because I had less chance of being recognized by anyone – the dinks were on Queen's today. I didn't want my mates accusing me of being a 'kit tyke', someone who hangs around Whitehall watching the troopers on guard. Believe me, that really happened.

I wasn't being a grump, although I was accused of being one, but there was no way I was going stand next to a dink for a photograph, Can you imagine what would happen if someone found out? Whitehall was busy, with swarms of people battling for their place as the four o'clock inspection started. I wanted to leave, but Pam insisted on watching it. I spent the whole time staring at my shoes to avoid being sussed out. The yellow gravel stones of Horse Guards Parade crunched under our feet as we made our way to St James' Park. It was a lovely sunny late afternoon. Sitting on a bench next to the lake, I glanced at Pam. To me, she was the one. I don't know why, but she was. I was 17 – too young to marry, some people would say, indeed many people did say – but I'd made up my mind: I was going to ask her tonight. Shit, not tonight, we were going to meet some of the boys in The Baker and Oven. I'd ask her – no, we'd talk about it – before she returned to Bristol tomorrow. As it turned out, I didn't ask her that weekend. We sort of decided it would be a good idea while we were sat in her Mini Traveller in a dead-end lane back in Bristol on our way home from the pub.

After accompanying Pam to Paddington station on Sunday afternoon, I walked back to the barracks through Hyde Park. We were now at the stage in riding school that the following week we would have our first ride in the park. We were learning sword drill too, so we'd been issued with service swords. These are different to our official state swords – they are sabres. British Army heavy cavalry swords, 1796 pattern (service swords), were just over a metre long and weighed around 3lb. That doesn't sound much, but when you're handling a stroppy horse at the same time you soon begin to feel it.

Captain Jackson was, as far as I any many others were concerned, a legend. He wasn't a big man, but his presence made not only everyone brace up, but even the horses changed their mood when he walked into the school. Even Sausage showed a little more effort when 'Jacko' was around. I recall one afternoon towards the end of our time in khaki ride when he took the lesson. The whole afternoon was unusual. Firstly, we were told to wear two-dress jackets, and secondly, the dreaded jumping lane had been set up. Most of us had by now altered the peaks on our SD caps. *Jacko* didn't like this tradition, even though he had probably slashed a peak or two on his journey through the ranks.

'Wallington!' he screamed while he was inspecting the ride.

'Yes, Sir.'

'Have you slashed your peak?' he asked as he checked the bit of Roupo, Quiff's horse, who was beside me.

'A bit, sir,' was the best I could come up with as he reached out for my cap.

'A bit? A bloody fucking bit? You've ruined it, you bloody fucking man.'

It's strange how naked and vulnerable you feel when everyone else is wearing a cap and you're not. Following close examination, he looked up at me; he was turning red with rage. I thought this was where I'd die – right here, right now. I couldn't see his eyes, ironically, because his peak was covering them. I didn't particularly want to, anyway. Suddenly, he turned and threw it like a frisbee across the school towards the jumping lane. Roupo beside me threw his head up in shock; even Sausage gave him a long hard stare. Will's mount reined himself backwards towards the door. We were on the brink of chaos. I followed my cap's progress as it just missed one of the jump stands and carried on its journey to the tongue and groove wall. When it hit the wall, it was like everything went into slow motion. I can remember the 'thud' when it made contact, then I watched in horror as the cap separated into two parts, the peak continuing its upwards trajectory while the remainder fell to the sand below.

'Dismount, and go and get the bloody fucking thing!' he shouted, as I began the tricky job of getting off when sandwiched between other horses and men. As I dismounted, I could feel the horse's stirrup next to me catching the back of my two-dress jacket, and it riding up towards my neck. Trying to run in sand in tight long boots, while at the same time trying to rearrange your attire, is no easy feat. The journey back was no better. It was humiliating, dancing back through the sand while trying to put my precious cap back together. The figure who caused all this mayhem was pacing about, slapping his whip against his boot like someone contemplating his next evil act. There was one, of course: the jumping lane. In a bid to humiliate me even more, he pulled me out of the line first to take on the lane.

'Right, get on with it!' he ordered, nodding his head towards the jumping lane. I nearly said, 'Get on with what?', but thought better of it. I didn't fancy spending a few nights in the cells and cleaning the parade ground with a toothbrush.

No instruction was given, so I just went for it. I dropped my reins as Windrush approached the first obstacle – one, two, three, four, I counted, as I fixed my gaze on the mirror at the end of the school. I swear I could feel my peak coming looser with every jump we cleared. The one thing about *Jacko* was that he never held a grudge. He would go ballistic and then act as if nothing had happened. I'm sure if he sat in front of a psychologist these days, they'd put a restraining order on him! Once our first pass was completed, Will ended up on the deck again in his favourite spot after *Jacko* had literarily chased him and Sausage into the lane. He was screaming so much I thought he might die. Still red faced, his next order was to unbutton our jackets. Even Lieutenant Who-Jimmyflip looked confused, though that wasn't difficult, given his past performances. As usual, I was first in the firing line. Windrush and I found ourselves standing in front of the riding master, jacket undone, tie badly tied – I didn't know I'd have to half undress in front of him, did I?

'Right, your next challenge,' *Jacko* calmly announced, as if we were children being taught to cross the road, 'is to ride down the jumping lane, taking your jacket off.'

I nearly asked him to repeat himself, but thank goodness my mouth was too dry to speak. In the British Army in the Seventies, if you were told to jump you wouldn't ask why, you would only ask how high, such was the discipline.

Okay, I thought, as I gently squeezed Windrush forward. I contemplated asking if I had to drop my reins, but I suddenly realized, after a quick rehearsal in my head, that taking your jacket off with two hands on your reins would be a tad tricky. I was lucky enough to have competed in a lot of gymkhana events when I was younger. I tried to focus on them and how they always looked harder than they actually were. Before Windrush had broken into a canter, I'd dropped my reins and was pulling my jacket from my shoulders. Four jumps came in quick succession as I struggled to extract my left arm from its sleeve. The riding school was 40 metres long, and I'd already covered three-quarters of it. Windrush must have wondered what the hell was going on, my jacket flapping around his ears only serving to make him go faster. Glancing up at the mirror, the image of my horse and I grew bigger with every millisecond that passed. Windrush was going too fast, I thought, as I dropped my jacket into the sand below. I was desperately trying to grab the reins as the lane came to an end, bracing myself, knowing that if he suddenly stopped, I'd be going out of the front door; and if he managed to get around the sharp left-hand corner, I would most likely be going out of the side door. Here we go, this is going to hurt, I thought, as I abandoned the reins and grabbed hold of Windrush's thick black mane as he took the corner option. Pushing my right leg as hard as I could into my right stirrup, I just managed to stay on board. As Windrush was by now beginning to enjoy the sense of freedom he felt from me having no contact with his reins, as we headed for the rest of the ride I was leaning as far back as I could, trying to pull him up with the end of the rein I'd managed to retrieve. Even *Jacko* took cover as I struggled to stop Windrush having another pass of the jumping lane.

'Well done,' *Jacko* said as he handed me back my sand-covered jacket. Will was visibly shaking as I asked him to hold Windrush's rein while I shook my jacket before putting it back on. I would say it was about a fifty-fifty split between those who fell off and those who stayed on that afternoon. That was, until Lieutenant Who-Jimmyflip's turn came around.

'Okay, Rupert, when you're ready,' *Jacko* said. He didn't order, like he did his other trainees, just politely asked if the lieutenant wouldn't mind having a jolly little jaunt down the jumping lane while at the same removing his posh khaki jacket. None of us realized what we were about to witness. It was always funny when officers fucked up, but this was off the scale. Good old Rupert started well enough, but as he turned into the lane his charger took a bit of a hissy fit. We observers quickly realized that there was no way, at the speed he was traveling, that the two were going to make the other end – as a pair, that is. He was over the first jump before he'd even started to remove his jacket. Everyone let out a quiet groan as, looking a bit like Jesus on the cross, jacket stuck on his shoulders, he hit the wall. I think his head actually hit the mirror, which was about 10ft above the ground. You know how in cartoons when whoever has splatted into a wall or something, it stays there for a second or two before sliding to the ground? Well this is how it looked from where we were sat. I could see shoulders begin to shake around me as everyone tried not to laugh. *Jacko* took off running in his fellow officer's direction to see if he was still alive, while at the same time ordering us to 'catch the bloody fucking horse'.

Lieutenant Who-Jimmyflip was just about conscious as *Jacko* attempted to sit him up against the wall of the school. His nose was bleeding and his once neatly combed hair was full of sand. By pure chance, as all this chaos ensued, Corporal Smith turned up. He ordered the ride to dismount and hold each other's horses so some of us could catch the officer's charger and restore some order. I had to check I hadn't pissed myself trying not to laugh at poor old Rupert's predicament. As he was finally helped to his feet by two of the bigger guys, I had the ironic job of picking up his now completely knackered posh officers' cap and plonking it back on his head as he was helped back to the officers' mess.

We were still giggling about it while sitting on our beds having a cigarette after returning the horses to their stalls.

'Give us a hand with my boots,' I asked Quiff as my calves began to cramp up in my over-tight boots. The cavalry method of removing your long boots was quite unique. Your mate or assistant would stand in front of you, facing in the opposite direction, while you sat on your bed or a chair. You then brought your booted leg up between his legs so he could take the boot by its heel, and your job then was to place your spare foot – booted or not – on his arse and push. The trick –just for a laugh, you understand – was, as he'd nearly got the boot off, to curl your toes up to hold the boot on and then, without warning, push his arse with the other leg and release the toes, watching with glee as your assistant shot across the room for the inevitable collision with the locker opposite. Of course, having performed this act of kindness many times, Quiff knew what was coming and was ready for it. You knew the same thing would happen to you almost immediately as you performed the same favour for someone else.

* * *

One early November evening when we were nearing the end of riding school, and I was busy cleaning my jackboots ready for the next day, Quiff walked in the cleaning room wearing a cavalry greatcoat over his civvy clothing.

'What's that for?' I asked as he inspected my spit-and-polishing efforts.

'Lord Mayor's Show. We're on it next Saturday. You've got to go down to the fourth floor and borrow one. I managed to borrow this one from a mussie, but no one's got a small one that would fit you. I've already asked.'

'Will you come down with me?' I tentatively asked as I finished off my boot.

'Fuck off! You've got no chance. I'm not going down there; you'll be lucky to get out alive.'

Cheers, mate, I thought as I slipped my pullover on and tried to sort out my curly blond hair. The corridor looked quiet as I nervously peered through the narrow glass panel in the door that would lead me to the dreaded fourth floor. I decided I'd just ask in the first room I saw with the door open. The trouble was that most of the doors were shut. I was at the stables end of the block, which I'd worked would be 3 Troop's end. Okay, just walk normally, I told myself as I made my way forward. It was seven o'clock, so some of them would be out, I thought, down the Paxton's. Suddenly, a door to my right opened. I couldn't believe my luck – it was harmonica man.

'Hello young man, what are you doing down here?' he asked as he stood in front of me, wearing nothing but an army green towel.

'Oh, I've got to borrow, if I can that is ...' stop waffling, I thought. 'I'm on the Lord Mayor's Parade on Saturday and I need a greatcoat.'

'I've got one that will probably fit you,' he replied, gesturing me into his lair – sorry, room. 'My name's Terry, by the way, Terry Skitmore,' he continued as he pulled his greatcoat from his locker. 'Try this on.'

It was a perfect fit. After thanking him – too much, I fear – I assured him I'd return it on Sunday and made my escape – sorry, exit. Back at the room, Quiff was impressed. I told him about harmonica man being Terry Skitmore, that now he was my best mate and that, if he'd had the bottle to come with me, Quiff might be his best mate as well.

The interesting fact is, though, that he did become one of both of our best mates, and remains so to this day. All three of us still talk regularly via the internet. The purpose of the recruit troop attending the Lord Mayor's Parade was, as it turned out, just to hold horses while the mounted cavalrymen took a break. It was good fun, though. I remember it was a cold day, so I was grateful for the warm greatcoat.

* * *

The routine of riding school only became more intense as we moved onto the kit ride. We weren't expected to turn out to the very high standards of the Queen's Life Guard, but our kit had to be in good order. The horses were in their ceremonial saddlery as well. You didn't have to clean all of the kit every day, but there was definitely a knack to it. Our instructors helped a lot by showing us techniques such as 'thumb bobbing', how to fit the sheepskins onto the saddles and things like that. I'm not sure that Pam quite understood or believed me when I asked her to save all her old tights for me, something I had to explain to her and I'll now attempt to explain to you, dear reader. Thumb bobbing is a very clever way of cleaning leather work on bridles and such like. The knack is quite simple, really. Firstly, though, I must explain that, unlike most soldiers, who had to supply their own cleaning kit, up town when carrying out state duties etc., all cleaning kit – polish (always Kiwi black, large tins), Brasso and white sap or white Blanco – was free. We cleaned so much and so often that we had to spend most of our wages on it. Cavalry blacks' head kits were originally designed with both function and protection in mind. The whole thing comes apart, leaving you with a headcollar, attached to the back of which is a chain – a 'bright chain' – which is attached around the horse's neck. In the field, this would be used to tether your horse whenever or whatever you were doing. The bridle has two bits, so it's what's known as a double bridle. The first bit is a snaffle and the second is a pelham, or a 'Banbury state bit'. Two bits means two reins, so all in all there's a fair bit of kit to clean. Back to thumb bobbing. All the head kit pieces are attached to each other by brass buckles, and hooks hang from the concrete ceiling in the cleaning room, with cleaning benches all around. There are loads of methods of cleaning kit; it can easily become an obsession. But if you hang your reins from a hook and place a bit of polish on your thumb, then gently rub it into the leather, and follow this with using the tights you've acquired to buff the polish up, then hey presto, you are thumb bobbing! The results are spectacular. I still have an old pair of tights in my shoe cleaning kit. I know, sad, isn't it?

It was mid-November and we were passing out of riding school just before Christmas, then we would go on leave and, in theory, join our troops and start state duties. We went out to the Gloucester for a pint or two one evening, and I left early because I wanted to call Pam on the way back to the barracks. I always used the same telephone box, just opposite what is known as Scotch Corner. I don't know why I used these particular boxes, because they always stunk of piss, so I used to hold the heavy door open a bit with my foot. The call – reverse charge as normal – didn't last long, and I was soon walking towards the large black iron gates to the guardroom.

The geraniums, which looked good in their pots during the summer, were dying back now. They needed to go in a greenhouse, I was thinking, as I pushed the button to call the lift. I wasn't really paying much attention. Instead, I was recalling Pam and my earlier telephone conversation when the lift doors opened. I was surprised to see a Life Guard trooper who I knew as 'Shandy'; he was called that because his surname rhymed with, I don't know, deer or queer, pick which you like, but they all end with him being a twat.

'Oh shit, I must have pushed the wrong button,' he announced as the lift doors opened. 'You're going to the sixth floor, aren't you?'

'Oh, yeah, thanks,' I said as I naively stepped into the lift. Little did I know as the lift started on its journey, firstly to the fourth floor and then onto the sixth, that I'd stepped into a trap. I quickly sussed it out, though, when we reached the fourth floor and the lift doors opened. In front of me were two Life Guards – one was a corporal and the other a well-known bully. The next thing I knew, I was being pushed in the back towards the bully. I can remember his eyes were sort of glazed over. He had definitely been drinking; I could smell it. I then saw a fist coming at me and I tried to duck away, but it was too late. He clipped the side of my head. I don't know why, but this massive feeling of rage then rushed through my body. In that instant, I remembered what my elder brother, Tony, had told me. He said if you are attacked by a few of them, just focus on one. Don't fanny about trying to hit all of them, just get the main man. The main man in my case was this trooper who was about to have another swing at me. Still raging with anger, I went for him. I got him in the mouth first, closely followed by one to his eye. He was backing away now, and strangely, the other two just stood there. I didn't want to stop; honestly, I wanted to kill him, finish him off. I hate bullies. I hate what they do and how they try to justify it. He had now backed into what I presumed was his room. He was a pathetic sight, sat on the floor with his arms covering his face for protection. Shall I finish him off with a good kick, I wondered. No, he wasn't worth it.

When I returned to the lift, I was crying with rage. The other two were backing away. The corporal was actually out of the door and hiding on the landing. I grabbed the wanker from the lift by his throat, pushed him up against the lift door and warned him that if he or any of his bully-boy mates came near me again, I'd kill them. I didn't bother with the lift, I just kicked the landing door open and took the stairs. As I started to climb the stairs, I could hear our brave NCO scurrying down them below me. I still sometimes see the bully boy on social media. I heard he hasn't been well. Normally, I would have some sympathy, but not for this lowlife twat – no way. From that night on, I never had any fear of going down to the fourth floor. Indeed, we had to move down there on the afternoon after the regimental Christmas lunch. Drunk troopers were grabbing the rookies as they entered their new rooms. I can remember one of them – Will, I think it was – being hung out of the window with his trousers and pants around his ankles while someone tried to stuff hazelnuts up his arse. If they had lost their grip and dropped him, he would have been dead, that's for sure. Strangely, I had a completely uninterrupted move there. The moral: if you can, stand up to the bullies; they're just cowards really.

* * *

Back to the kit ride. Two sessions a day in the school, breaking in your kit, takes its toll on your body. Imagine for a moment what it's like. Your jackboots are so rigid when you attempt to walk or march in them that you can't help but develop a sort of wobble in your stride. You are constantly relying on your heels for balance, while being aware of the swan-necked spurs that are just waiting to trip you over and send you crashing to the floor. When you are sat astride your charger, wearing state kit, your ability to move freely is severely restricted. You have no real feeling in your legs. If you lose a stirrup you can't replace it yourself because if you look down to locate it, your plume drops in front of your face and obscures your view. The white metal and brass helmet – named the Albert helmet after Queen Victoria's husband's redesign of it in 1842 – has a 20in plume attached to the spike on top of it. The chinstrap is worn differently by each regiment. The Blues and Royals wear their chinstraps under their chins, whereas the Life Guards wear theirs on their bottom lip. Life Guards wear a white plume with an onion formed into the top of it, while the Blues have a red plume with no onion. Inside the helmet is a leather skull cap, if you like. They have a cord running around the bottom of them, so you can do those final adjustments to make your helmet fit, yet no matter how well you adjust them they seem to have a mind of their own. The peak constantly tries to flatten or even rearrange the shape of your nose, especially while trotting. Cuirasses restrict your upper body movements to a minimum, especially when returning your sword to its scabbard. Imagine it; you are contorting your upper body around to the left as much as is humanly possible, and your gauntleted left hand – which has a bunch of reins in it – is getting in the way as you try to get the tip of your sword into a 2in slot. And of course, while you try to perform this act, the bloody plume makes you do it through a thick fringe of white nylon. With all that said, practice makes perfect. Hours in the riding school pay off; it's an art to be mastered.

During the last two weeks of riding school, we spent a lot of time in the park – Hyde Park – carrying out drill moves on Rotten Row. It was cool showing off to onlookers. Rotten Row was established by William III at the end of the seventeenth century. He created – well, I doubt that he did it himself, but someone under his orders created – this broad avenue in 1690 so he could have a safer way to travel from Kensington Palace to St James' Palace through Hyde Park. It was lit by 300 oil lamps, making it the first artificially lit highway in Britain. The track was called Route du Roi – French for King's Road – which was eventually corrupted to Rotten Row.

When we were out there on the morning ride, there always seemed to be some guy in judo kit. He looked like he was wearing army-issue pyjamas without the stripes. Anyway, this chancer insisted on showing off his Kung Fu moves while standing right in the middle of Rotten Row. Maximum attention spot, I guess. One morning, our instructors had had enough. They formed the whole ride across the wide sandy avenue and ordered us to charge. There he was, with probably fifteen cavalry blacks thundering towards him. As he turned during one of his fancy spin kicks, he suddenly noticed the line of red, blue and silver approaching him at speed. I'll never forget the sight of him running for the protection of the trees, holding up his pyjama pants as he went.

As I have already mentioned, cavalry blacks are canny devils. Some of ours became so adept at escaping that they had to be stabled in one of the loose boxes at the bottom end of the stable room. Sausage, for instance, was so good at undoing his headcollar rope that no number of complicated knots would stop him. The horses living in stalls had a rope attached to their headcollars, on the end of which was a cylindrical lump of wood with a hole through it. You passed the headcollar rope through a galvanized ring which was fixed to the wall at the front of the stall, then through the lump of wood. The next job was to tie a knot in it, which allowed the horse a certain amount of free movement of his head so that he could easily reach his hay and water trough. The alternative to this neat little idea was to leave the headcollar rope loose or slack, but that posed the danger of them getting it caught up in their front legs. There was always a stable guard on duty down in the stables. When we were assigned our troops after passing out, we would also join that rota of night guards. During the day, each troop had a stable guard, but at night three of you would do stags with two hours on and four hours off. The two not on stags were accommodated in spare cells in the guardroom. One morning, Quiff and I were walking into 4 Troop's stables at six o'clock. The stable guard was stood by the feed room door, looking a combination of angry and perplexed.

'What's the matter?' Quiff asked.

'What's the matter? What's the fucking matter? That fucking Sausage got loose during the night. He's then broken into the feed room and now we can't get him out!'

I couldn't help smiling as I observed Sausage's fat arse jammed in the feed room door. Not only had he untied his headcollar rope, but he had also then waited until the night guard had done his rounds and moved to another troop room. He probably waited until he went up to the Blues floor, so he had more time, then made his move. The first problem facing him would be the door handle; it was one of those handles you grabbed in your fist and turned to the left. How he managed that beggars belief. He must have got it in his teeth and turned it until he could push it open. The feed rooms in the barracks weren't that big – about twelve by six at a guess. On three sides of the room sat large metal feed bins:, one contained crushed oats, another contained bran and the one at the end of the room contained horse nuts. They were identical, with heavy lift-up lids on top that were often stacked with empty feed bowls. Not only had Sausage successfully gained entry, but his next mission was to open one of the bins. He must have again used his mouth, teeth and head to somehow lift the lid past the vertical so it leant against the wall behind. The chosen bin was at the end of the room, the one with the horse nuts in. In order to do this, he would have had to avoid wheelbarrows and various hand tools that were kept in the corner opposite the door. He'd obviously been in there some time because the bin was nearly empty. Trouble was, the cake-like feed that was in the bin was now in his belly, and it didn't take the brains of an archbishop to work out that he wasn't coming out of there anytime soon. The situation was resolved when a senior NCO turned up and a plan was formed. Firstly, one of us had to squeeze in there. Being the smallest, that job fell to me. With help from a leg up, I managed to get on Sausage's rather broad back and literally crawl far enough up his neck to grab his headcollar rope and secure it safely around his neck. I couldn't shut the lid of the bin yet because I couldn't move him back far enough. The last thing I wanted was a ton or so of horse kicking off in this small area. Next to go were the empty feed bins. Now I had to get down on the floor on his near side, from where I could pass brushes and other paraphernalia under his belly to waiting hands. The last to go were the wheelbarrows, which was tricky as they were heavy and would have to go over his back. Picture the scene. The area I now stood in was quite a bit larger, large enough for him to swing round in my direction and trap me against the breezeblock wall. I tried lifting a barrow, but it was impossible.

'It's too heavy,' I explained. 'Someone else is going to have to come in and give me a hand.' My request was met with silence. No volunteers then, I thought. However, a head then appeared between Sausage's back legs – it was Jarvo, holding Sausage's tail to one side like he was peering around a curtain.

'Alright, mate. If you push his arse over towards me, I reckon you could crawl between his legs.' This would be nothing unusual – they made us do all sorts of tricks like that in riding school.

I was pleased and relived to see Jarvo's black curly hair appear under Sausage's fat belly. I could feel his stomach rumbling as I held him steady. Don't get colic, I thought, as Jarvo started getting to his feet by grabbing my leg and nearly pulling my trousers down. As he got to his feet, Sausage's stomach rumbling reached a crescendo and he let out an enormous fart!

'Fucking hell!' I shouted, as Jarvo and I turned in unison to face the corner of the feed room. I could hear the laughter coming from the corridor outside, but I couldn't see anyone. They'd all done the best thing and stepped back for a while.

Between us, we managed to pass the two wheelbarrows out over Sausage's hind quarters to the guys outside. There was a lot more room now, and we were able to shut the feed bin and get a bucket of water in for him. Now, there was no way that we could turn him in the space we had, so our only option was to back him out. Cavalry horses – even Sausage – are taught to walk backwards, or rein back as it's officially known ,so we knew he could do it. The question was, would he?

'Okay, mate, nice and steady,' I suggested as we began to move him backwards towards the door. One of the guys on the outside was directing him, pulling his tail, but that didn't work. All it served to do was make him fart again, so once again they all took cover for ten minutes. Jarvo and I had to put up with the smell as we coaxed him into the doorway. I had my hand over his nose, gently trying to guide him, while Jarvo had his shoulder into his chest and pushed. I played rugby with Jarvo in juniors and knew he was strong, but not strong enough to move this lump. We managed to get him out as far as his stifle (the bit where his back legs meet his belly), so about a third of him was out. Trouble was, it was clear to see that his belly was just too fat from all the cake he'd necked during the night. Everyone was assessing the situation when he started a familiar move by padding his rear legs back, sort of stretching them out.

'Watch out, he's going to piss,' I quickly informed Jarvo as we both backed away from the splash zone. The smell in that small room was intense again as a thought came to mind.

'We need to take the door off,' I said. 'Without the door we would have another six or eight inches.'

'Good idea,' Corporal Smith said from the other side of the door. 'Who's got a screwdriver?'

I heard some sarcastic twat say, 'Oh, I've got loads, what colour do you want?' Another voice suggested ask the dung rat – the civvy who worked moving the large containers under the dung shoot. 'I'll go and ask,' another voice said. This had been going on now for about half an hour and people were beginning to turn up to see what was going on. Even the orderly officer appeared in his deep blue frock coat, trying to look intelligent I was hoping Sausage would fart again. I even contemplated giving him a sneaky dig in the belly to see if I could make it happen.

'Pull him back in, Wol,' I heard someone from outside say. 'I've got a screwdriver.'

I'd spent hours of my childhood lifting and holding things for my dad while he carried out his DIY exploits, so I had a good idea of what to do. It was clear that the door was heavy by the size of the hinges that held it in place. I could tell it would take two of us – one on the outside and one on the inside – to get it off and out of the way. The voice I just heard turned out to be Stinch. If anyone was going to get that door off, Stinch would. I suggested that he start at the top, leaving one screw in place to hold it. Sausage didn't seem to give a jot about all the activity that was going on around him. Stinch stood on an upturned feed bin so he could get enough traction on the screws to get them out. Eventually, three hinges later, it was crunch time. I'd been in there with old smelly arse for an hour now – I mean

Sausage, not Jarvo, by the way – but he didn't care. He even started looking around for more food at one stage.

'Okay, slide it this way,' Stinch suggested as he got to his feet.

Jarvo managed to help slide the door out of the way from the inside as I stood at Sausage's head. If he doesn't fit this time we're really up shit street, I thought, as Jarvo and I started the backwards-coaxing once again. Like last time, his hind quarters went out a treat; now for his fat belly. There was definitely more room, but it was still tight. Jarvo assumed his previous position, like a second row forward in a rugby scrum, while I tried to shoo him away from me by waving my hands around like a demented fool. He reacted to my waving by throwing his head back, as I hoped he would, and 'pop', like a cork from a bottle, he was out. A cheer went up from the assembled onlookers as the farrier who was waiting outside checked him over for any injuries. Apart from Sausage having to attend vets parade later that morning, all ended well.

* * *

The London traffic was busy as we stood in the passageway that ran along the bottom end of the stables above the dung tunnel. Through the gaps in the high brick walls, you could see people walking past. We were all having a well-earned cigarette when we heard a shout from some twat lance corporal from 1 Troop. We were near the end of the very intensive course that was riding school, so most of us were feeling quite cocky. As the corporal made his way towards us, Quiff didn't even move from his position leaning against the wall.

'Oy, you three, no smoking out here!' the corporal shouted as he got closer.

As I turned towards Quiff, I noticed one of those red signs about 6 inches above his head which read 'No Smoking'. It was too late to tell him, as the corporal was already there.

'Any problems, Corporal?' Quiff cockily asked as he took a drag on his cigarette.

'Yes, this is a no smoking area. Can't you read?'

'Read what?'

'The sign above your fucking head, you twat.'

We could see the blood shooting into Quiff's cheeks as he straightened himself up and quickly made his way back into the troop, closely followed by Jarvo and me.

As passing out parade was in a couple of days, we only had a khaki ride today. Sausage was given the day off, so Will 'the skull' was tasked with putting the feed room back together while we were out in the park.

* * *

It's amazing how many times we have to change in a day, I was pondering to myself as I dabbed white sap on my white kit. You would go down for morning stables in denims, then after breakfast if you were on kit ride you would have to return to the stables and get your horse mostly ready for your morning lesson – saddle, breastplate and most of the head kit. Then you'd return to the sixth floor and start the long job of getting your state kit on. Buckskin breeches started the job, army-issue braces holding them up over a t-shirt. It was supposed to be a cuirass shirt, but most people didn't bother with that. Sword belt followed, and next was your tunic, buttoned and hooked at the neck. Your cuirasses would be ready to slot over your head, with the white buckskin cuirass belt hanging from one side. It was then you'd have to engage the help of a friend. The trick to fastening a cuirass belt was to stand with your back on a doorframe while your mate would push the cuirass into your stomach, at the same time attaching the eye-shaped opening to the brass button on your back cuirass. A good stretch was now required to get your tunic straight and, if it was possible, comfortable under the cuirass. Next was your cartouche belt, which had to lay over your left shoulder, under your tunic's epaulette. Again, it was easier if you could get someone else to help you with doing them up. Getting ready is very much a joint effort. Finally, there were the gauntlets. You'd find them, if you left your kit ready, sitting on top of your sword, which would be slotted into the top of the radiator at the window end of your room. Then you'd attach your sword to the sword belt and lean it against the pointed inside of your jackboot. This was dressing for riding school or a state escort, not for the Queen's Life Guard, which was slightly different – I'll explain that in the next chapter. It's best to carry your helmet when you are descending stairs in jackboots, I've always found. Even though you've got both hands full with sword and helmet, at least you've got half a chance of seeing the next step without your vision being impaired by your plume. Walking in jackboots is an art in itself. They were designed to protect you in battle, on a horse, not for walking or marching any distance. It's a bit like walking in Wellington boots that are too big for you, or waders even. If your spur chains aren't tight and correctly fitted, you end up sounding like a troop of Morris dancers, not a troop of cavalrymen.

Eventually, bearing in mind we had to do this twice a day, you arrived at your charger's head, with gauntlets still on top of sword tucked behind left jackboot, helmet on now, the remainder of the head kit in your right hand. Don't fuck about, you remind your mount, as you 'offer' the snaffle bit to his mouth. If your horse isn't willing, this can be a nightmare when wearing state kit. Luckily, most of the time there will be someone less restricted around to help. Snaffle bit in, now the pelham. That done, secure all leatherwork at the browband, both sides, and you're good to go on your second walk to the mounting block. Getting mounted in state kit is a challenge in itself. Inevitably, you end up standing beside your horse wondering what you should or shouldn't hold. If you don't hold your sword, your gauntlets will fall off the hilt as you swing your leg over, yet if you put your gauntlets on, you can't really hold your reins well enough to keep your increasingly impatient horse from moving away from the block. What you need is a helpful instructor, or even a passerby, to hold your horse to the mounting block while you somehow climb aboard. Once in the saddle, ask your helper one last favour, to put your left boot in your stirrup. Once you've shuffled yourself into the sheepskin that surrounds you in the saddle, it's quite comfortable. The big sheepskin lump in front of you is actually an old state cloak which is tightly packed into a sausage shape and strapped to the saddle. One of the most important bits of saddlery you have looks pretty insignificant – it's a small leather ring known as a rein stop. It fits over the end of the pelham rein, and basically slides down it to lock your rein in your gauntleted left hand. The tighter the fit, the better.

Imagine four highly polished reins neatly arranged in your left hand, your right hand holding your sabre, gripping the handle with your first three fingers and thumb, with your little finger behind the handle. Why do it like that? It's a neat little trick: when your sword is in the carry position (pointing straight up), it keeps the sword vertical. If you take the finger to a normal grip, it will lean back slightly towards your shoulder. You can, when you get more confident with riding in the kit, sit the hilt of the sword in or on your left hand/gauntlet to adjust your helmet or pull your rein stop tighter. Talking of helmets, I'm sure the bridge of my nose has been reshaped by my state helmet's peak trying to chisel its way into it. They are strange and complicated things to master. Life Guards, who traditionally wear their chinstraps below their bottom lip (I'd like to meet whoever thought that one up – probably an officer), have virtually nothing to hold them on, unless of course you are able to lift the chinstrap with your tongue into your mouth and grip it with your teeth. When your mount kicked off, losing your helmet in the Seventies was a 'no no'. If you wanted to see *Jacko* have heart palpitations, you could lose your helmet. Danger moments included your horse playing silly buggers, you losing control and your grip on the reins when your horse was playing silly buggers, other horses around you playing silly buggers; in other words, literally anything could cause the shit to hit the fan. Horses are strange and wonderful creatures. You can ride your usually bombproof horse past the same manhole cover every day, then, without warning or reason, he or she stops, stares and snorts at this inanimate object like it's just come down from space, and shies left or right – or even sometimes backwards. And he or she won't tell you which of the three options they are going to take. That's when, if you're not paying attention, you end up leaving your comfortable sheepskin saddle out of the side door. Falling off in any riding wear is no joke, but when wearing state kit it is potentially very dangerous. It's never happened to me, thank goodness. I suppose you would get rid of your sword on the way down, but if you're in amongst an escort, you might not have enough room to. It doesn't bear thinking about. It still happens to this day, and knowing horses as I do, it will continue to happen well into the future.

Our final practices over, tomorrow – Friday – we were finally passing out of riding school. The hardest course in the British Army, they used to say. In my opinion, it wasn't that tough, but I'd been riding for years. A tough course to me would be something like the SAS course – now that would be tough. All Thursday afternoon and evening, apart from a quick couple of pints down the Paxtons, was spent cleaning horses and kit. Brass and metal wear polished, head kit thumb bobbed and polished, boots bulled and whites, white sapped; it felt a little bit like being back at the depot the night before a room inspection. A bunch of parents and family, including Pam, came to the passing out parade. It was performed in the riding school, with the small audience observing from the gallery. Everyone who started the ride successfully passed out. Even Will got through, though he'd been bounced (thrown off) more times than a Wimbledon tennis ball. Will, by the way, is still a mate of mine and continues to be a very involved veteran.

The last act in 4 Troop was to return our horses to their troops and find out which troop we were going to before becoming a proper Piccadilly Cowboy.

'Wallington!' our riding school instructor called out.
'Corporal of Horse,' I answered, eagerly awaiting my fate.
'Swamp Troop.'
'Swamp Troop? What's Swamp Troop?' I nervously asked.
'Three Troop, the one you've just taken Windrush back to.'
Perfect, I thought. My mate Terry Skitmore was in Swamp, sorry 3 Troop. At least I would know someone. Onwards and upwards. We were on Christmas leave for two weeks from tomorrow. Happy days!

Chapter 6

First Queen's 'Troughing'

THIS IS SO weird, I thought, as I quietly made my way along the corridor on the fourth floor. It was 3.45 am, my second night on the fourth floor after leave. For the first time, I caught the milk train – as it was known – back to Paddington station. The bloody thing stopped at every station between Bristol and London, but at least it was quiet so I could stretch out over the long bench seats and get some sleep. I managed to get a room sharing with Terry and another guy, a proud Yorkshireman whose name I hadn't got my head around yet. All I can say, though, is that first impressions weren't great. The room was dark, warm and, apart the sound of breathing, quiet. No one was in my bed, and all padlocks on my lockers were still intact. I gingerly pulled the bed away from my locker, trying not to disturb anyone and just got my head down. It was two hours to reveille, but I'd barely shut my eyes before I was aware of people moving about. Terry was at the sink, cleaning his teeth, and the Yorkshireman was sitting on the side of his bed, rubbing his eyes.

'Good Christmas?' Terry asked as he noticed me in the mirror.

'Great, thanks. Do you by any chance know what I'm doing this morning?'

'Yes, watering order. If I remember correctly, you're on your old mate Windrush.'

That sounds okay, I thought, as I pulled on my over-tight long boots. I'd managed to blag a greatcoat from *Polly Perkins* before going on leave. I was grateful I did, as it was cold out there. The stables was a hive of activity as Terry and I walked along the corridor towards 3 Troop. I noticed Quiff and Stinch in 1 Troop as we passed; their room would be further up the corridor from us on the fourth floor. I made a mental note to catch up with them at breakfast.

The three-bar who was in charge of 3 Troop was Corporal of Horse Murray. He seemed alright when I met him on the day of our pass out. Everything felt much more professional now; you could tell immediately that the focus was on the horses and Queen's Lifeguard. It would be a while before I would be on Queen's, I'd been told. I would be learning the ropes on watering order and suchlike. Windrush recognized my voice when I arrived at his stall. Saying 'hello', after placing his saddle on the left-hand stall divider, I squeezed my way past his belly to put his head kit on. As I finished off tightening his girth and surcingle, I took a second to look down at my boots and admire my new spurs – they'd been hard-earned and I was proud of them.

When I'd settled in the saddle and pulled my greatcoat straight, Terry handed me my lead horse. He was stable guard this week, so wasn't on watering order.

'This is Panorama,' he told me as he handed over this lovely-looking black. 'Everyone calls her Pan Am.'

Watering order takes its name from the historic daily routine of troops being ordered to ride their horses to one of the several watering troughs located around Westminster. A lot of the troughs are still there, probably full of flowers now. By 6.30 am, in control of two horses for the first time in my life, I followed the ride through the triangular stone entrance to Hyde Park Barracks, the only bit of the old barracks that stood here to be incorporated into the new one. I could clearly see the officer leading the ride. It was our troop leader, Lieutenant Crispin Paket or something. We'd turned right out of the barracks and headed down South Carriage Drive towards Mayfair. Before too long, we could see him put his right arm, while bent at the elbow, towards the sky and pump it up and down like he was cheering at a football match, or in his case a polo match. This was the cavalry order to trot, rising trot on watering order. Although the morning was cold, the heat generated by the horses soon warmed us up. I was loving this. It was quite a sight, with all the hooves clattering around the narrow streets of the West End. I noticed the guys in front of me not paying much attention to what was going on ahead of them, but looking up at the windows above us. It turned out they were looking for curious people suddenly drawing back their curtains in various stages of undress to see what the noise was about. Windrush and Pan Am were behaving themselves as we carried on to I don't know where. The streets around that part of London early in the morning were surprisingly busy. A few of the porters cheered as we rode past Covent Garden Market – it was still a busy fruit market in those days. Before I knew it, nearly an hour had passed and we were heading down Park Lane towards home. Steam obscured my view as it gently rose from the horses' necks and quarters as the ride walked back to the barracks. The early-morning sun bounced off the windows of our accommodation block as Lieutenant Crispin Paket brought the ride to a halt. Green denim-clad guys gathered at the top of the ramps, waiting to take our lead horses back to their stables, where breakfast was waiting. After feed-away and a final tidy up, it was our turn to go for breakfast and our morning confrontation with 'one sausage Henry'.

'How's 1 Troop then?' I asked Quiff as we finished our food.

'Yeah, it's alright. That one you had a run in with in the lift is a bit of a gobshite though.'

'Don't let him get to you, mate, he's just a low-life bully. He'll soon crawl back into his hole, I expect.' As I said this, I spotted him on the other side of the canteen. It looked like he'd copped another black eye. Some people will never learn, I thought, as we got up from our table and made our way back to the fourth floor for yet another change of kit.

The routine in the troops was completely different than what we'd become used to in riding school. After breakfast, at 7.30 am, we returned to the troop to either groom or, if it was a Queen's Life Guard that day, assist anyone who was on it to prepare their horse before they disappeared upstairs to get themselves ready.

Queen's Life Guard is made up of two parts. In my day, the guard changed every day at 11.00 am at Horse Guards, named after the troops who have protected the sovereign since the restoration of King Charles II in 1660. It is the official entrance to Buckingham Palace and St James' Palace. The first part is a long guard, which was mounted when the Queen was in residence. The long guard is made up of an officer, a corporal major – who carries the standard – two NCOs, a trumpeter and ten troopers. The second part is a short guard, mounted when the sovereign wasn't in residence, consisting of ten troopers and two NCOs. If the Queen left while the guard was mounted, or returned to Buckingham Palace, the guard was 'made up' or 'made down' accordingly. An average of three or four troopers were on Queen's from each troop every other day. The trooper was responsible for his own and his horse's turnout. Guard relief stags were given out by merit. The best turned-out combinations received mounted sentries, so the four best got the four 'box' reliefs, number one box being the best and so on. Their stags were one hour on and one hour off between eleven in the morning and four in the afternoon. When they had finished, although they couldn't go anywhere, their time was their own. The Horse Guards guardroom at that time was the only guardroom in the British Army to have a bar, so the 'box men' could sit all evening drinking and watching the telly while those on foot sentry duties, 'tabbing it', had to do two hours on and four hour off for the twenty-four-hour guard. The incentive was thus definitely to be a box man. Next down the metaphorical ladder were the gate sentries – three of them – whose job was to guard the arch that allows traffic from Horse Guards Parade through to Whitehall. The traveller had to be in possession of, and be able to produce, an Ivory pass. Only the Royal Family was exempt from this. On the rare occasions I was a gate sentry, we were always briefed that a white light in a car's windscreen allowed it through. Finally, the grot reliefs were the three under the arch, known as the 'chicks', hidden under the arches that fronted the stables and guardroom. It was lonely back there and mostly went unnoticed. The real attraction was those at the front on the horses. In the Seventies, the gates shut at 10.00 pm and the foot sentries carried on their stags throughout the night, guarding the stables.

At 4.00 pm, the Four o'clock Parade, also known as the 'dismount parade' or '"punishment parade', takes place. This was started in 1894 when Queen Victoria found the entire guard drinking and gambling while on duty, and as a punishment ordered that they had to be inspected every day at 4.00 pm by an officer for the next 100 years. Although the hundred years finished in 1994, Queen Elizabeth II wanted the parade to continue as a tradition. This parade also ends the mounted sentries' duties for the day.

Back in the troop stables, if your mate or someone had asked you to bring his horse up for Queen's, at 10.00 am you'd finish off putting the remainder of his horse's head kit on, always having your tights in your pocket for last-minute fingerprints or anything else untoward. You'd remove the horse's tail bandage and lead them up to the parade square when your man was ready. As it was January, we were still in winter order so he would be wearing his state cloak, normally carrying his jackboots in one hand with his sword in the other. He would mount in stocking feet, and when he was comfortable you would carefully slot each boot into place before placing then in the stirrup irons. After a quick check around, straightening his cloak as you went, and the odd tickle with your tights, you'd wish him good luck and go for your NAFFI break.

The new guard would leave Hyde Park Barracks at 10.30 am. At 10.45 am, it would pass Buckingham Palace to arrive at Horse Guards as the clock above the arch chimed eleven.

After NAFFI break, we'd return to the stables for an hour's grooming. This was a great time to spend with your designated guard horse, if you had one. Being new to the troop, I was told to stick with Windrush for the time being. Terry had told me that Pan Am was going spare now, as her previous keeper had just left the regiment. I really liked her. No disrespect to Windrush – he'd really looked after me through riding school – but Pan Am was a better fit. She was around 16-2 in height, not too big for a short arse like me. It's all about the look, you see. We had one horse in 3 Troop named James Pig; he stood at nearly 18 hands, and if you put me on him in state kit it wouldn't be a good match. Don't get me wrong. 'the pig', as he was known, was great. I rode him many times on watering order and really enjoyed it. After I'd finished Windrush, I went on to groom Pan Am. I can still see her now, bending her neck to greet you as you entered her stall. She had a white star on her forehead and two white socks on her hind legs. She had the letters 'LG' branded into her off fore hoof, and on her near fore her military number, '52'. All cavalry horses were marked like this, the reason being to identify them both here in the regiment but in the past on the battlefield. The farriers carried an axe in battle. If a horse was injured, he could dispatch it if beyond saving with the sharp pointed side of his axe, then chop off the two front hooves with the axe bit and keep them to record losses.

Not all the blacks were as even-tempered as Pan Am. Will ('the scull') Freedman had been posted to 3 Troop out of riding school with Jarvo and I. On this particular day, the troop two-bar must have been feeling spiteful because he told Will to groom a horse named Rockingham. He was alright, but you had to watch him, as he kicked out if you walked behind him and, given the opportunity, would bite your balls off! Will wore his normal clueless-looking face as he entered Rockingham's stall. I could see the horse wasn't in a good mood – he was already dancing on the spot before Will had even shown him a brush.

'Shorten his headcollar rope. He'll bite you if you don't,' I shouted as Will took absolutely no notice and began grooming him with a dandy brush. Like a lot of the guys, Will hadn't worked with horses before joining the regiment. Most, if not all, the learning came from your mates or in riding school. It's not cruel to say that Will wasn't the sharpest tool in anybody's locker. In riding school, he looked after Sausage. Sausage was a plug – you could do anything with him. The most harmful thing he would possibly do when you were grooming him would be to fall asleep and crush you as he leant on you. Rockingham was a different beast; 'beast' being the operative word. His main purpose in life was to inflict as much damage as he could on whoever was in range. Deep down, like a lot of these things, it probably wasn't his fault. Because he reacted, some twatish troopers constantly goaded him, which obviously made him worse. Back to Will, it's difficult to describe him. He had what my mum would call a gormless look on his face. He definitely wasn't listening to any advice offered. I'm sure most of the troop went into pretend grooming mode as we all waited for the inevitable. Sure enough, a piercing scream rang out as Will shot out of Rockingham's stall, clutching his lower back. What he didn't realize was how close he also was to getting a kick up the arse as the horse lashed out. As Will pulled up his KF shirt, we could already see the red-blue bruise appearing. Corporal of Horse Murray lifted Will's shirt with the end of his whip, as though something was going to jump out and bite him.

'Right, that looks nasty. Get yourself to the medical centre. Wallington, go with him.'

When he said 'medical centre', I pictured an extensive suite of white-tiled rooms, maybe with a pretty nurse or two around, but when I knocked on the door opposite the guardroom marked 'Medical Centre' I was surprised to enter a room – singular – that felt pretty full with the three of us standing in it. The nurse was an Army Medical Corps bloke dressed like a slop jockey in white attire. As I made my excuses and left, I spotted the door to the barbers shop. I needed a haircut, but could I cheek it while Will was being seen to next door? Fuck it, why not, I thought as I pushed the door open. In front of me, sat in the barber's chair, was our regimental barber, affectionately known as 'Jimmy the Fish' – don't ask me why, because I don't know. All I do know is he was cheap and didn't do a bad job. He was a civvy, so could charge you for his skills. If you were lucky, he might just do as you asked. We were allowed to have our hair a little bit longer than other regiments in those days. Some said it was so we would blend in more when we were out in civvy street. That's great, I thought, look at me blending in nicely in my neatly pressed trousers, blazer, shirt and tie!

My hair at that time didn't grow down; it was so curly it grew out. If it was too long at the side, it sprung out like it was trying to escape from underneath my SD cap. I think anyone could have cut it and it would still look the same. After my sneaky haircut, I cautiously opened the door to the medical room to see Will having his torso bandaged. He was even thinner without his shirt – if he had turned sideways, I think I might have missed him.

'Fucking hell, mate, you'll get a biff chit for that, won't you?' I said as I closed the door and leant against it. Biff chit is army slang for a sick note.

'Probably,' the medic agreed. 'He will have to go to hospital to have a doctor take a look.'

'Okay, good luck with that, mate. Catch you later,' I said as I made a swift exit. It was nearly scoff time and I was starving; there was no way I was going to miss that.

'Update?' Corporal of Horse Murray asked as I walked back into 3 Troop.

'Looks pretty bad to me, Corporal.'

'Pretty bad? Pretty bad – is that the best you can do?'

'Well, the medic said he'd have to go to hospital, and he would probably be on a biff chit for a week or so.' I thought I would embellish it a bit, being as he was so pernickety over my diagnosis.

'Great, just what I need. Alright, finish off what you were doing, we're late for feed away.'

I quickly gathered my grooming kit together, gave Pan Am a pat down the neck and took up my position by Windrush's feed bowl to wait for the orderly officer to inspect. After lunchtime scoff, everyone apart from the stable guard had a couple of hours off. Afternoon stables started at 3.30 pm, so you could do a number of things. I spent most of my spare time cleaning my kit. We were issued with our guard boots when we passed out of riding school, and if you were lucky you could keep your other boots for escort boots. Getting a pair of jackboots to Queen's Life Guard standard wasn't easy; it involved literally hours of bobbing, spit and polishing or whatever you want to call it. A tab guard (Foot Guard, or 'wooden top') bulled his boots with two fingers with a damp duster wrapped around them, whereas we used our whole hand, four fingers wrapped in what was known as a silvet duster. It was an expensive duster you could buy from Harrods (just across the road). You learnt to treasure your silvet duster. Never lend it out – no offence, but please don't ask to borrow my silvet, was the watchword. Overall cleaning kit and state kit was fairly safe in Hyde Park Barracks. So long as you kept the nickable kit locked in your locker, you'd generally be alright. Getting a pair of guard boots 'there' was an art in itself. The trees to hold the boots' shape were massive; even my size 8s centre tree was like a cricket bat. When the trees were in place, you could 'bone them out', a process of removing or smoothing out the creased leather with a polish tin lid. The creases naturally formed in the foot and ankle area of the boots through movement, which was why you wouldn't put your boots on until you're on your guard horse and you don't move your feet until you've been inspected. Boneing complete, you would brush the boot. You would use a toothbrush to clean and polish welts out, then after a final brush off, you're ready to go.

On the long cleaning benches that were next to the toilets in Hyde Park Barracks, you'd have your large tin of polish, with the lid containing tap water, your diddly (a yellow duster used for bulling boots) or silvet on whatever hand you favoured, and away you'd go. I preferred to start from the bottom up – toe, heel and ankle first. Depending on how good you were, you could easily spend a few hours on your boots. It could be longer if you'd sustained some damage on guard, or especially an escort. The key to cleaning the kit was focusing on the bits that could be seen, so you wouldn't over-polish the inside of the boot, the bit that sat by the horse, for instance. I quickly sussed the theory of 'first impressions' and the fact that bullshit baffles brains. On Queen's, for instance, if you are in winter order, cloaked up, the focus would be on the bits Lieutenant Tiddly-Push could see. Helmet and plume immaculate, tick; cloak in good order, tick; boots so clean that the officer inspecting could see his lovely wavy hair appearing from underneath his forage cap; horse and his or her kit in good order. When you were in summer order, you would spend ages brushing up you sheepskin saddle cover. When cloaked up, what's the point? No one can see it. Spend your time on the bits he could see. Also remember, the officer had an NCO with him who actually knew what he was looking at, and they were at ground level so you had to imagine it from their perspective. When I first started in the troops, I always volunteered to help mounting the guard. It gave me a chance to study the box men, study how they did it. Your guard horse was also key to your success and how long you could sit in the bar that evening. Height-wise, you and your horse had to match. I mentioned James Pig – if I had taken him on Queen's, I would have looked like toddler on a shire horse. The best guard horses had plenty of white on them. There's no better sight, in my opinion, than four white socks washed, dried and chalked up, with ermine marks blacked in with polish (ermine marks occur when the contrasting black of your horse's coat meets the white, forming above the coronet band at the top of the hoof). Black against white always stands out. Your white girth and white brow band will ping if they are well white-sapped. Like a lot of things in life, it's a knack, one I was determined to learn.

* * *

My first Queen's Life Guard was in mid-January, a little sooner than we expected due to manpower shortages – one of 3 Troop was in nick and Will Freedman was still nursing his poorly back. As it happened, it was Quiff's first Guard as well. I thought my kit was alright. I was riding Windrush – he wasn't my preferred choice, but I liked him and he would have to do. Like I have said, turning out on Queen's Life Guard was a knack, one I clearly hadn't got yet, because I ended up second relief under the arch, or second chicks, the second-worst relief on the Guard. The stags on that relief were 1.00 pm until 3.00 pm, then 7.00 pm until 9.00 pm, in the kit, then every four hours throughout the night not in the kit on stable guard, until the gates opened again at ten the following morning. Of course, the whole thing was exciting. Just being a part of it was an achievement. We'd been working towards it for years by now, and at least standing in the chicks gave me the opportunity to recce the place out. Two hours in one area about 10 or 12 metres long soon became pretty boring. You could patrol, of course, like a caged lion, up and down, up and down, doing the famous jackboot swagger, sword sloping on your right shoulder. A minute soon feels like ten, then ten minutes feels like an hour. It was a dull January day. Most of the people scurrying about were civil servants or high-ranks in their civilian uniform of pinstriped double-breasted suits and regimental ties. It soon became quite confusing: do I come to attention and salute by carrying my sword or not? That one coming out of the big black door wearing a bowler hat's got to be an officer. I decided to adapt the old military adage, 'if it doesn't move, paint it', to 'if it does move, salute it'. You could tell if you were right by the way they lifted their hat in recognition, or not.

The highlight, of course, was the tourists. There weren't many at this time of year, but when they did venture as far as the chicks, curiosity having got the better of them, I figured they deserved to be entertained. So a quick photo opportunity, then a surprise patrol. It's amazing how shocked they were when you actually moved; young girls especially shrieked and ran when you suddenly sprung to attention and began to patrol. They all, without fail, tried to make you laugh, which was a challenge in itself. I found if you just fixed your gaze into the peak of your helmet and mentally removed everyone from your field of vision, you could blank everything out for as long as you needed. Over the years, Quiff, Terry and I have attended many meetings in and around Whitehall in our quest for justice. We would make time to go and 'check the boys out'. From my personal perspective, I understand, to a degree, their frustration at being under relentless social media scrutiny, but they are fortunate enough to be in the best two regiments in the British Army. We were always taught from day one, that if you couldn't take a joke, you shouldn't have joined. You've got to remember that back in the Seventies, there was a real threat from terrorist attacks. We had no protection from armed police, no chains or white painted boxes to 'protect' us. We just used our dignity and sense of duty to drive us through. Hitting the alarm as a mounted sentry was considered a sin, an admission that, between you, you couldn't handle the situation. Granted, we didn't have cctv cameras everywhere and mobile phones, but tourist had cameras – lots of them. I remember taking over a box sentry one summer morning. When I emerged into the sunlight from the dark of the box, the whole of Whitehall was packed with people. Traffic couldn't move, such was the number of people setting off cameras and trying to get a better view. The box doors were always closed behind you. Why they leave them open now beggars belief. Surely that's not going to help your horse feel secure. They are flight animals; just look where their eyes are set on their heads. Anything going on behind them has got the potential to spook them. I did hear that having the doors open was for ventilation – come on guys, you're only there for an hour, so grow a pair.

It was nine o'clock that evening when my second stag in the chicks ended. The clock above the arch in Horse Guards chimed every quarter of an hour, but from where I stood, no matter how much I tried, I could not see it. I could, however, hear a lot of movement in and around the stables behind me. A chill ran down my spine as I imagined what was going to happen when the gates shut at 10.00 pm. Still cold from spending two hours in the winter air, I was getting out of my kit at the far end of the long room that the troopers slept in. There are/were many traditions in the Household Cavalry. Most are historic and cherished – in those days anyway. One was the order of beds in the barrack room at Horse Guards. As you reached the top of the rickety old staircase and opened the squeaky door, you'd see ten or so military beds all in a row down the room. The first bed was for the number one box man, the second for second box, and so on until you reached third chicks at the bottom. Another tradition was the initiation affectionately known as 'troughing'. This happened to all troopers on their first Queen's Life Guard. Firstly, the guys who had sat in the bar all evening, drinking and watching the television, didn't use the toilet. Instead, they pissed in the buckets that had been bought in from the stables for that purpose. The noise I could hear going on behind me during my stag was several troopers digging large holes in the dung heap – ideally they should be deep enough to bury your victims up to the neck. The idea was, and we all knew it was going to happen, that when the gates shut at ten o'clock, the victims – Quiff and I on this occasion – would be buried in the dung heap and the contents of the buckets and any kitchen scraps would be tipped over our heads. Following much ridicule, we would be dragged out of the dung heap and unceremoniously thrown in the freezing cold trough.

'I'm not looking forward to this,' Quiff said as we both got into the taggiest kit we had. We felt like condemned men as we heard the footsteps coming up the stairs to get us. Quiff was grabbed first, rapidly followed by myself, and dragged down to the yard below. The ancient cobbled yard, with its tying rings attached to the walls, was dark, the only light that escaped from the stable room beside it. The light could escape, but we couldn't – eight against two doesn't really work in your favour. By now, Quiff was up to his neck in all kinds of shit in the dung heap. The focus was mainly on him, with most of the contents of the foul buckets now running down his head. If I stay in the background, I thought, I might at least get away with some of it. Not a chance! The next minute, I was in the shit pit as well. The smell of shit and stale piss was overwhelming. Quiff was desperately trying to clear his throat as I copped the remainder of the last bucket, my curly hair caked with 'something' – I didn't want to think what. Like a well-rehearsed drill move, before I knew it I was desperately fighting for breath as I landed in the freezing cold water of the trough. After one quick dunk under the water, I was dragged out. As one of the guys led me to the hot showers, I could hear Quiff's screaming as he took his turn in the trough. A hot shower, change of clothes and a bacon sandwich, and it was all over. We were now, officially, state troopers – Piccadilly Cowboys!

It all sounds very cruel and bullying, but it really was not. As well as being humiliated, in a funny sort of way you're looked after. I remember a future troughing when Quiff and I were on the other side of it. This crow who was on his first Queen's really – I mean really – didn't want to go in the trough. He was whinging so much, that great consideration was given to possible alternatives. Finally, after lengthy debate, he agreed to streak from the back gates of Horse Guards up to the Whitehall Theatre and back again. I reckon it was around 200 metres each way. It was 10.00 pm on a busy evening in central London when we prepared to open the 10ft-high black gates and send him on his mission. He really didn't think it through, because when he was sprinting, naked, back towards the safety of the yard, we shut and bolted the gates and went back to the bar to carry on our evening. To this day, I don't remember who let him in or how long he was out there, banging on the unscalable gate, pleading to be readmitted.

I read in the tabloid press sometime in the Eighties that some young trooper had complained about his troughing to his mum. She told the press, and as they always do, they destroyed a tradition, a regimental tradition that had probably been taking place for centuries.

Needless to say, both Quiff and I survived to take part in many more Queen's Life Guards. I managed to blag Pan Am as my guard horse and went on to become a bit of a box man myself. Pan Am and I spent many an hour watching the strange goings-on that some folk get up to when they visit Horse Guards.

Chapter 7

Tying the Knot

PAM AND I had planned to get married for some time. Trouble was, we hadn't discussed it with anyone else. I say 'anybody else', but I'd talked to my mum and my mates. They all knew Pam well and liked her. The only consensus of opinion, though, was that I was too young. Pam was four years older than me, which seemed strange to some people, but not to us. I was nearly 18, I thought to myself, I shouldn't still be afraid of the 'old man', as dad was known in our house. Don't ask him, tell him, I thought to myself. No, don't tell him, present your case in a calm and controlled manner. Just remember how it was having to take the daily orders into the RSM's office at Pirbright, how I slipped and fell on my arse in front of the most senior NCOs in the depot. I survived that; I even received a credit (a day's extra leave) for my week's work. I should be able to talk to my dad, God damn it.

'Where is he?' I asked my mum, as Pam and I visited on a Sunday evening before I was travelling back up town (London) on the milk train.

'He's in the conservatory,' she indicated by nodding her head in the direction of the other door in the kitchen.

Baugh Farm was a strange building. Over the years, bits and pieces had been added on and some, no doubt, taken away. Anyway, I had to negotiate three doors to get into the extension known as the conservatory. It wasn't a conservatory as we know it today, it was actually a flat-roofed room with a long row of windows on three sides. I say three doors, it was actually two proper doors and a dog gate. You had to perform pirouettes like a ballet dancer to make your journey through them, especially if you were carrying a drink, like I was. I could see through one of the window he was sitting in his usual seat listening to some music – Beethoven, I seem to remember.

'How do,' he said as I crept in and sat opposite him. His gold half-moon glasses had made their way so far down his nose they looked about to fall off.

'Dad, I need to talk. Do you want a top up?'

'If it's what I think it is, yes please.'

'If this is what I think it is.' What does he mean by that, I was thinking, as I struggled to open the door back into the kitchen. I was visibly shaking as I poured some whisky into his glass and made my way back. Time is of the essence, strike now and don't take 'no' for an answer. All these thoughts were spinning around my head as I took my place opposite him.

'Pam and I want to get married. I know you're going to tell me I'm too young, but I've done everything you told me to do. You know, joining up and all that. I've got a good career ahead of me, so why can't we?' I blurted out, hardly stopping for breath.

'Well, I can't stop you. You're 18 in a few weeks. You know your mum and I like Pam. It's your decision.'

I think I was in shock as I tried to bring my glass of cider to my lips to refresh my over-dry throat. The old fella wasn't that old, but he looked tired. He'd been busy all afternoon directing my brother Mark and I in splitting and storing logs for the fires. His daily cigar jumped up and down as he tapped the pockets of his waistcoat in search of his matches. He shouldn't have been smoking. He'd suffered with severe rheumatism since he was a child. He'd joined up – volunteered – during the Second World War and served in the Royal Air Force as an aerial photographer in the Far East. He had such bad rheumatic fever while he was in India that the doctors in the hospital he was in said he would never ride a bike again. Little did they know that he had one parked against the wall outside, ready to go. He smoked (cigars or a pipe) when he shouldn't have. He didn't earn a great deal of money, so he made his own alcoholic concoctions, such as cider, which in our house was known as 'cripple'. He also made wine in old oak barrels, which he turned into punch for parties we regularly had in the large vaulted cellars of the farm. He was my hero, but I was too scared of him to tell him. That's one of my biggest regrets. As we grew older, our relationship got easier. I like to think that, deep down, he was proud of me.

As I sat there, Beethoven had done his bit, so all I could hear was that rhythmic clunk every time the record completed each revolution of the player. The door to my left tentatively opened and Pam poked her head through, looking apprehensive. All it took was a gentle nod from me for her to know everything was okay. After giving dad a big hug, Pam went off to see her pony. I stayed drinking with both mum and dad until she returned, and I went to get my kit together to return up town.

* * *

It was quarter past three in the morning as I walked along the wide corridor that led to 3 Troop. It was quiet, and only a few lights shone in each troop room that I passed. Standing by the feed room door with a handful of horse cubes in my hand, I could see Pan Am's head up, waiting for me. After any time away, I would always go and check she was alright before I got some kip. Standing there taking in the scene before me, I suddenly heard, 'Wol. Wally.' What the fuck, I thought, as I tried to gain the courage to look for where the sound came from.

'Wol, over here in the hay store,' the whispered voice continued. 'Help me, I'm stuck.'

'Stuck where? Who the fuck is it anyway? I think I've shit myself, you twat, whoever you are.' I whispered back. I don't know why I whispered; I didn't need to, as there was no one else about. As I walked towards the stack of hay bales in one of the spare stalls, I could just make out this figure. It was very confusing – I thought for a moment that I'd drunk too much of dad's cripple, because the figure in front of me was upside down. I could see now it was a skinny figure, and he/it was wriggling about like a fish on a hook. As I got closer, I could see who it was and what the problem was. It was Stevo, the dink from Bristol that I first met when we joined up at North Camp railway station. Somehow, he'd caught his ankle in a piece of bailing string, which had formed a sort of noose around his lower leg. For a minute, I thought of leaving him there because of the way he had just made me look and sound like a frightened girl.

'How did this happen?' I asked as I looked at the orange twine that was trying to cut off his lower leg.

'I was having a quick doss on the hay when I heard footsteps coming down the corridor. Well, I panicked, didn't I? I thought it was the orderly dog, so I tried to get down sharpish like. But it wasn't the orderly dog, was it? It was you, knobhead.'

Charming, I thought, as I lifted his shoulders to try and take the weight off the noose. As I was doing that, we both heard footsteps coming along the corridor towards us. I could hear spurs jingling as the steps came closer. We must have both doubled our efforts, because when the shadowy figure came into view, Stevo was free. I don't even want to know what the orderly officer must have thought as he dissected the image in front of him – two troopers, one in civvies, the other in stable dress, with hay in his hair and all over his heavy-duty jumper.

'Er, I've just got back from a thirty-six-hour pass, Sir, and I just popped down to see my horse before bed. I saw Stevens here sorting some hay out for one of the restless horses, so we were catching up.' I was going on to say that because he was a dink, we didn't see as much of each other as we used to, but I thought waffling on like that wouldn't further our cause.

'Exactly as Wol – Wallington – said, Sir. Couldn't have explained it any better myself.'

Luckily, Household Cavalry officers weren't the sharpest, and he soon turned on his heels and clinked his way back to wherever he'd come from.

'Thanks, mate,' Stevo said as I stood in Pan Am's stall and fed her the horse nuts that were now in my jacket pocket. I took a quick look at the massive blackboard on the way out to see what I was doing in about an hour-and-a-half's time. Panorama single exercise in the park, it read. I had a feeling I knew what that was all about as I made my way to the fourth floor.

A cold, frosty morning had turned the park opposite white in the dawn sun as I climbed onto Pan Am's back. As I'd thought, the troop Corporal of Horse, Corporal Murray, was a bit concerned that Pan Am might have a touch of Azoturia, or Monday morning disease. She was apparently a bit stiff around her hind quarters on Sunday when she was led out of her stall. Sunday was a rest day and also bran mash day. Azoturia was common after a day's rest. It causes severe muscle cramps, especially in the hind quarters. In very severe cases, the animal can't even get up from lying down. Pan Am's condition – Equine Exertional Rhabdomyolysis (ER), or tying up as it's also known – didn't affect her too much, thank goodness. Good husbandry was what she needed, and that's what she got. If she had been sent out on watering order, she could well have 'tied up' fairly rapidly and wouldn't be able to move. All that was needed was a gentle walk to get the muscles warmed up before they were asked too much of. I was glad of the slow start, as it had been one hell of a weekend. Pam and I – mostly Pam, I have to confess – had a lot of planning to do before our proposed wedding in February. My ears were freezing as we made our way towards the Serpentine Lake in Hyde Park. Pan Am's back was beginning to drop now as she started to loosen up. She wasn't an easy ride. When fit and well, she'd pull like a train – a proper little pocket rocket, just my type of horse. The sight that was beginning to unfold as we reached the far end of the lake always fascinated me. Members of the Serpentine Swimming Club were out. Mainly old fat men in Speedos, they would swim in the lake most mornings. It was always fun to watch. The sheer stupidity of it fascinated me. One of the swimmers I spotted was a disgraced ex-Tory MP named Ian Harvey. Quiff and I had struck up a conversation one morning while out on exercise. Quiff occasionally went out with his daughter. We were playing a lot of squash at the time – there were two squash courts on the very top of Peninsular Tower, the massive block of married-quarter flats that towered over West London. George often invited us to give him a game at his club, the RAC Club in Pall Mall.

* * *

Pam and I had finally set a date, 15 February 1974. Being near Valentine's Day was a pure coincidence – it was just when the regiment would allow us some leave. Quiff and Jarvo were ushers, and Terry and Stinch were there to make fools of themselves, basically.

'Do you think this thing will make it all the way to Bristol?' I asked Stinch as we rattled down the M4 towards the south-west. I'm not sure where he got his Vauxhall Cresta, but two of the four forward gears didn't work.

'Of course it will. Have faith,' he replied, trying to spread the faith throughout the overloaded car.

Quiff, Terry and Jarvo were squeezed into the back, with our freshly cleaned tunics over their laps. All the rest of our kit was in the boot, while I got the front seat because I knew the way. As I recall, none of us could drive. I don't think Stinch had passed his test. I knew he had a motorcycle licence, because he got that when we were at Summer Camp, when I got the first aid course. The Vauxhall Cresta was a big old car, and the lane into Baugh Farm was a narrow one. I explained how my dad negotiated the narrow entrance in his big Rover. The entrance was a gravel lane between two houses on a housing estate. Once you were successfully in, you'd have about 6in of space either side for about 30 metres between garden and garage walls. After negotiating the narrow bit, the lane opened up, with green fields on the right and a small copse of trees on the left. Ahead of us, about a hundred metres away, stood the large white farmhouse that was Baugh Farm. A large barn filled a lot of the skyline to the right as the lane made its way downhill. As I directed Stinch to park outside another barn, I could see my dad and brother Mark in the yard that lay before us. It was around 4.00 pm on Friday when we struggled out of the car. My neck was a bit stiff, probably from the tension of the journey. With stretching finished, we were greeted by the old man and Mark. It's always awkward to introduce your dad by his Christian name. To be fair, most of them – well,

Terry and Quiff – had met before, so it was Jarvo and Stinch that would be meeting Reg for the first time.

The five of us occupied most of the bedrooms at the front of the house. I was chuffed to see I had been given the room with a double bed and not my regular bedroom at the back of the house. All settled in, kit hanging clean and ready, we decided to have a quick livener with mum and dad. A large jug of cripple greeted us as we filed through the narrow passage into the large kitchen. If you've never drunk cripple before, you have to approach it with caution – a bit like poison, really. The first sip, even if you're used to it, can be brutal. Your eyes will narrow and your cheeks will suck inwards; you want to puff them out, but your face won't let you. While all this is going on, your ears make funny noises, like they're laughing. It's alright, though, it doesn't last long, and with each sip it becomes easier. For mid-February, the weather was wonderful, so we stood in the back garden with our wine glasses of cripple, having a cigarette while watching the Friday evening traffic on the M4 in the distance. Our plan, to avoid Pam and her mates on their hen night, was to just go to our local, the Golden Heart, for a few drinks and then get a fairly early night. The pub was packed, and people were insisting on buying us drinks – lots of drinks. Pam knew where we would be, so, as superstition or whatever it is says, she knew not to come in this particular pub. I think we'd progressed about two-thirds of the way through the crowded bar when a joyful scream rang out and Pam and her mates burst in. I could see the joyous sparkle in her eyes, even from where I stood some distance away.

'It's still Friday, so it doesn't count,' Pam whispered into my ear when we finally met. It was always the best moments when I held her, so I didn't mind one bit.

The evening ended with us waving Pam and her mates off from the pub car park before we returned to the farm to resume drinking. Mum being mum, she had prepared several plastic bowls that we could take to bed with us, in case we were sick in the night. Dad was in his usual place at the head of the long kitchen table. A jug of his famous punch, with a few empty glasses surrounding it, sat in the middle of the table, and I didn't have time to warn my fellow cavalrymen before they were lured into 'trying a drop'. When I left to go to bed at about one in the morning, I can just remember that Terry was fast asleep under the kitchen table, Stinch was in a similar state by the range – with his head half in the dog's basket – dad was asleep, leaning on the table with head in hands like he was meditating, and Jarvo was asleep half on the chair at the opposite end of the table.

'What shall we do?' I asked Quiff as we stood in the doorway that led to the hall.

'Fuck it, leave them. They'll be alright.'

For a moment I had trouble working out where I was the following morning. I'd never slept in this bedroom before. The sun was casting coloured shadows from the leaded light top windows on the cream blanket on my bed. Baugh Farm, as I've explained, was a massive house. The front half – the Victorian bit – had large, tall rooms typical of its time. At some time in their history, the large upstairs bedrooms were divided in two so they could be used as bed and breakfast rooms, which was handy for us because there were bodies everywhere. Some had made it to their bed, but others hadn't. Mother was in a big, flap scurrying around the kitchen trying to feed people. Relatives were also turning up. To be honest, I didn't expect it to have been that busy. The boys and I spent most of the morning at the front of the house, out of the way. Being squaddies, we were all used to drinking. I had the advantage of having been on the wrong side of my dad's punch several times before. Pam wouldn't touch it after having a glass one bonfire night, when dad had to drive her home she was so pissed. Trouble is, it tasted so nice. Like Rockingham back in 3 Troop, it would creep up and bite you in the arse!

By midday, Quiff, Jarvo and I had our kit on: one-dress trousers, welly boots with spurs, state tunic buff belt with sword slings, white gloves and forage cap. There were people I didn't really recognise – relatives from Northampton, aunts and uncles I hadn't seen for years. My brother Tony, who was an officer in the 2nd Royal Tank Regiment, was outside talking to dad. The whole thing was amazing. The best place for us, I decided, was the pub. The wedding was at 3.00 pm about a mile away in Downend Church. There was a pub close by where we could have a drink and wait, so we all agreed that was the best plan. Stinch was in civvies, so he didn't draw too much attention to the three scarlet-clad troopers squeezed on the back seat.

I thought I had a lot of relatives there, but I think Pam's outnumbered us by two to one. There was her aunt and uncle who had travelled from Canada to be here, and Uncle Knobhead from Kingswood was there. We were lucky on our side, as our Uncle Knobhead couldn't make it'

As you would expect, Pam looked stunning. I don't know what the vicar thought of being referred to as padre by the people with military connections who were there. He reminded me of the interrogation – sorry, meeting – we had with him at the start of this process, the reading of the banns and so on.

That was Pam's gig, I'm afraid. She lived literally round the corner from the church, whereas I was in London serving Queen and country. We were so lucky with the weather, considering it was February. Pam's bridesmaids looked wonderful alongside her when they posed for pictures. I suddenly realized how much effort everyone had gone to, to make this day happen, let alone be the success it was. Quiff was working very hard to hook up with one of our friends, Helen, rather than doing his actual job of being an usher. I wouldn't have trusted him to usher a group of blind people into a dark room!

After the reception, which was also fantastic, we ended up, changed this time into full one-dress – blue tunics rather that the red state tunic – back in the Golden Heart. I have to say, even as a fit 18-year-old I was knackered. I had to return to London the next day with the others and, because the army hadn't found us married quarters yet, use my spare time to find us somewhere to live. Pam was working in Bristol for the Royal Mail by now, and they'd agreed to transfer her to London, so time was of the essence and I had to find some sort of temporary accommodation. Back up town, armed with a copy of the *Evening Standard,* I sat with Terry – or was it Quiff, one of the two anyway – in our local Wimpey studying the 'bedsits to let' section when one of us came across a room to let in Crystal Palace – Farquhar Road, to be exact. It was a double bedsit close to the bus route. I went to the phone box to telephone to make an appointment to view, and the following afternoon found Quiff and I on the number fifty-two bus heading for Crystal Palace.

'What's that all about?' I asked Quiff as we stepped down from the bus.

'What's what all about?'

'That thing,' I observed with much intrigue, as I pointed at what looked like a mini-Eiffel Tower.

'That's a radio and television mast, tit head,' he replied, politely as ever.

'Right, no fucking about when we meet the agent. I didn't bring you to fuck it up for me, understood?'

'Er, yes Sergeant,' he sarcastically replied as we walked towards Farquhar Road. The large three-storey house was in the corner of a row of the same, not far from the pub – check, I thought, as we approached the young lady we assumed to be the estate agent.

'Hi, I'm Simon, we've come – sorry, not we, I've come to see the bedsit you've got to let. He's just along for the ride, as it were.' This wasn't going to plan, I thought. It didn't help that Quiff had quickly latched onto my nervousness and was trying to hold my hand.

'Sure, follow me,' the agent said as she opened the large front door. 'It's on the second floor – follow me,' she continued as we climbed the wide old staircase typical of this age of house.

It's very hard to stay focused when Quiff is continually fucking about. He had his arm in mine now. He was coming close to getting thumped, I can tell you. The room was large enough for Pam and I, and was about £10 a week all in, if I remember correctly. The shared bathroom was right outside, and it had a tiny kitchen to cook in. The double bed looked okay. We were at the back of the building, so didn't have the lovely views of Crystal Palace Park that you could see from the front. I decided to take it, making the decision without Pam seeing it. I had been assured by the housing officer that we should get our married quarters fairly soon, so this would be a very temporary measure. The bus back to Knightsbridge along Slone Street passed the Gloucester pub, so we decided to have a quick beer before returning to the barracks for scoff. London buses, in those days, had the open exit/entrance at the back. If you were able, you could exit while it was still moving, but what footwear you were wearing was important. Quiff was very proudly wearing his new trendy Chelsea boots. That's all very nice, I thought, but will they give him the same firmness and grip that a pair of lace-ups do? Very much in the military method we had been so meticulously taught at the depot, I went first. The thing is, you've got to quite literally hit the road running. For that split second you're between the bus and the road, or sometimes pavement, you have to start running. You start with a sprint, then quickly slow down to end up in a casual walk as if nothing had happened. A quick check of the tie always seems a cool conclusion to the manoeuvre, I thought. I have to admit, I wasn't expecting what I saw when I turned to check on Quiff's progress. He'd made his exit from the bus and I could see his was looking for his landing area, but his feet weren't correct. Adjust, adjust, I thought as the tarmac fast approached. Too late; he was nearly flat on his face, his left ankle giving way through lack of support in the footwear department. His arms started flailing like a swan trying to take off. It was obvious he was going to hit the deck and it wasn't going to be pretty. I suddenly realized he'd borrowed my best blue sports jacket. I didn't give a shit about him, but what about my jacket? Rather than attempt to help him, I stepped back between two parked cars and, along with everyone else in the vicinity, waited for the inevitable. As I reached him, he was struggling to his feet. His left boot was off by now, revealing a hole in the big toe area of his sock. I grabbed the boot as I passed it, holding it up by the pull tab like it was a grotty sock your squad sergeant had found in your locker during a room inspection.

'Yours, I believe,' I smugly said as he finally straightened himself up. 'If you've damaged my jacket, you're a dead man. Now let's get in the pub, you're embarrassing me.'

On his return from the toilet, I inspected the jacket thoroughly before allowing him the pint I'd bought him. The palms of his hands were grazed, and the knees of his trousers looked a bit worse for their ordeal, but apart from that all looked okay.

Pam was delighted when I called her that evening. We agreed that I would collect the keys on Saturday, then get the train down on Saturday afternoon and move her kit up on Sunday. The sense of pride and happiness I had as I watched Pam get out of the taxi was palpable. This was a new chapter for both of us. Pam had left home for the first time, and was starting her new job in a couple of days. I'd managed to blag a couple of days off in exchange for a Queen's next Saturday, so we had a little time to settle in. I was to become very familiar with the number fifty-two bus over the next few months. I liked riding on the top deck, preferring the front seats if possible. Even with Pam's two large cases, I insisted on struggling them up to the top deck. The journey took about an hour; an hour of worrying whether she would like the place. I was rehearsing in my mind what I would say if she didn't. I'd reassure her that it wouldn't be for too long, that I was pushing as hard as I dare with the housing officer for quarters. Pam, as far as I was concerned, had given up a great deal to be with me. She'd sold her beloved pony, Shane, which had been bought for her to keep in the stables at Griffin Farm where we'd first met. She'd also given up her job in Bristol and a comfortable home life with her parents. I'd told her in my drunken state on our wedding night at the Golden Heart that she should strap herself in because she was in for one hell of an adventure. At the time, I honestly didn't know just what an adventure it would be.

Needless to say, she liked the room and we enjoyed a great month or so there before moving into our first married quarters just down the hill at Anerley Court in Penge.

Chapter 8

Horse Guards (Friend or Foe)

THE HOUSHOLD CAVALRY Regiment's legacy dates back to 1660. It is formed from four antecedent regiments: The 1st Life Guards, 2nd Life Guards, Royal Horse Guards and 1st (Royal) Dragoons. Horse Guards, where we carried out ceremonial state duties guarding, in our case, the Queen, is packed with history. There have been many books written about the place. I'm going to take you inside our bit of the regiment and tell you, from a trooper's perspective, what it was like and what went on during my time serving there. Genuinely, until I arrived in Horse Guards on my first Queen's Life Guard, I'd never been behind the scenes, as it were. I'd been there with Pam as a tourist, but nothing else. In the Seventies, the guard changed at 11.00 am every day in the courtyard behind the main gates. The new mounted and foot sentries would change, and when the old guard had left the remainder of the new guard would dismount and lead their horses through the arch into the stalls behind the chicks. As you entered the stable room, it was like stepping back a few centuries. The stalls, the wood, iron and brass dividers, were original, as were the worn stable bricks beneath your feet. Large arched windows at the end of the building looked out over Horse Guards Parade and St James' Park beyond. Opposite the stalls were saddle and bridle racks, again original. Windows on that side looked over the small yard where the trough and dung heap were. By the time you had got your horse's kit off and stowed it, the guard van would be in the back yard dropping off your overnight kit and collecting the old guard's stuff before returning to the barracks. As a newbie, the best thing to do was follow somebody who knew what they were doing and take advice where you could get it. As I said earlier in the book, Queen's was all about the knack – the knack of turning out to the highest standard that would get you a box sentry; the knack of keeping your state kit safe and undamaged throughout the guard and not making yourself work between guards. On average we did two or three Queen's a week. If you did them one after another, that was known as 'trotting guards', which could be quite challenging, especially

171

with me now married and living out in married quarters. I soon learnt that the best way to look after your jackboots was to avoid walking in them. One and two box sentries did stags from eleven until twelve, one until two and finally three until four. With those stags, you wouldn't have to tab it on the four o'clock inspection, just march in after the dismount. It's no wonder we wore out socks quicker than most with the amount of time we spent walking in them. We had to try not to walk up stairs with boots on, as that really cracked the creases on them.

With your guard horse in his or her stall, you would then make your way upstairs to the guard barrack room to change into stable order. The best way, I found, was to leave your boots downstairs while you took your overnight bag up and changed. Everything in that ancient building either creaked, rattled or groaned. The windows of the barrack room were of the old sash type. They opened out onto a narrow balcony above the chicks overlooking the courtyard below. Also on the second floor were the kitchen and dining area and the toilet block. The place was like a warren of creepy passages, especially on a windy winter's night.

As I mentioned earlier, the week after getting married I copped a Thursday and a Saturday long guard. These were mounted when the sovereign was in residence at Buckingham Palace. The guard would comprise an officer, a corporal major who carried the standard, two NCOs and ten troopers. Technically there were eleven troopers because one of the reliefs was a stable guard; he would still turn out in the kit for inspection and be given that relief. He would then rein back and his horse would be returned to his troop, and he would grab his bag, go and get changed and travel down to Whitehall in the guard van. His main job throughout the guard was to look after the officer's and corporal major's chargers while the long guard was on. The stable guard relief was considered the fifth box sentry really. Trouble is, it was the last relief to be called. The reliefs were called out in strict order: first were the four mounted sentries, box men, then the three gate reliefs – not too bad if you had to tab it, at least you had a bigger area to patrol – then the three chicks reliefs were called – 'shit order' – and finally stable guard. It was a terrible wait when you knew your turnout was good enough for a box but were overlooked and you thought you'd be tabbing it. The relief of hearing 'stable guard, Wallington' called out was immense.

This Thursday guard, I'd just cheeked fourth box, so my first stag would be at twelve. When you were a box sentry, it was not worth taking your buckskins off between stags. They were a pain to get on and off at the best of times. I even left Pan Am's saddle on, such was the short time between reliefs. I grabbed some scoff from the kitchen, quickly eating it before getting ready. Getting ready was just a matter of doing up my tunic and throwing on my cloak, going downstairs with helmet in hand and stepping into my jackboots before the stable guard, in this case, brought Pan Am to the mounting block. Once on board and your cloak was buttoned up and correctly spread over the horse, your helmet and sword would be handed to you. You were now ready to follow your fellow box man and the NCO out into the courtyard to take your place behind your sentry box and await orders to replace your relieved box man at the conclusion of his stag.

As the doors behind you shut, you settled down, sword sloped on your right shoulder, and your hour's stag would begin. The drill was, at about two minutes before the hour you would hear the big black double doors behind you open. This would be the time to let your horse know that you were soon going to do a bit of work. When ordered by the guard NCO, both box men would ride forward into Whitehall and circle towards each other to form up as a pair, follow the guard NCO back into the courtyard and form up ready to dismount. For the dismount, the lead one would move forward one stride, then the NCO would order us to return swords. When wearing cloaks, this involved undoing a couple of buttons and tossing it backwards – a bit like a flasher, I suppose – then your man at the front, along with the NCO, would continue with head signals until your sword was safely returned to its scabbard. Now you have two, in this case gloved, hands available, the lead sentry then – and this looks worse than it is – slaps his horse on the neck with his right hand. This alerts your horse that you are about to dismount. When in state kit, the change in weight can be significant, so you are telling your mount to be ready. You then pull the Pelham rein up, using the rein stop to keep if tight, and on the signal toss it away. Then comes the tricky bit, the bit when you hope and pray that the gate sentry hasn't loosened your girth while putting your boot back in its stirrup When you're on box duties, you have two means of communication. The first is a black iron bar that protrudes from the inside wall of your sentry box, which rings an alarm in the guardroom and assistance will come. The other is getting the eye of your gate sentry so he comes over to assist you. Out of boredom, sometimes you would deliberately kick your stirrup iron off as an excuse so he'd come over for a chat. Obviously he would have to appear as if he was doing something while chatting, so before he replaced your boot he would check your horse's girth and surcingle, either tightening or loosening it.

Who's going to know? You can't feel or see anything from where you are, and you won't know until you swing your leg over your horse and stand with all your weight in the left stirrup, waiting for the signal to drop to the ground below. If your gateman, for a laugh, has loosened your girth, there's a good chance you're going to end up on the deck, looking at your saddle hanging under the belly of your horse. This has happened, I can assure you. Not to me, thankfully, but I can remember one incident. I won't mention any names, but needless to say, I don't think the gateman expected what he saw. When safely back on *terra firma*, on the command you lead your horse back into the stables, and so it goes on.

There was always stuff going on, mostly in the evenings, especially during the summer months when we were cooped up and bored. The kitchen overlooked Whitehall. It was staffed during the day by a civvy chef, but when he had gone we could use it to make sandwiches or a brew. Quiff and I were up there one evening boiling a kettle. It had been a hot day, so I lifted the sash window and poked my head out to see what was going on. It wasn't that busy, but there was a steady flow of people below, making their way to wherever they were heading. No one looked up; they never did. But if they had done, they would have noticed two young troopers hatching a plan.

'Have you got a ten pence piece?' Quiff asked.

'Yeah, why? What's your plan?'

'If we heat it up on the gas until it's really hot, then we can throw it out the window onto the pavement and see if anyone picks it up.'

I rifled through the pockets of my denim trousers to find a coin. You have to bear in mind, back in those days in the bar below where we were standing, a pint of beer was about twenty-five pence.

'Are you sure you want ten pence? Why not two pence?'

'Because no one will see a copper coin – it's got to be a silver one.'

After reluctantly handing over the coin, Quiff proceeded to clamp it between a pair of tongs and heat it up. Both of us watched as it changed colour several times before returning to its original state. 'That's it. It's ready,' Quiff announced as he turned the gas off and moved towards the window. A gentle breeze hit us as we resumed our positions to carry out this operation. The footpath below was clear – check; launch – check. The coin bounced as it hit the stone paving slabs. For a moment I thought it was going to ricochet into the road, but luckily it settled right in the middle of the pavement, plain for all to see. Now all we had to do was wait for our first victim. The first looked a bit dodgy, one of the Whitehall suits (civil servants), but fortunately he just kicked it slightly with his shoe and carried on. Next was a tramp. We used to see loads around here; they slept under the arches on the embankment close by – cardboard city, as we used to call it. 'Here we go, stand by,' Quiff whispered as the old boy bent down to grab his prize. Well, I bet he hadn't moved that fast in years. His grubby wrinkled hand shot skywards like he'd had an electric shock. Fair play to him, he persisted and eventually picked up the coin and put in his pocket. Our next idea – or should I say Quiff's next idea – was to fill a condom, that conveniently he had in his wallet, with water and launch it like a bomb on some unsuspecting passer-by. Quiff held the thing open while I operated the tap. The stainless steel sink was a large one, but still the condom was taking on so much water that it was filling the sink. 'That's enough,' Quiff suggested as I attempted to tie a knot in the top of the thing. I think it was me who started the giggling fit that followed as we tried to get the bloody thing out of the sink. We had clearly overfilled it, because there was no way it was coming out of there. If we tried to sort of roll it out of the sink into our arms, it just threatened to slide through our arms onto the floor. I managed to undo my knot and let some of the water out, which made it slightly more manageable. Still giggling uncontrollably, we managed to get it onto the window ledge, ready for launching. As I looked up and down Whitehall, I heard footsteps on the stairs just down the corridor. 'Who the fuck's that?' Quiff asked, like I was supposed to know. 'I don't know – just get rid of it.' The footsteps were getting louder now. By the sound of them, they were heavy boots, so more than likely it was an NCO. In the end, we had little choice but to let it drop onto the wrought iron railing below and maintain a position as though we were just looking out of the window, watching the world go by. Heaven knows what the guys in the bar thought as this massive wobbly bomb exploded outside their window. The footsteps did indeed belong to an NCO; it was the corporal of the guard doing his evening checks.

I'm pretty accustomed to living in creepy old houses. Since being a young child, I'd lived in two old farmhouses that were allegedly haunted. It never bothered me. Maybe I'm not susceptible, I used to think. Maybe I just can't connect with the spirits or something. Horse Guards, however, was different. It had that feel about it. The history of the place was incredible. Right opposite where Quiff and I were innocently gazing out of the window stood the Banqueting House, outside which Charles I was executed in January 1649. The whole place was connected by windy corridors with creaky floorboards, and the windows rattled in the wind, causing curtains to move curiously. It was as though Horse Guards was never totally asleep. There was always someone on duty – be it was the guard commander in the guardroom or, as on this occasion, me on stable guard. It was a long guard, so we had an officer on the guard. Traditionally, he walks from Horse Guards to St James' Palace to have dinner with the officer commanding the Foot Guards at Buckingham Palace at St James' Palace. His journey would take him across Horse Guards Parade, down The Mall a bit to St James'. Most of us wouldn't see him leave or return. The gates are shut and locked at 10.00 pm when the last foot sentries finish their stags. The bar shuts at 10.30 pm, when the civvy barman is let out of the back gate to go home. Everything quietens down fairly quickly after that, unless there's a troughing going on. This particular evening, my stag was due to finish at midnight. I was in the stables, checking the hay nets and things. It was dark; only the light from the yard outside filtered through the windows. The windows overlooking Horse Guards Parade were set quite a bit higher than normal, as the parade ground outside was higher than the stable floor I was standing on. I could see the dark image of the large statue outside becoming lighter and darker as clouds passed across the nearly full moon. In such situations, I found the best thing to do was to keep busy and take no notice of what was going on around me. I could hear chains rattling, but I knew that was just the horses tugging on their hay nets and rattling their headcollar chains. Suddenly, my focus was disturbed by a tapping sound. For a moment it put me right on edge. Was someone winding me up? It wouldn't be out of the question, after all. I looked around – nothing there. Then it went again. It seemed to be coming from the far end of the long room, the end where the parade ground was. As I looked up towards the large windows and the statue, I saw it – a dark shadow kept appearing in the bottom left-hand corner of one of the windows. Tap, tap, tap, it went again. I thought whoever or whatever it was, it was likely armed and I wasn't about to go any closer. Some of the horses lifted their heads and started to anxiously move around in their stalls. I quickly checked my watch; it was midnight, time for me to go. As I raced up the stairs towards my bed, I saw the next guy on stag wandering towards the kitchen. 'All quiet down there, mate,' I said. 'See you tomorrow.'

The following morning, as I sat eating my porridge, the junior NCO of the guard sat opposite me with his breakfast. The big smug grin on his face told me he knew something about last night.

'Your last stag last night – alright was it?'

'Yes, Corporal, why do you ask?' I replied, desperately trying to remain calm.

'No one knocking on the window at the end of the stables?' I sort of knew he knew, but I couldn't work out how he knew.

'I can't be sure of it, but I might have heard something. I just thought it was a chain banging the side of a stall or something.'

'Well, it wasn't a chain, it was Captain Crispin Paket trying to get back in after his dinner at St James' Palace. Because of you, the poor twat had to walk the long way around and come in the main gate, which incidentally, he should have done in the first place. Well done, Wol. Fuck 'em, aye?'

I must say that I tried not to catch the officer in question's eye as I held his charger to the mounting block later that morning!

The following Saturday, I got two box on Pan Am so didn't have to hang around the stables late at night. It was great to see Pam walking up from Westminster, to see her venturing out. She had started her new job and was really enjoying it. When my stag finished, she was allowed to come into the yard and stables and meet the horses before returning to Farquhar Road for our last weekend in the little bedsit. They had finally found us our first proper married quarters, not far from where we were in Crystal Palace at Anerley Court in nearby Penge.

Chapter 9

Trooping the Colour

PAM AND I were settling into married life well. We'd bought our first dog – she was a lurcher-type rescue dog from Battersea Dogs' Home named Susie. Getting to Hyde Park Barracks was a bit of a pain. We had to catch a train from Penge East station at 5.15 am each morning. I say 'we', as also living in the redbrick C-shaped block towards the end of Anerley Park Road was another cavalryman who was an old mate from our junior days, Colin Galagher. He and his wife lived in the flat above us, so we would make sure either of us was up and ready for the half-mile walk to the station. Living out, as it's known, wasn't all it was cracked up to be, especially when you didn't have your own transport. I couldn't wait to be offered a flat in Peninsular Tower in the barracks, but Colin was happy where he was. His wife was expecting their first child, so I sort of got where he was coming from.

Our first Trooping the Colour was soon after we passed out of riding school in 1974. I always remember the Trooping dates because it's around Pam's birthday; that year it was on 15 June. We weren't married yet, so I was still living on the fourth floor, slowly gaining experience in carrying out state duties. I didn't officially have Pan Am as my guard horse yet, so it was a case of cajoling the troop three-bar into allocating you a half-decent horse both for guards and escorts, which included the Trooping. Your first Trooping the Colour, or state escort for that matter, is very much a learning curve. You learn how to turn out, how to control your horse while all around you appears to be going to shit. It's a bit like the calmness of the duck on a pond theory; it should all look calm and controlled to the viewer, yet under the surface all hell's being let loose. At a trot, you have to perform complex mounted drill moves while you and your mount are fighting for space and having several shades of shit knocked out of you by the guys and their horses either side of you.

Not many people know that for each Trooping you watch on the television on Saturday mornings, there have been three full rehearsals in the preceding weeks. The first is a khaki rehearsal when, starting in the early hours of the morning, West London is woken by the clatter of hundreds of hooves as they make their way to Horse Guards. Although you are wearing khaki riding kit, you also have to wear your state helmet and carry your state sword. The choreography is a sight to be seen. When we arrive at Horse Guards, having pretended to escort the pretend Queen from Buckingham Palace, we form up with our backs to the Guards Memorial to sit and watch the pure theatre of several Regimental Sergeant Majors, all under the command of the Garrison Sergeant Major, London District, drilling and screaming orders at half-asleep wooden tops dressed in their equivalent of khaki order, complete with bearskins and rifles. The massed bands of the Brigade of Guards is represented by four guardsmen manoeuvring a long – very long – rope that formed a square to match the band's dimensions as it carried out its somewhat tricky manoeuvres. While sitting observing the spectacle, I often wondered why they just didn't get the mussies out of their scratchers and down here on parade. Our band was on parade, so why wasn't theirs?

Jacko, the Household Cavalry's riding master, was involved. He was in a huddle of mounted officers getting in the way, it seemed, in the middle of the parade ground, pointing their whips at various landmarks around the vast gravelled expanse. Dawn was breaking as our turn to perform came. Most of our horses were half-asleep by now, so had to be gently reminded what we were here for. State helmets aren't easy to wear, especially for a long time. They're alright for an hour or two when you are on guard duty, but trotting in state helmets is a whole different kettle of fish We'd gained a lot of experience during riding school, but this was feeling very real now. I was sat next to a lance three-bar who was on his fifth Trooping; it was a bit like being allowed to play with the bigger boys at the park! The walk past was fine. The Queen was being represented by some wooden top officer named Rupert, I expect. Even though the parade ground was large, I could still spot *Jacko*'s beady eyes drilling into each and every one of us. On the second 'lap' we were in a trot, which meant you wouldn't get back to where you started from before the next call was blown. It was a dinks (Blues and Royals) parade, so they led. I was in the last rank, the only thing behind us being the farriers. It's a bit intimidating, I have to say, being followed by two large, muscly men carrying axes. From where I was, I could hardly hear the trumpeter's call to trot. It was very much a case of doing what the man in front or beside you did and 'winging' the rest. We had our saddles fitted with their sheepskins, so the sitting trot was a doddle really. However, a lot depended on your horse's gait to determine whether it was comfortable or not. Some horses are just uncomfortable in trot, like some aren't so good in canter. The trick is to relax your hips while sitting as deep in the saddle as you can. All well and good in theory, but you have to take into account the constant bashing from your cohorts and the constant change of pace. When you are wheeling around the corners of Horse Guards, those closest to the middle of the square will be barely moving, while the poor bugger on the outside will be cantering, holding his right leg in against his horse's belly while trying to keep his dressing. As all this is going on, your helmet keeps digging itself into the bridge of your nose as if to remind you 'I'm still here but really what I want to do is fall off'!

When the khaki ride is finished and the horses are fed, everyone goes for breakfast. Henry would have a right cob on because we all turned up at the same time. I often wondered just what he expected. While any rehearsals took place – and I can assure you, there were a lot of them – the Queen's Life Guard would go on as normal. The next rehearsal was the following Saturday, in full state kit. The only thing different to the actual thing was that the Queen wasn't the Queen. In our time, it was usually one of her ladies in waiting, who would be mounted, as our Queen was in those days. Spectators would line The Mall and Horse Guards Parade, just like the actual Trooping. It was a good opportunity for more people to see it. In fact, as Junior Guardsmen, we were taken from Pirbright to watch one of the rehearsals.

* * *

The following year, 1975, Pam and I were married and living in Penge, South London. Two things happen when you are married and living in married quarters. Firstly, you're not entitled to use the mess hall, unless you are on Queen's. Secondly, you no longer have a bed space in the living block – what you have is a locker in a large cleaning-cum-locker room next to the forge. All that's fine when you've got a nice new flat in Peninsular Tower – the Tower Block, as it was known – as you were a five-minute walk away from your locker. That is, of course, if the lifts were working. If not, it was a ten-minute walk. When you live over an hour away, it's a different story. There was no way, unless we got a minicab – Colin and I, I'm referring to – that we could get into Knightsbridge for the early hours of the morning. So what could we do? Well I managed to blag a bed in Terry and Liz's flat in the Tower Block. We hadn't seen Terry for a while because he had been posted to the cavalry's hunting stables at Melton Mowbray in Leicestershire. While there, he met his future wife, Liz, who served in the Royal Army Veterinary Corps. Although he was still in 3 Troop – you never leave the Swamp Troop – we didn't see much of him because he was now a State Trumpeter. Apparently the regiment was short of trumpeters, so both Quiff and Terry put their names forward. The regimental corporal major allegedly asked Terry if he could play a musical instrument, and he replied that he could 'tinkle on the piano a bit'. 'That will do,' he was told, 'get down the music block and learn!'

Terry was the trumpeter for the 1975 Trooping the Colour. Both Quiff and Terry turned out to be decent trumpeters, but this year Terry got the gig. A year on, I was a lot more prepared. I'd ridden in one or two escorts, including the state opening of Parliament, and Pan Am was my regular mount now, so all seemed good. I was working hard on achieving box sentries on Queen's, doing all the things I'd been told to do to get put on a farriers course at Melton.

As I've explained, you effectively do three rehearsals for every Trooping you take part in. What I didn't mention was the Monday after Trooping weekend – 16 June that year – the regiment had to take part in the Order of the Garter parade at Windsor Castle. It was the same every year, and every year it was a pain to do. The regiment was knackered. We'd just completed a month of ceremonial duties, including Queen's in between, and then we had to go to Windsor to line the road at Windsor Castle while a load of old farts wandered past in tights and very valuable robes. I remember trying to manoeuvre myself up the isle of a coach in state kit to try and sit on a seat for what seemed like the endless journey to Windsor.

The summer of 1975 was a hot one, as I remember. Everyone was already hot as we lined up for the colonel's inspection for the Trooping. You are so tightly packed in on the relatively small square in Hyde Park Barracks for a parade like this that you could get away with checking your escort kit. Let me explain. All the inspecting officers and NCOs could see in the limited time available to them was the front and back of yourself and your horse. A little tap with your spurs as they approached also helped. With Pan Am, she thought we were about to move so started tossing her head about – there's nothing like a bit of snot flying about to encourage Colonel Tiddly-Push and his entourage to move on by. I was lucky enough by then to have acquired a second pair of jackboots – escort boots, as they were known. They weren't bulled to the same high standards as your guard boots. They were clean, of course, but the main effort would be on the bits they could see, i.e. the front and back. That applied to everything really – your horse, horse's head kit, brass wear and whites. To the untrained eye, everything appeared to be gleaming.

Sitting there waiting for the off, I was aware that something wasn't quite right with my helmet. It felt like someone was pushing their thumb into my right temple. It was too late to adjust it because the regiment was starting to move off. The pain was becoming quite intense as we paraded along South Carriage Drive towards our first landmark, Wellington Arch. I'd worked out what I thought it was by now. Inside the helmet was a leather concoction that sat on your head; it had a lace around it that you could either loosen or tighten according to your needs. Once you've got it correctly fitted, there's no need to touch it. Trouble is, the spare end of the lace thing was knotted at the end, for no obvious reason. This isn't normally a problem, as you make sure you shake it to the top of the inside of the helmet before putting it on. Somehow, on this occasion, the bloody knot had managed to make its way down and lodge between my helmet and temple. The pain was really beginning to affect me now. I had plenty to think about for the next few hours without having to put up with this torture, I thought, as I tried to come up with a plan. Tipping my head back and forth didn't help, in fact it made it worse as the knot seemed to lodge itself deeper into my temple. I couldn't adjust it in plain sight – there were people everywhere. However, the police had held up the traffic as we crossed the road towards the Wellington Arch at the top of Constitution Hill. This is my only opportunity to fix it, I thought. If I could take it off and shake the knot back to where it belongs in the two seconds it will take to travel under the arch, I might be okay. Timing was key. Ranks had to close slightly as we travelled under the arch. As soon as we walked into the shadows of the arch, I took my opportunity: with reins and sword in my left hand, I reached up and removed my helmet. My hair was sticky with sweat, so I could feel the lace unstick itself from my forehead. As quick as I could, I shook the helmet towards the ground and in one swift movement planted it back in place. Success! While everyone else was focused on the arch, I'd managed to free the offending knot and everything appeared to be back to normal.

The sun was intense now as we sat waiting at the bottom of The Mall. In front of us lay one of the most famous sights in Britain, if not the world.

Union flags stretched ahead as far as the eye could see, with thousands of people squeezed up against the temporary barriers on either side of the wide thoroughfare, a line of scarlet tunics of the Guardsmen who were on street lining duties covering both sides. On this Trooping I was on the right-hand side of the rank, so found myself close to the foot sentries on that side. The trees on the edge of St James' Park provided much-needed shade to both the spectators and those of us on that side of The Mall. Waiting in that situation is strange; you can hear people in the crowd talking and cheering, flags are waving, and behind you the band is playing. Our signal would be when we heard the national anthem finishing. We knew then that the Queen would be in place, sandwiched between her two companies of Life Guards.

I could feel Pan Am brace herself up slightly as the various commands were called and we began the procession towards Horse Guards. The next bit of entertainment for us guys on the outsides of the long rank of horses that filled The Mall was to see if we could kick the magazines of the wooden tops (Guardsmen) as we rode past. Because the Queen was behind us, they were ordered to present arms as she passed. This involved – with a SLR rifle as it was in those days – literally presenting it by offering it out in front of your chest whilst at attention. The magazine protruded from the weapon at just about the same height as our boots. I wouldn't do it if I was wearing my guard boots, but with escort boots on the fun could begin. The tab guards knew what was going on – you could see their eyes straining to look to their left without moving their heads as we approached. This little game was like tent pegging. You had to keep your eye on the target as you approached, then 'bang', got one. I couldn't look back – that's physically impossible while wearing state kit – but a gasp from the crowd tells you you've scored a strike!

Once the escort completed that part of the parade, we formed up with our backs to the park just in front of the Guards Memorial. Once you have been ordered at ease, your sloped sword hand rests on top of your left rein-holding hand and you sit there and relax. The mass bands of the Household Division never fail to impress. The bass drums echo off the buildings that surround the parade ground as the Guards wait to be inspected. They've probably been there for over an hour by then. The sun is roasting hot, and this is where the next game begins – spotting the Guardsman who is about to faint before he actually does. It normally starts with a slight swaying back and forth. The bearskined head may twitch a bit, then, without any other warning, he's gone. The best scenario is falling backwards, but that's rare. Normally its forward, straight on their face. Back in those times, there were no niceties like bringing a stretcher on to help the victim out. No, he was dragged off to the nearest perimeter fence without ceremony and later put on a charge for not asking permission to leave the parade! I was always impressed by this parade. All the rehearsing was worth it. It was literally timed to the second, and after doing it so many times we knew when to start waking our horses up ready for their first lap. The mounted band took up their position in the middle of the parade ground first. My mate Terry was sitting in front of me in his ceremonial gold coat, trumpet in his right hand whilst it leant on his right thigh. If only the vast crowds could have seen him this morning, I thought, running around the married quarters changing room in his pants.

It was good to get moving. I could feel the sweat on my tee-shirt and under my buckskin breeches. The first ride past went well, as I was on the outside, the side nearest the Queen. I didn't have to give her the eyes right salute; I had to keep focused on the dressing, both ahead and to the left of me. Ahead of me I could see Terry bringing his trumpet to his lips in preparation for blowing the call to trot – not an easy thing to do. Horses are very intelligent beasts. His trumpeter's grey would know exactly what Terry was doing and would start jigging about, ready to comply. Despite this, the call was perfect and we were off. Whereas on last year's Trooping I was on the inside of the line, this year I was on the far outside. This would require me to get quite a shift on – a canter, I mean – in order to keep the dressing correct as we performed the wheel turn in each corner of the parade ground. This wasn't a problem. Pan Am was as sound as a pound, and the faster we went the better as far as she was concerned. When the parade had finished, I was at the back of the escort now instead of the front. The shade under the trees was a great relief as we waited on the slight gradient that led to The Mall. I was probably 3ft away from the barriers that contained the spectators, and could hear the cameras clicking and people talking. That's when the next problem began. First, I could feel Pan Am's back rising under my arse. Oh shit, no, I thought. I knew what was coming; she was about to pee. When a mare pees and you're on board, you are supposed to take the weight off her loins by standing up in you stirrups. Of course I did this, at the same time praying that she wouldn't take long as the escort was about to move off. The crowd beside me thought it was highly amusing as the pee ran towards the gutter beside them. Like an old man, it seemed to take forever for her to finally finish and give a wink or two to her spectators.

The ride back to Hyde Park Barracks went without a hitch. After safely delivering Her Majesty home, we arrived back on the parade square to perform the mass dismount and order to 'dismiss'.

Pam and her parents, who were staying with us for the weekend, had attended the parade, although I hadn't spotted them. I didn't expect to really, as it's very difficult to pick out individual faces in a crowd that large. The day was exceptionally hot, even for June. After taking off Pan Am's saddlery, I took a few seconds in her stall to compose myself before waddling back to the locker room to change. I can't explain the feeling when Terry released my cuirass belt and I could breathe freely again. My tunic had become one with my tee-shirt underneath it. The heavy woollen lining was soaked with sweat. I've always found it was easier to hang and store your state kit as you took it off. I left my tunic hanging on the outside of my locker to hopefully dry out a bit while I took on the mammoth task of getting my buckskin breeches off. Bearing in mind that I would be wearing them on the following Monday in Windsor, I couldn't preserve any of their pristine whiteness as I wrestled, kicked and stood on the bloody things until they were in a heap on the changing room floor. I wasn't on my own; everyone in the locker room seemed to be having the same dilemma. Eventually, sitting there in my pants getting my breath back, I noticed the letters 'NOTGNILLAW' tattooed into my left thigh. Well it looked like a tattoo, one of those homemade jobs. It took me a while to work out what had happened. Upon examination of the inside of the corresponding leg of my buckskins, I noticed where I had written, in marker pen, my name 'WALLINGTON' on the inside. The morning had been so hot that my sweat had transferred from leather to skin. It was there for a few days before it finally washed off. When we had finished stables and were satisfied that the horses were okay, I changed, yet again, into civvies, including shirt and tie. Even though the sun was still blazing down outside and we'd all lost several litres of sweat, rules are rules. I then walked down to the Paxtons to meet up with Pam and her parents for a much-needed pint.

Chapter 10

The Edinburgh Escorts

LESS THAN A month later found most of us from the mounted regiment on the move, heading for Redford Barracks on the outskirts of Edinburgh. Once home of the Royal Scots Greys, it was a large military barracks in the suburbs of the city. The barracks sat in 70 acres of land. It was designed and built just before the first war. As well as being a cavalry barracks, it was also home to various infantry regiments. The three-storey cavalry barracks, with its tall domed clock tower, had a large annexe of stables and various other outbuildings. This would be our home for around three weeks. The journey up took hours – all day in fact. I travelled in a commercial horse box. I obviously didn't know it at the time, but as fate would have it, I would be driving one myself two years later. The logistics involved for this escort were immense. Horses, men and all their kit, farriers, saddlers and tailors all set up their workshops and forge in the buildings that surrounded the stable blocks. Our horses were in stalls similar to Hyde Park Barracks, and we lived in large barrack rooms that reminded me of Pirbright. The escort was to take place between the 8 and 10 July for the Queen and her guest, King Gustaf XVI of Sweden.

Pam and Susie, our dog, remained in Penge on their own, with basically no easy means of communication other than letters while I was away. For a fairly newly married couple, it was pretty shit really. But Pam was committed, as I was, to my career, so we just muddled through. Terry was in the same situation, having to leave Liz back in their flat in the Tower Block. There was some Scots infantry regiment on site, but the powers that be kept us apart by providing a small NAFFI bar for us in the evenings. I know the weather in Scotland can be, let's say, harsh, but every time I've been there – then and since – it's always been glorious.

The first morning, the sun was flooding through the mullion windows of our barrack room. I'd just woken and was in the process of working out where exactly I was. I'd become accustomed, apart from Queen's once or twice a week, to waking up next to a lovely lady, and here I was in a bed next to Terry's and around fifteen other Swamp Troop urchins.

'What's that noise?' a voice from the other side of the room inquired as we all strained our ears to work out what the screeching sound was.

'It's the pipes,' another voice observed.

'What do you mean, "the pipes"?' another voice chipped into this now riveting conversation.

'Bagpipes – fucking bagpipes!' Terry confirmed as he sprung out of bed and started to remove the trees from his jackboots.

'What are you doing?' I casually asked as he stepped into said jackboots, picked up his trumpet and made his way towards the door. Of course, pure curiosity got the better of us and we all followed. On the landing of our second-floor accommodation, through a set of double doors, stood a balcony looking over a large quadrangle. We could see the piper now, poncing up and down in his fancy skirt on the other side of the quadrangle. Without hesitation, wearing nothing but a pair of blue Y-front pants and a pair of jackboots, Terry raised his state trumpet to his lips and blew the cavalry reveille. The piper's pipes made a sound like a dying pig as the mouthpiece suddenly dropped from his mouth in surprise. As Terry finished the call, a loud cheer went up and we all started getting ready for the day ahead.

The first couple of days were spent acclimatizing the horses after their long journey. The escort would be through the centre of Edinburgh, about 4½ miles from the barracks. It was going to be quite a challenge for both horses and men. It was Thursday when we arrived, and the escorts were due to take place the week after next. Ninety per cent of the mounted regiment were here; even 'one sausage Henry' had been persuaded to take a rare trip out of London to what he considered a foreign country. Well he wasn't wrong, was he? Despite living in the vibrant West End of London, I'd never been in a chip shop that had deep-fried Mars Bars on offer. And pretty much all that was available in our makeshift bar was Tennent's lager, which wasn't bad if you drank enough of it. Quiff wasn't here with us, as he'd somehow blagged staying back in London., The King's Troop, Royal Horse Artillery – or 'the pony club' as we referred to them – were carrying out Queen's Life Guard in Whitehall. They were due to carry on with that for a few weeks, because we were off to summer camp at Stoney Castle not long after we finished in Edinburgh.

Edinburgh remains one of my favourite cities. Apart from the hills, that is. A few of us decided to get a bus into the centre on our first Saturday night there. Princes Street was buzzing with people enjoying themselves. Once we were in one of the bars, it didn't take long before people started to sus out who we were and what we were doing there. On the whole, everybody was friendly and a good night was had by all.

'Where would be a good place to visit tomorrow?' I asked one guy I was talking to.

'Aye, well, you'd be better getting out of town, especially on a Sunday. I know, you should go to the beach.'

'The beach?' I somewhat over-excitedly replied, picturing golden sands and a lovely blue sea in my naive mind.

'Aye, Portobello beach. You can get a bus from where you're staying.'

Decision made. The four of us – Terry, Jarvo, Jonny and I – would go to Portobello tomorrow afternoon. The weather was still hot; if anything it was getting warmer by the day. The mental picture I'd built in my head of Scotland was turning out to be completely wrong. Not only was it friendly and you could get deep-fried anything, it even had a beach!

The walk from the bus to the beach wasn't what I'd imagined. The deep azure blue sky meeting the sea wasn't what I'd imagined either. What first caught my eye was the massive oil refinery, belching smoke and goodness knows what else out of its enormous chimneys into the sky. The bloke in the pub didn't mention that, I thought, as we reached the sandy area they called the beach. It was packed with people – locals, I guessed – enjoying their Sunday afternoon. I convinced myself and the others that it couldn't be that bad, given the amount of people there. Jonny, ever enthusiastic, was the first to mention 'going in for a dip'. It seemed like a good idea, and we'd all brought out gym shorts and army green towels, neatly rolled up, as taught back at the depot.

'What's that floating in the water?' I asked Terry as we cautiously dipped out feet in the surprisingly warm water.

'Haven't got a clue. Ask someone.'

'It looks like some sort of seaweed to me,' I observed, while still moving further out into the bay. The water wasn't blue, as I'd imagined; it was shitty brown. I was up to my neck now, about to start swimming, when I spotted a guy swimming towards us, on his way back in, I guessed.

'What's this stuff, mate?' I asked as I pointed to a larger bit which was floating towards my face.

'That's muck,' he replied in his strong Scots accent.

'What do mean, "muck"?' I naively continued.

'It's shit, son, from the sewage works over yonder. They must be pumping it out right now.'

'It's shit, guys!' I shouted to my mates. We all scrambled back towards dry land. I swear I saw a used condom floating around as we doubled towards the shore like we were being pursued by a shark.

'Who told you it was shit?' Terry asked as he tried to remove some of the bits from his legs.

'A bloke swimming in it. At first, he said it was muck, so I asked him again and he confirmed it was shit from the sewage works. Check the back of your thigh, Jarvo, it looks like you've got a piece of bog paper sticking to it.'

Luckily there was a solitary shower at the top of the beach that we could clean up under. It was freezing cold, but nobody seemed to care. Sitting back on the beach, well away from the water, I couldn't help but keep sniffing my arm, just to check, you know? I was amazed how many people still continued to go in and have a dip. We did intend to stop and have a pint on our way back that evening, that is until we discovered the strict licensing laws in Scotland at that time, meaning pubs couldn't open on Sundays.

The following week found us doing rehearsal after rehearsal. The first three were in khaki kit, like most rehearsals were. As I have said, it was just over 4½ miles to Holyrood Palace in Edinburgh from Redford Barracks. The powers that be decided early starts were the order of the day, so the three khaki rehearsals were on the road by five in the morning. Hyde Park Barracks was deliberately built just three-quarters of a mile from Buckingham Palace – enabling officers and soldiers to be available to respond speedily – which was the starting point of most state escorts., Bearing that in mind, 4½ miles was a big ask both of soldiers and especially their horses. It took forever to get to the escort's starting point outside Holyrood. Portaloo's – or turdisses, as they were known in the military – had been installed at our starting point. Tea urns gave us the welcome opportunity to dismount, give our horses a drink and have a pee, fag and tea – in that order – before beginning the escort proper. I worked it out in my head during the endless hours of watching Pan Am's head nodding up and down in front of me as she diligently plodded the streets of the city, that the complete escort would cover at least 10 miles in the baking sun in state kit, but no one complained. That was our job, our commitment to our role as ceremonial soldiers.

The following weekend, we decided against Portobello beach but did highly recommend it to everyone else, especially the swimming. saying not to be put off by the appearance of the water and that it was only a bit of old weed from further up the river. We instead found a way up onto the roof of our barrack block. Between the slate-covered roof ridges, we discovered a flat leaded area perfect for a spot of sunbathing. Wearing only shorts, and with towel and newly discovered favourite game, backgammon, tucked under my arm, we set off for our Sunday afternoon recreation. The view from up there was amazing. We could see Arthur's Seat, the large hill/mountain that looked like a military saddle overlooking over the city. The buildings of the city itself seemed to glow gold in the summer sun as Terry and I settled down for a game or two. The way we sat meant that Terry's back got the sun on it, as did my front. We didn't bother with sun cream or anything – we didn't have any anyway. It was roasting up there. The reflection of the sun off the slate and lead must have intensified it, and when we decided to return to our room an hour or so later, we soon discovered the gravity of the situation. My chest, shoulders and face could only be described as red. The same applied to Terry's back, shoulders and neck. If we'd stood close enough, we'd have looked like one red glowing torso and head. I was sore, I grant you, but Terry didn't take it at all well. To put it bluntly, he whinged like fuck. Rather than go for scoff, he just laid on his stomach on his bed, whimpering like a petulant child.

'Are you coming down the NAFFI for a few beers later?' I asked him when we returned from doing afternoon stables and having some much-needed scoff.

'Fuck off, this is all your fault. Fucking backgammon,' he unfairly whinged. He'd found the place and suggested it, after all. I was going to tell him that Jarvo had a sunburned cock, but thought better of it. Still glowing like a belisha beacon, my red face starkly contrasted against my short blond curly hair. The sunglasses hadn't been a good idea either, as I now looked like an albino panda.

It was 4.00 am when were rudely awoken by our troop three-bar. It was the last rehearsal before the first of two state escorts. After breakfast and a few snide remarks from others, our troop three-bar latched onto the fact that a few of us were in a little pain.

'You know it's an offence in the army to get sunburnt? It's classed as a self-inflicted wound,' he said as he slapped me on the chest.

'Yes, Corporal, understood. No problem,' I replied, just managing to keep my composure as the pain shot from my chest to my shoulders.

Terry kept well out of the way as he struggled with his now blistered back. It was 9.30 am when we started mounting for the long day ahead of us. Riding 10 miles in a conventional saddle wearing conventional riding kit would be a challenge for most people, let alone doing it in state kit in the middle of a heatwave. I remember once being on a state opening of Parliament, riding alongside the wheel of the carriage carrying the crown jewels. We were cloaked up because it was so wet. The rain didn't stop the whole time we were out there, black clouds continuing to throw sheets of it at us as we trotted down The Mall towards Parliament. I remember the rain running off my helmet and finding its way inside the collar of my cloak, sending a shiver down my spine as it trickled down my back. What really struck me though was the light radiating from the jewels within the carriage beside me. Even in this grey, shitty wet day, it looked like they were illuminated from below. They were a sight to behold. Everyone involved was so wet that the Queen ordered that we should all have a tot of navy rum on our return to barracks. When our horses were safely back in their stalls, we were lined up along the long corridor between the troops and given said rum. To be honest, I'd have preferred a nice mug of tea urn tea.

I felt like I had a fever or something as I sat on Pan Am waiting for the off from Redford Barracks. My face was burnt red anyway, without adding the burning fever I was experiencing. Don't worry about it, I told myself, all you've got to do is sit here and try to chill out. Pan Am will do the rest. The rhythm of the steady walk was quite mesmerizing as we made our way to Holyrood. I'm sure at one stage I actually nodded off for a second, only coming 'back in the room' when my head twitched so violently my helmet nearly fell off. The further we travelled, the larger the crowds were getting. The union flag contrasted starkly with the light blue and gold of the Swedish flags that were being waved either side of us. Pan Am was a wonderful horse; she knew when it was work and when it was play. When she took off on Rotten Row, for instance, you couldn't hold one side of her, let alone stop her, but on escorts or Queen's she was a total darling. I loved the fact that I was the one that rode and looked after her.

Even returning my sword was a painful challenge as we reached our first stopping point just outside Holyrood House. Pan Am took on copious amounts of water, while I managed a plastic cup of tea that was so hot I had to put one of my gauntlets back on to hold it. We had about ten minutes to drink tea and have a smoke; it must have been a strange sight, seeing me standing there, helmet sitting on the ground between my jackbooted legs, tea in my gauntleted right hand and cigarette in the other, trying to decide which one to tackle first. The over-sprung doors of the turdisses (Portaloos) behind me sounded a bit like someone pooping balloons. I contemplated going for a pee, but decided I couldn't face the challenge of trying to release my horse – or maybe pony – from its stable, especially in state kit!

The escort itself, went off without incident. Princes Street and The Royal Mile were packed with people as we escorted the various state carriages to and from the castle. By the time we had finished – some trotting, some walking, some just waiting – my nose was sore from the combination of sunburn and a constant bashing from the peak of my helmet. I could smell the sweet aroma of horse sweat rising from all around me. My right hand was cramping from constantly pushing the hilt of my sword into the sheepskin saddle covering to try and keep it from waving about like a deranged orchestra conductor. My shoulders and chest felt like they were on fire; I was convinced that when eventually I was able to remove my tunic, most of my burnt skin would come with it. The reflection of the sun above us was bouncing off the cuirasses, nearly blinding me. In the heat of the moment, in the thick of it, I always found the best way to survive the torture of it was simply to relax – sit into it and focus on the end goal, which was getting yourself and your horse back home safely. It took eight hours to complete the first escort, eight hours – apart from two short breaks – sitting in the saddle in the unseasonably hot Edinburgh weather. The sense of relief was palpable as I dropped to the floor of the parade square back at Redford Barracks. My mouth was as dry as a nun's do-dah as I sucked my cheeks in, trying to draw any moisture I could to my throat. At first my legs didn't want to work. Standing in jackboots is a bit like standing in a narrow box that reaches just above your knees, like wading through about the same level of water; it's tricky to start with but becomes easier as you become accustomed to it. I was doing the old trick of wiggling my toes back to life inside my boots as Pan Am tried to empty the water trough. I forgot my troubles for a minute as I watched her swallow every gulp, her ears flicking slightly as if recording the amount of fluid she was replenishing herself with. The long troughs were packed with blacks all doing the exact same thing, a sight to behold. The next tricky bit was stopping your horse from dribbling water all over your state kit as he or she licked their lips.

Back in our room, most of us just sat on our beds, still in full kit, and rested a while. Terry, opposite me, looked completely spent. He was the trumpeter, remember, so he had a lot more to do than us sword-carrying followers. He had to respond to the commanding officer's orders by blowing the correct calls at the correct times. Finally, peeling the sweat-soaked tunic from me was, as predicted, excruciating. My army green tee-shirt was several shades deeper in colour due to the amount of sweat it was holding. I was surprised at how well my skin had help up. My neck looked like a noose had been held around it from the tight high collar of my tunic constantly irritating it. As I said earlier, most escorts were done and dusted in an hour or two; these ones were unprecedented, a whole different experience. There were no water stops or anything in those days. Yes, the horses' welfare was paramount, but ours less so. Talking about welfare, we had to get straight back down to the stables to finish off and feed away before we could get some scoff ourselves.

The final escort was tough again, but we got through it. I was really looking forward to getting back to London and Pam. My journey back was by train. After making sure all the horses were boxed and on the way, we were driven to Waverley railway station on a coach and put on a train to London King's Cross. We train travellers were back in Hyde Park Barracks way before the horses, so, because of the distance Colin and I lived away, we were allowed to go as soon as we'd finished getting the troop stables ready and our kit unloaded from the three-tonners that had left the day before.

'Your missis must be due soon?' I asked Colin as we sat on the bus that was crossing the Thames, making its way towards Streatham.

'Yes, it's due sometime in the next week or so.'

'Good luck with that then. I wouldn't have a clue about any of that lark,' I reassured him as we headed towards our stop at Crystal Palace. There was very little clean kit left in my holdall. We'll have to go down the laundrette on Saturday, I thought, as we walked the final few yards to the entrance to our flats in the corner of the block. This was a nice area, but Pam and I still had our hearts set on moving back up town to a flat in the Tower Block. Susie, our dog, went crazy as I fought to get through the front door of our flat. Pam looked lovely with a nice tan she'd got following a weekend in Bristol, but she wasn't so impressed with my efforts – red on the front, white on the back! After quickly dropping my kit in the spare bedroom – we didn't need to sleep with that stuff – we took Susie for her walk in nearby Crystal Palace Park, then finished with a couple of pints outside the Bridge House pub at the end of our road.

Chapter 11

Summer Camp

BECAUSE THE SUMMER of 1975 – the escort season – had been so intense, everyone was looking forward to having a break at good old Stoney Castle. We only had a couple of weeks back in London before we were heading back to the Surrey countryside for summer camp. The sight that greeted us was a familiar one as we turned in through the large galvanized farm-type gates into Stoney Castle. The grass was in most places a burnt yellow, with just a few areas of green that had been saved from the hot summer by the trees surrounding the camp. The horse box I was travelling in belonged to Foxtons, the same horse transport company that had taken us to Edinburgh a few weeks earlier. The camp was identical to the one we left just a year ago. The forward party had done a great job preparing the rows of stalls known as troop lines. The chosen bedding was straw; much better, I thought, than the shavings we used up town, as sawdust would be a nightmare to deal with if it rained. The construction meant 1 Troop's horses faced those of 2 Troop, separated by a narrow walkway down the middle, while 3 Troop's lines faced 4 Troop, or the riding school – they'd come as well, although I wasn't sure how they were going to deal with their kit ride down here as we only had an arena made out of metal stakes and rope. I walked Pan Am and Octave, another troop horse, from the horse box towards their temporary home. They both sniffed the air, drawing the sweet scent of summer into their lungs as they walked. This must have been a great feeling for them, as for the majority of the year all they had to look at was a white brick wall in the troop rooms. Having said that, while we were away, contractors were due to fix up a radio system down in the troop rooms at Knightsbridge, so when we got back they would have music to listen to during the day.

Pan Am was doing her usual trick, trying to knock my SD cap off my head with her nose as I packed straw around her water bucket so it wouldn't fall over. I noticed my old mate, Sausage, in the stall opposite her. Whoever had put his hay net up hadn't done it correctly, so every time he tried to grab a mouthful it slid from one end of the bar it was thrown over to the other. Of course, this didn't deter Sausage – he just kept going, it was food after all.

By mid-afternoon, most of the regiment's horses were here. The accommodation tents that ran alongside the big hedge that separated us from the road were filling up, and the horse lines were pretty much full. Even the drum horses were here, at the bottom of 4 Troop's line in specially adapted stalls.

'There's a tea urn over at the scoff house – are you coming over?' Quiff shouted from 1 Troop's lines.

'Yep, be there in a minute,' I replied as I battled to get Pan Am's hay net over the corner bit of her stall so it wouldn't slide around like Sausage's opposite.

'How did you get down here?' I asked Quiff as we drank our tea and had a cigarette.

'I came down with Mick *Flemming* in his car.'

'That's handy. Maybe he'll give us a lift back up town later in the week.'

'Yeah, I'll ask him. See you in the bar later. Where's Terry, by the way?'

Oh, he's mincing about in the troop lines as normal.'

Unlike the horse lines, our accommodation at summer camp was very much a case of grabbing the first bed you could find. A lot of the old rookie crew from last year got back together. Apart from Terry, Stinch, Jarvo, Quiff and I from last summer camp when we joined the regiment were all back together in the same tent. I'd blagged a bed in the corner, with Quiff on my right. That oh so familiar smell of canvas and Quiff farting filled the air as I managed to crawl on my belly out of the bottom of the tent to escape the smell. I couldn't believe it had been a year since we were last here. Life had definitely moved on, for me at least. I was married for a start, while box sentries were a regular feature of my ceremonial duties. My future thus looked set to progress just as I'd imagined.

The bar at summer camp was run by the guys who worked in the messes at Knightsbridge. I remember they had a beer dispensing system which they held like a shower head while pushing whichever button was required for the customer's chosen drink. It goes without saying that this was often used as a weapon to spray anyone who was in range with lager or whatever. In the middle of this large tent stood a pool table, and all the military-issue benches and tables were set up around the canvas walls. Plastic glasses made it tricky to sit on the grass outside without them falling over, so a bit of thought had to be given to making temporary tables. I have to admit that although I wasn't too chuffed about having to be away from Pam again so soon after coming back from Scotland, I was looking forward to the events that were planned. And I reckoned I could blag a couple of nights back in London during our time here.

The next morning, Tuesday, found us out on watering order. The ones who rode, rode, and the others mucked the lines out and filled up hay nets from the haystack at the bottom of the lines. We always worked as a team while completing these tasks. Filling hay nets, for instance, would be done by a team of four. Two would be filling them by standing on the bottom entry point of the net and scooping the already shaken hay into the net, while the other two were shaking the hay out if its slices and stringing the full hay nets together into a long line so that we could drag them up to our troop line. The grass in between was raked clean three times a day, a straw muck heap growing by the day nearby. After morning stables, the routine would be pretty much the same as up town, the only difference being that we had various events and activities to get ready for. Some of these were planned by the hierarchy, while others were organized by the lads themselves. The last Sunday of camp was always an open day, when family and friends could come down for the day and watch troopers compete against either other troopers, NCOs or even officers in various weird and wonderful mounted events. As it was my first year being allowed to ride, I fancied both the handy hunter event and the showjumping event. Pan Am jumped like a stag and she was quick too; the only trouble was if she got her head down and took a hold, you couldn't hold one side of her. It had happened to me a couple of times in the park back in London, but it didn't bother me too much as I'd been riding thoroughbred racehorses since I was kid. This was one of the things that really made me to want to ride and look after her.

The troop officer for 3 Troop was a young floppy haired man named Lieutenant *Bruton*. He was probably around the same age as us young troopers, but, like his peers, obviously came from a somewhat privileged background. He drove a little blue Lotus Elite, which stood out from the other ranks' Fords and whatever old bangers they'd managed to acquire. Lieutenant *Bruton* rode his officer's charger every morning. He would head watering orders and various activities both in London and down here in Surrey. Recently, I'd been tasked with getting his charger ready for him to ride, his groom if you like. I didn't mind, as it was a cushy number really. It meant I was able to exercise Pan Am on my own after everyone had gone off on watering order. One morning, as I was holding his horse for him to mount, he mentioned that he was going back to Knightsbridge that evening and that if I wanted a lift, I was welcome. That will do, I thought. It was about 40 miles back to London, and he'd do it in no time in his car. If we were late in the morning, it wouldn't be my fault, would it? Anyway, lots of guys travelled back at night, so if he didn't turn up in the morning I could always blag a lift with someone else.

As instructed, I was waiting by his car at 5.00 pm that evening. I didn't have a driving licence at this point, but I was still interested in cars, especially flashy cars like this one. I'd never seen him as a nerdy type, but he was about this thing: 'Well yah, it's a mid-engine rear-wheel drive, you know', he was saying in his posh public school accent as we made our way to the tent at the gate that was the guardroom. As he pulled up outside, the car's powerful engine rumbling beside us, I noticed Pablo King extract his massive frame from inside the tent and make his way to the officer's window. Pablo King was a cavalry legend, a three-bar Life Guard farrier who even had a cavalry black named after him. 'Pablo' was quite a lumpy horse, not small by any means. Legend had it that when he was a remount, having just joined the regiment from Ireland, he was being a bit of a handful during his first shoeing. Pablo got so frustrated with him constantly spinning around that he put his shoulders underneath him and, like a gym lifting bar, lifted him up. From then on, they both shared the same name. Pablo King wasn't particularly tall, he was just muscular and wide. It took two standard stable belts stitched together to fit around his belly, and they reckoned all his state kit had to be re-tailored out of two kits to make them fit his massive frame. Anyway, he was now bent double so he could peer in through the small window to talk to the young officer. Following a quick conversation exchanging pleasantries, he tap-tapped on the car – I thought the roof was about to cave in! We were ready for off as the gate began to open. I was looking forward to seeing what this thing could do as the officer engaged first gear. I heard the engine tone rise, but nothing happened. 'That's strange,' the young officer protested. 'I wonder what the problem is.' The only thing I could think of was why I was leaning further forward than I was a second ago. I turned in my seat to look out of the small rear window, but all I could see was a massive heavy-duty jumper. It was Pablo; he'd lifted the back of the car completely off the ground, drive axle included. I'm just glad he didn't let it drop, because if he had, it would have shot off like a greyhound out of the traps. It was eight in the evening by the time I got back to our flat in Penge. You might think it was not worth all the effort, but it was worth it to me.

'How did you get on with old Houton, or whatever his name is?' Terry asked as we eat breakfast the next morning.

'He was alright actually. You heard about Pablo, I suppose?'

'The whole regiment's heard about that one, mate,' he concluded as we walked back to our tents.

The next day was the troopers' and junior NCOs' handy hunter competition. The course included the woods that surrounded the campsite. It was run in pairs, working together against the clock. I was paired up with Jonny Barrett, a mate from 3 Troop. I was happy with that as he was a good jockey and his horse – which had the unfortunate name of Randy – was fairly tidy as well. The race started in the afternoon just after lunch. I checked the blackboard to roughly work out our start time. I reckoned we'd be on about 3.00 pm. The riding school were in the woods for the kit ride, finishing off their drills. A scream then rang out and everyone around the blackboard seemed to look in the direction of the shriek at the same time. Suddenly, out of nowhere a red and white (Life Guard) emerged from the trees. The trooper on board had already abandoned his sword and was doing the only thing he could – hang on for dear life. His helmet was hanging off the back of his head, only staying there because he had the chinstrap between his teeth. At least one stirrup had gone. I cringed at the thought of falling off at that speed in that kit – it could be catastrophic. I couldn't recognize the horse, but it was on a mission, and that mission wasn't about to stop any time soon. The next to emerge from the darkness of the woods was one of the riding instructors in khaki kit hunting him down. Trouble is, the bolting horse seeing another chasing him would only make things worse. That's when the figure everyone was dreading appeared from one of the admin tents. It was *Jacko*, Captain *Jackson*, the Riding Master – God. I could see his rage from 50 metres away. I thought he was about to explode, his face the same colour as one of our state tunics. He kept looking like he was about to chase after them, then thought better of it, but his legs were visibly twitching.

'Go and help, you bloody fucking lot!' he screamed in our direction.

What the fuck can we do, I thought, as we all pretended to look lively and run towards the scene of the impending disaster. The rookie, still on his horse, was at the bottom of the camp by now. His horse still had its head down, fighting the bit. It may seem strange – and believe me, it's not an easy thing to do – but the best thing to do in that situation is to give your horse its head, drop your reins, concentrate on staying on board and let him or her come to a halt in their own time. After a couple of circuits of the football pitch, he did exactly that. He stopped, put his head down and started munching the long grass that had grown around one of the goal posts. By the time the rescue party arrived – me and two others – the rookie was in that place where you think you've shit yourself but dare not check. His top lip was quivering as he continued to grip onto his chin strap like his jaw was locked shut. He was clearly in shock as he struggled to dismount from his now secured charger.

'Just say he was spooked in the woods,' I advised him as *Jacko* and his crew came into view.

I knew he was in the shit. Everyone there, including him, knew he was in the shit, but this was when the unpredictable *Jacko* emerged. Everyone was waiting for him to explode – even the horse was ready for it – but he simply asked if the lad was alright and if the horse was sound.

I have to say that incident didn't fill me with confidence as I walked the rookie's horse back to 4 Troop's line. In about an hour's time, I'd have to get onto the pocket rocket that was Pan Am and race through that same bunch of trees at full pelt, alongside Jonny.

I felt grateful that the army had provided such good PPE (an extra chin strap to hold your SD cap on!) as Pan Am and Randy danced on the spot waiting for the signal from the timekeeper to go. Jonny and I had agreed that I would lead and he would follow. We would have to be in single file anyway because the tracks through the woods were too narrow for two. Pan Am didn't need any encouraging. As the flag dropped for the off, she leapt like a stag towards the first two jumps in the makeshift arena. Within seconds we were approaching the tiny downhill entrance into the darkness of the trees. I knew where the jumps were – we'd jumped them many times before, but never in a race. Trouble was, Pan Am knew exactly where they were too and what we were doing. It was if she said, 'Come on, dad, stay with me, I'll look after you' – and she did. All I could do was try not to do anything that could, potentially, kill the two of us. I could hear Jonny behind us. Jump after jump appeared in quick succession. A large fallen tree trunk that crossed the path was jumped with ease as we headed for a sharp right turn that led us back uphill towards the light that would see us exit the trees. I could hear a loud roar go up as we appeared into the sunlight, galloping towards the last few jumps. To be honest, I might as well have just dropped the reins and left her to it. Her ears were pricked forward all the way around, and her mane had a look of silver about it as it danced in the afternoon sunshine. It felt like forever, but it was over in minutes. We had no idea how we had done as we slowly let our horses come back to a walk. I think I was breathing as heavily as my horse as we walked, on a long rein, back towards the start to see how we'd done.

I could see our names chalked in first position on the blackboard as we tried to quieten down our mounts. Both of them were white with sweat and still breathing heavily as we dismounted and made our way to the water trough. The event was still continuing, and we hadn't won yet. I honestly thought we didn't have a chance. We were up against members of the riding staff, riding instructors, guys who went to Melton every winter hunting. All we could do now was go and deal with our horses and hope for the best. I couldn't be more delighted with Pan Am, and I knew Jonny thought the same about Randy.

'Bloody hell, we're still in front,' I said to Jonny as we approached the scoreboard.

'How many more to go?'

'Two, by the look of it.' I allowed a little excitement to flow through me as I saw who the teams were. One of the pairs were two of the three who attacked me on the fourth floor when I was still in riding school. As these thoughts were dancing through my mind, a lone horse galloped out of the wooded area in front of us. Someone else was out of the running – I wondered who it could be. I looked at the blackboard to check. Oh shit, it was Will, Will Freedman from riding school. I could see now, he'd been riding Rockingham. Luckily, a few seconds later, he and his teammate emerged from the darkness. Will looked like he'd been dragged through a hedge backwards, but apart from that he seemed okay. There was one pair to go now. Twat and bigger twat were in the collecting area, waiting for their signal to start. It was common knowledge how much I despised these two. I'm not normally like that, but I made an exception for these two. It wouldn't have bothered me at all if they never emerged safely from the trees at all. They did, of course – emerge, that is – but not quick enough though. Jonny, Randy, Pan Am and I had won the junior NCOs' and troopers' handy hunter competition.

The following day was the turn of senior NCOs and officers. Lieutenant *Bruton* decided that he too could win on Pan Am. I wasn't so keen. She'd walked out sound that morning, but I thought she needed an easy day. Yes, I was being selfish – I wanted to keep her sound for the showjumping competition on Sunday. But who was I, a nobody young trooper; I was told in no uncertain terms to tack her up in his civvy saddlery ready for the competition. Our troop three-bar and Lieutenant *Bruton* lined up on the start line that afternoon. It was obvious Pan Am was up for it; the thing was, was Bruton? I watched, anxious about what could go wrong, as they disappeared into the darkness of the wooded section of the course, the tricky bit. He had every advantage: civvy saddles are a lot easier to ride in than our slippery military ones. I was a little concerned that he'd insisted that he use his civvy bridle, complete with eggbutt snaffle bit. He's got no chance of holding you in this, I whispered to Pan Am as I gently slipped it into her mouth while getting her ready. All appeared to be going well until they exited from the trees. As predicted, Pan Am was first to emerge. He clearly had no control of her. At least I could keep her head up and looking in the right direction, but he seemed to be leaning too far forward and clinging onto her mane. The next thing that happened scared the shit out of me. She stumbled as she reached the top of the slight rise coming out of the trees and sent the good officer 'out the front door', as they say. I can still see it now, how he was buried into the grassy ground in front of him. It's all a momentum thing, because as he started to slide and bury his head in the deck, Pan Am, still with that dreaded forward momentum, sort of rolled over him. The only saving grace was the civvy saddle. If he'd had her regular one on, I reckon the weight and shape of the saddle would have broken *Bruton*'s back. I was pleased to see her gallop off, kicking and farting, as though nothing had happened. I followed to wait for Pan Am to calm down; when I caught her, I hopped on her back and walked her back to the scene of the carnage. And it was carnage. He was smashed to fuck. His nose was bleeding and both his eyes were turning black in front of us. His fancy officers' shirt was irreparably ripped and his lovely khaki cap was completely flattened – again it looked beyond repair. While he was carted off to A&E, I returned Pan Am to her stall. 'Extra nuts for you tonight, my darling,' I whispered in her ear as I went to get my grooming kit to tidy her up a bit.

That evening was pretty much the same as any other, with a couple of pints in the bar, maybe a game of pool and a quick visit to the horse lines to check Pan Am before bed. I was a little worried about her back legs; they could swell up after severe exercise, but all looked okay at the moment. The sun was setting in the west, and was just about to disappear behind the trees as I made my way back to our tent. As I walked in, Terry was sat on his bed playing his mouthorgan, Quiff was laying on his bed just listening and Jarvo was having a can of beer. As I sat on my bed and lit a cigarette, I was wondering what Pam would be doing back in London. She would probably in bed by now, with Susie the dog by her side. She was enjoying her job and living and working in London, and if she was happy, I was happy.

As I made my way to the wash house (the growlers) to clean my teeth, I could just make out the sound of sirens going off somewhere. It must be at the depot, I assumed – it was only a mile away as the crow flies. Probably a fire drill, I thought, as I returned to the tent for a much-needed kip. It had been a strange but amusing day.

It must have been around three in the morning when the explosion went off. All I can remember is coming to my senses laying on the grass, sandwiched between the side of our tent and my upturned bed. I could hear panicked shouting outside and see the shadows of people running about outside.

'What the fuck's going on, Quiff? Are you there?' I blurted out as I tried to extract myself from the carnage that surrounded me. It was still dark, but not that dark. As I peered over my upturned bed, I could see everyone else's beds scattered around the tent. It seemed like forever, but shadow-like figures started to extract themselves from their predicaments and look around. Quiff was rubbing his head, and Terry was leaning against the canvas behind him in a sort of dazed state.

'Is everyone alright?' I asked. 'Where's Jarvo? Jarvo, are you alright?'

'Shit – I'm okay. What was that?' Jarvo's voice came from the corner of the tent.

It couldn't have been more than two minutes before we heard someone unlacing the tent flaps and letting some light in. It was one of the troop two-bars. All I can remember thinking was why he was wearing pyjama trousers. Who wears pyjama trousers while camping?

'Is anyone injured?' he shouted. 'If you're not, then go and wait in the NAFFI tent. Understood?'

I managed to locate my heavy-duty jumper from amongst my scattered kit and pull it on as we walked the short distance to the bar. The night guard were dragging fire hoses into the tent next-door to ours. It was the saddlers' tent. As I glanced in as we were ushered past, all I could make out was mangled metal, which I soon realized were beds. The bar was buzzing with talk as we sat on the pool table and began to work out what the hell had just happened. 'It was a bomb,' someone suggested. 'Where the fuck would a bomb come from?' another voice pointed out. It was clear everyone was stunned and confused at what had just happened. We could hear the sirens of fire trucks, police and ambulances in the distance. Eventually, Squadron Corporal Major Varley turned up with a sitrep (situation report) and informed us that, at the moment, they were treating it as a hostile situation. The powers that be had been informed, but they thought the incident was confined to the saddlers' tent. There were no saddlers in the tent – they had returned back up town that evening so, as far as they knew, at the moment there were no casualties. Varley added that there had been an incident over at the Guards Depot earlier, a possible IRA terrorist attack, which could be linked to this.

The following morning, having had very little sleep, the camp was awash with rumours. Terry was whinging because he couldn't find his mouthorgan. We'd managed to put our tent back into some sort of order before going to attend to morning stables. Thank goodness, the horses were none the worse for their experience, so after finishing and feeding them we made our way to the mess tent for breakfast.

'Do you reckon they'll cancel open day?' I asked Terry as we tucked into bacon sandwiches.

'I don't see why they should. The civvy and military police will do their thing over the next day or two. It will be alright. Have you seen my harmonica, by the way?'

'For the last time, I haven't seen your bloody mouthorgan. I'm sure we'll find it later. Failing that, we'll tell the police that they should be looking for a dodgy Irishman playing a harmonica!'

None of last night's events had sunk in yet as I sat on the ground while I let Pan Am munch on the grass around the perimeter of the camp. If it was the IRA, I figured, they must have abandoned trying to plant it in the depot – the security over there was always pretty shit hot – and decided to dump it on an easier target. Let's face it, a tented camp full of drunken cavalrymen was an easy target. It was just pure luck that they chose the wrong tent, and the fact that it was a tent and it absorbed most of the blast. If they had gone for the one next to it, I doubt that I would be here to tell the story.

Pam and Colin's wife from the flat above ours travelled down together from Penge for the open day. The weather was fantastic; we'd been lucky and hadn't had any rain the whole time we were there. All the usual events took place – tent pegging, mounted tug of war and my event, showjumping. The junior NCOs' and troopers' showjumping competition was nearly as notorious as the handy hunter which Jonny and I had just won. There was an officers' and senior NCOs' event, but my focus – along with my trusty steed Pan Am – was on winning our event. I'd competed in many gymkhanas while I was younger, riding my loan pony, Phantom, and Pam's pony, Shane. Like Pan Am, Shane would jump anything that you pointed him at, and also like Pan Am, he pulled like a train. The showjumping started after lunch and would be followed by the officers and that lot. The whole day's competition would culminate with the tent pegging. The first thing I had to establish with Pan Am was that she was sound. She'd had a busy camp and was beginning to show signs of it, but after a little trot round – bareback – before breakfast, all looked and felt good. I was up against the same old faces we'd taken on the other day, except this time it was an individual event. The army coaches that were ferrying guests up from nearby Brookwood station began dropping people off at around 10.00 am. When the mounted regiment put on these types of events, they always did a great job. There was a fair amount of interest in the tent where the bomb had gone off. There was nothing to see really, and it was still cordoned off. If they could have got in there to have a look, all they would have seen was mangled metal beds amongst a scorched canvas interior. As I walked the jumping track, I found it difficult to believe that just twelve months ago I had stood in this very arena, putting fallen poles back in place during the same event.

Pan Am was on good form. As I leant forward and grabbed her ear while we waited in the collecting ring, I tried telling her that because it was against the clock didn't mean she had to go mad. Like Pam's pony, she was near impossible to hold in this situation. I'd paced the course out – three strides between these two jumps, one stride in the double – all with the best intentions. Of course this was all a load of bollocks, for as soon as the bell rang to start she was off. I had to leave all that technical stuff to Pan Am and concentrate on steering her in the right direction. Amazingly we stayed upright and together as we turned to start the last two combinations of jumps, which were placed diagonally across the arena. Safety, obviously, was at the forefront of my mind as we tore across the makeshift ring of rope towards the crowd of my colleagues' wives and children who were enjoying their ice creams without a care in the world. Holy shit, I thought, as we landed from the final jump, turn her to the right. Oh God, please turn right before we completely wipe all of them out, I was thinking as the crowd got closer. I could plainly see their eyes getting wider with horror as we thundered towards them. I noticed Lieutenant Bruton backing away towards the entrance of one of the tents, his arm still in a sling following his last encounter with this enthusiastic girl. Finally, at the very last second, she obeyed my right arm that was tugging at her rein and began to drop her head and circle around the arena. I remember it took two circuits to get her fully back on the bit. It was a quick round and would take some beating, I thought, as I nodded at my nemesis, the fourth-floor bully, as we exited the ring. Indeed, no one did manage to beat our time. A remarkable double, they called it; never been done before, they said, as we enjoyed our last evening in the bar before we started the move back to London in the morning. I couldn't wait to return with Pan Am to defend our titles. I would return, but not as I thought I would. Read on, dear reader, for nobody knew what was coming next – definitely not me, that's for sure!

Chapter 12

SIB (investigated)

LIFE WAS GOOD. The autumn was setting in, changing my view of London as I took my regular train journey back to Penge East railway station. I bought Pam a bunch of flowers from the lady outside the station. The nights were drawing in, so if we wanted to get Susie out for her walk while it was still light, we'd have to get a bit of a wiggle on.

'I've got to start clipping tomorrow. That means I'll be off Queen's for a week or two,' I mentioned to Pam as we walked through Crystal Palace Park in the late afternoon sunshine.

'That's good. I won't have to worry about getting home so early. There's loads of overtime going at the moment at work.'

'Okay. I'm going to do one in the morning and one in the afternoon. That should get me home at about five, I reckon.'

The following day, after solo exercising Pan Am in the park and managing to blag a breakfast, with the help of Quiff I began stepping into the green boiler suit that the troop three-bar had 'borrowed' for me and began to examine the clippers I'd been given to complete my task of clipping the thirty or so 3 Troop horses. The cooler nights at summer camp had caused some of them to start their coats wooling up ready for the winter. Selfishly, I did Panam first. I knew she'd behave and it would give me a chance to get my eye back into clipping. I learnt this skill while working with the thoroughbreds Pam and I looked after back in Bristol before I joined up.

'Full clip is it, Corporal?' I asked our newly out of riding school Corporal of Horse that had been posted here some months ago from the armoured side of the regiment.

'Yes, that's what I've been told. Do you mind if I watch for a while – I've never seen this done before?'

'No problem, Corporal. Fill your boots.'

The trouble with clipping is two-fold. The first is that the clippings get everywhere. Even with my boiler suit buttoned right to the collar, I knew I'd be itching like crazy all the way home. The second is keeping your clipper blades from getting too hot. Corporal of Horse *Collier* had managed to find me a spare set, so I could swap them over while they cooled down and save some time. Over the noise of the clippers, I noticed my voyeur making strange hand signals in my direction.

Turning off the clippers, I asked: 'What's up, Corporal?'

'Well, I don't want to interrupt...' Well you are, aren't you, I thought, but didn't say anything.

'Well, wouldn't it be easier if you used the clippers in the same direction as the coat? Just a suggestion.' Even Pan Am looked at him in amazement.

'What, like this?' I replied as I switched the clippers back on and ran the clippers over Pan Am's hind quarters. 'How's that going to work? Like your own hair, you clip against it. Can I make a suggestion, Corporal?' I didn't wait for a reply. 'Why don't you go and see if you can find a Land Rover or something to play with? You understand them, whereas I understand horses.'

I only had Pan Am to do on the first day, so was thinking where I could skive until going home this afternoon. I was sitting with Quiff eating my NAFFI sandwiches when one of the regimental police two-bars put his head round the door.

'Wallington, you need to report for an interview this afternoon at 1300hrs in the empty office downstairs.'

'What for, Corporal?'

'Haven't got a clue. Just make sure you're there.'

'In the shit again, Wol?' Quiff encouragingly chipped in.

'Can't think of anything. I wonder what the fuck it's all about?'

I'd only ever been on one 'charge', and that was withdrawn within an hour, when I was late one morning after my train was cancelled. On that occasion, as soon as I walked past the guardroom, rushing to get in, I was grabbed and locked in what they used to call 'trap one', the first cell in a row of cells in the guardroom. Despite protesting my innocence, within an hour I was marched in front of the current Colonel of the Regiment, Lieutenant Colonel Bertie Fuck-Wit, or whatever his name was.

'We've checked with the railway company as to whether or not your train was cancelled, and they informed me that it wasn't. What have you got to say for yourself?'

'Well, Colonel, sir, could I ask you to check again please? The train was cancelled.' I was quietly shitting myself by now. What if I'd got it wrong, I was thinking, as he reluctantly picked up his telephone and began to ring the number he had somehow obtained.

'If you're lying to me Wallington … oh hello, my name is Lieutenant Colonel Fuck-Wit. I command the Household Cavalry Mounted Regiment here in London.' Too much information, I thought. 'One of my troopers travels in every morning from Penge East and he's telling me the train he was due to catch this morning was cancelled. Can you confirm to me whether this is correct or not?' Long awkward silence. 'Oh hello. It was, er okay – thank you for your time. Good day to you. Right, Trooper Wallington, it appears you were telling the truth. Get back to your troop. All charges dropped.'

No 'sorry', no 'you're presumed innocent until proven guilty'. No jack shit. Just 'get back to your troop'. What a wanker, I thought, as I was marched out of his office and dismissed.

Bang on time, I knocked on the usually empty office door. A fairly large guy in civilian clothes opened the door and invited me in.

'I want a word in your shell-like. We represent the SIB, the Special Investigation Branch, part of the Military Police.'

I supressed a laugh. I've never heard that one before, I thought, as the, I suppose I'll have to describe him as officer, though I'd rather refer to him as twat, carried on his 'bad cop' routine.

From the get go, because of this guy's attitude I found it hard to take the whole thing seriously. How wrong I was going to be!

'What do you want to see me for? What's this about?'

'Sit down. We do the asking, you do the answering, understood?' bad cop continued, getting a bit irritated now.

I did as ordered, still not knowing what this was all about. I'd had no prior warning, my mouth was dry and I could feel the anxiety rushing through my body. The other guy in the room – 'good cop', as it turned out – hadn't said anything at this stage. My main concern, believe it or not, was how long this was going to take. I was more concerned with getting back to Penge so I could let out Susie, our dog, than answering these monkeys' questions. I was pretty sure I hadn't done anything wrong; not bad enough to warrant an interrogation by the SIB anyway.

'Where do you drink?' bad cop asked as he took his place opposite me.

'A pub at the bottom of our road in Penge. The Bridge, I think it's called.'

'No, what I meant was, where do you drink close to here?'

At this point I began to understand what he was getting at. Terry had been interviewed by the SIB a couple of weeks ago. I remembered him telling me about the questions he faced. Right, I thought, let's have a bit of fun here.

'Oh, close to here? I don't. I live in Penge.'

'Okay, let me rephrase the question,' he said, getting angrier by the second. 'Where did you drink when you lived in the barracks?'

'Ah, understood. Loads of places. There's the Gloucester, the Baker and Oven, the Paxtons – I wouldn't recommend the NAFFI bar though, it's shit.'

Good cop looked up from his scribbling. 'Just answer the questions as they're put to you.'

'I just did.' I was getting more confident now, even though I'd been thrown into this potentially terrifying situation without warning or representation.

Bad cop continued. 'When you drank in the Paxton's, did you talk to civilians?'

'Sometimes, if they talked to me. Not talking would be rude, don't you think?'

Good cop: 'Just answer the question as it's put to you.'

Bad cop: 'Why did you talk to these civilians? Were they gay? Are you gay?'

'I've just recently married, and if I did, why shouldn't I talk to them? It's not against the law, is it?'

This form of questioning went on for another hour or so. I was getting as irritated as they were. If it sounded as if I was being impertinent, I was, because I was telling the truth. Some of the questions were unbelievable – 'is there a telephone line into the saddlers' workshop?' or 'who's running the vice ring?' I honestly didn't have a clue what they were on about. I was six months into our marriage, happily living in South London, working hard doing my job. My wife had a job with Royal Mail which she loved. My ambition was the same as it was when I joined the cavalry, which was to complete my training as a farrier, serve the nine years I'd signed up for, then leave and set up my own business.

Good cop: 'I expect you want to get home, don't you?'

'Of course I do. I don't know why I'm here anyway.'

Bad cop: 'Well, sonny, we've got other people to interview. Will they be mentioning your name? Because if they do, you'll be back in here faster than your bloody horses can carry you.'

I confidently nodded at both of them – as confidently as I could anyway. I felt sick to the core. I'd never been in this environment before. I had a feeling of relief, firstly at getting through it, and secondly that I could go home.

It was getting on for five o'clock as I walked out of the big metal gates that led onto Knightsbridge. Loosening my tie, I quickly made my way towards the tube station on the corner of Slone Street. At this rate Pam, would be home before me. Should I get the train or the bus? The number fifty two was waiting at the traffic lights as I crossed. That would do. The sign on the front told me it was terminating at Crystal Palace. Hobson's choice, really, I thought, I'll get this one.

Top deck, at the front, my favourite spot. As the bus rumbled towards Chelsea and the River Thames, the evening sun felt hot on my face. Rolling my ticket up as tight as I could between my fingers, my thoughts turned to the last three hours. Where did they get their information from? All their accusations were untrue. Well, I think they were untrue – I certainly didn't know anything about them.

'Crystal Palace!' the conductor shouted. 'The bus terminates here – off the bus please.'

I'd done it again, fallen asleep. Staggering to my feet, I made my way down the steep steps from the top deck. It was nice to feel the breeze on my face as I stepped from the bus. A ten-minute walk and I'll be home, I thought, as I started walking down the hill towards Anerley Park Road. Walking down the path towards the corner entrance to our married quarters. I noticed my mate Colin standing at the entrance, lighting a cigarette. As we were in the same regiment – he was in 2 Troop – we travelled in together most days.

'Hi, mate. What's happening?' he asked as we met at the communal door.

'Hang on, I'm just going to get the dog; she needs a pee.'

When I got back downstairs, I let Susie onto the large grass area in the middle of the block.

'I've just spent two hours being interviewed by two tools from the SIB,' I informed him as he offered me a cigarette.

'Oh, they had me in last week. I wouldn't worry about it. What did they ask – did you drink in the Paxtons and all that shit? Really, it's just bullshit.'

His reassuring tone made me feel a little better. 'They said they had more to interview.'

'Like I said, don't worry about it. Are you in tomorrow?'

'Yep, see you at five. Don't be late.'

After finishing our cigarettes, we returned to our respective flats. Susie, remarkably, had behaved herself so there was no mess to clear up. A short time later, I heard the key in the door. Pam was home.

'Had a good day?' she asked as she walked into the living room of the very 1940s-style flat. The military-issue furniture didn't help – a green vinyl three-piece suite and a black and white television rented from Radio Rentals stood in the corner.

'No, not really. A bit of a strange one. I'll tell you when we go for a walk.'

'Okay, won't be a minute. I'll just get changed.'

Our evening walk took us through Crystal Palace Park. I had two things to tell Pam – one was good, the other I'd sort of dismissed already as something weird that would just, in time, go away.

'Fancy a drink on the way back?' I asked.

'Okay, why not. You're quiet. What's up?'

'I'll tell you at the pub.'

It was a nice evening, so we sat outside. As I sipped my beer, I could hear the Bay City Rollers blaring out of an upstairs window close by.

'First thing, good news.' 'What's that?' Pam asked. 'There's a flat available in Peninsular Tower up town. If we want it we can move at the end of the month.'

'That's great. Can we go and have a look?'

'Yes, I'm trying to arrange it for this Saturday. Then I thought we could meet Terry and Quiff in the Paxton's for a drink. I need to talk to them about what happened to me today.'

'Oh yeah, what's that?'

'I've spent two hours this afternoon being interviewed by the SIB.'

'What's the SIB.'

'It's the army's Special Investigation Branch, part of the Military Police.'

'What did they want?'

'Well, I'm being accused of being involved with running a homosexual vice ring in the barracks.'

'That's ridiculous. Why are you being accused of that?'

'That's why I want to talk to Terry and Quiff, away from the barracks. There are loads of rumours floating about. I just need to know what they know.'

'Okay, we'll go up on Saturday then. I can't believe this. Come on, let's go home.'

I spent the rest of the week working, clipping the 3 Troop horses. Two a day was the target, and I was managing to stay on course. I left the dodgy ones like Rockingham and Windrush until last. I'd have to have help with some of them, so I decided to tackle that the following week. Before leaving to go home on Friday afternoon, I collected the keys from the admin office to the flat we'd been offered. I'd spoken to Terry, and he'd been interviewed while he was on Queen's at Horse Guards. The hardest one to track down was Quiff. Hyde Park Barracks wasn't that big, but somehow Quiff managed to avoid most people almost all of the time. The one place you could almost guarantee to find him was at scoff time up in the cook house. I was right – there he sat, in his usual place by the window, dressed in civvies.

'Alright, mate. Why the civvies?' I asked, having managed to avoid the eyeline of 'one sausage Henry' and nick a sneaky coffee.

'I'm training. You know, the trumpeter thing. I'm a musician now, mate.'

'Fuck off, you're a twat. A twat that does no more than blow a few calls here and there, then sits around all day doing jack shit. Anyway, have you been interviewed by the SIB yet?'

'Yeah, a couple of weeks ago. They came up to my room; went through everything.'

'Do you fancy meeting up at the Paxtons Saturday, early evening? Terry's coming down, so we can try and sus out what's going on.'

'Okay, I'll be there.'

* * *

'Fourteen A', the tag on the bunch of keys read. I was fiddling with it in anticipation as the lift stopped at our floor. Susie wasn't bothered by the lift. That's good, I thought, as we walked from the lift and turned right. Terry and his wife, Liz, lived two floors above, so we had both been in a one of the flats before. The Tower Block, as it was known, was at the time in the top five tallest buildings in the capital. The flats covered thirty-odd floors and the building was topped off by two squash courts at the very top. It was, and still is, an impressive landmark on the West London skyline. The flat itself was great – very modern, with fantastic views over Knightsbridge and westward towards South Kensington. Like all army quarters, unless you requested differently, it was fully furnished. You had everything you needed, right down to knives, forks and spoons.

'I love it,' Pam said as she stood looking out of the window onto the roofs of the posh Knightsbridge townhouses below. 'When can we move in?'

'About a week, I reckon.' The whole thing was ideal. Some married guys, like Colin for instance, preferred living away from the job, as it were, but not Pam and I. We had the park next door to walk our dog, and a modern flat right in the West End of London. Terry and Liz weren't particularly concerned about the SIB thing. Liz was ex-military herself, so knew a bit about it all. We were both troubled by the way it was sprung on us and confused by their same techniques and questions.

'Let's go and see what Quiff thinks,' I suggested as I looked out over the riding school to the parade ground ahead. The trees were beginning to change colour as autumn crept in over the park. The Paxtons was busy, as it normally was on a Saturday early evening. Quite a few troopers were hanging around the bar, already pissed after their afternoon session. As we sat in the corner out of the way, I noticed Quiff come in and join the drunken melee before coming over to join us.

'So, what did they ask you?' I asked Quiff as he sat in a chair close to the stairs that went down to the bar below.

'Oh, the necky fuckers went through all my kit. They even went through my address book. They spotted Ian Harvey's name and wanted to know why I had his number, so I told them about me and his daughter. They accused me of being gay. They wanted to know who I drank with in here, all that kind of stuff. What about you two?'

'Pretty much the same – where do you drink? When I told them the Bridge in Penge, one of them got quite pissy. They wanted to know who I met in here – all that crap really.'

Terry's account, strangely, followed the same path. All three of us had gone through the same interrogation script – we were still at a loss as to why. A vice ring in the barracks? A telephone connection to the saddlers' shop? There wasn't even a telephone in the saddlers' shop, as far as we knew. In those days, if you needed to see a saddler you'd walk down there and knock on the door. As for gays in this place, yes, of course there were. Everyone knew this was a cavalry pub. Before marrying and moving away, I used to get continual hassle from a little Spanish girl named Carmen, who hung around most evenings and at weekends. She called me 'Gringo' because of my blond curly hair. They didn't want to know why she hung around me, did they? It was obvious that the investigation was a gay thing, but we didn't know why. Up town, they were known as 'tykes'. You soon learned how to recognize them. There were different types: some just wanted to buy you a drink and chat, to be seen with you; some, known as 'kit tykes', would be out on escorts or at Horse Guards taking photographs, and they would bring them in the pub to show you and hand them out. If I remember correctly, at least one of the photos in this book was given to me by a 'kit tyke'. This didn't make you homosexuals, as we were being accused of. American tourists would come in. On one occasion, a young attractive American girl had stuffed a bar of chocolate along with a note saying where she was staying down Quiff's jackboot when he was on a box sentry. He had met up with her and brought her to the Paxtons. Was that a reason to treat us the way they did? Or was it the anti-gay thing that nobody seemed to want to address. There were a lot of questions about famous people drinking here as well. This was a public house in Knightsbridge. Famous people? No shit, Sherlock! I walked past Peter Sellers and Britt Ekland one evening when returning to the barracks. They were having one hell of a row in the doorway of one of the houses next to the stables end of the barracks.

'At least we'll be able to go to the Stock Pot when we're back up town,' I mentioned to Pam as we boarded the fifty-two bus heading back to our South London flat. The Stock Pot was a small Italian restaurant in the back streets of Knightsbridge. Most evening, when the pubs had shut, it would be full of cavalrymen – not a civvy in sight. Bread rolls would fly in your direction as you opened the door. It was worth it though, as they served the best 'Spag Bog' in London. It was good value as well.

The following two weeks were hectic, to say the least. The lads – Quiff, Stinch and Terry – helped us move. We'd got so fed up with our army-issue three-piece suite that we'd bought a new one from a store in nearby Croydon. It was a lumpy thing – so it required a bit of muscle to shift it – consisting of a large sofa and two equally large armchairs. The sofa wouldn't fit in the lift.

'If you think I'm carrying that bloody thing up fourteen flights of stairs, you've got another thing coming,' Quiff helpfully informed the rest of us.

'Twenty-eight,' Terry added.

'Twenty-eight what?' I was getting pissy now.

'There are twenty-eight flights of stairs to the fourteenth floor, two flights for each floor.'

'Oh, thanks for that invaluable piece of information – not!'

'What about the coffin door?' Stinch chipped in.

'What's a fucking coffin door?' I really couldn't believe what I was hearing.

'It's a door at the back of the lift that opens up so you can get a coffin in the lift. You wouldn't expect undertakers to carry your coffin down from the thirty-second floor would you? That's sixty-four flights of stairs, by the way. You're welcome!'

He was right. There was a door there, but who had the key? What good is a coffin door if you can't open it, I was thinking, when I suddenly remembered the tiny caretaker's office behind the laundry at the bottom of the building.

'Wait there, I'll be back,' I ordered as I jogged round the corner to this laundrette. I was right, I'd remembered correctly. It was Saturday, so there weren't many people about. One of the machines was rumbling away as I made my way to the office – well, more like a large cupboard really. To my relief, the door was unlocked. I was I looking for a large triangular key-type thing. There it was, hanging neatly on two nails on a wall full of various tools in neat rows. Whoever presided over this place was very organized, I thought. They'd even drawn around each tool or key with a marker pen to remind them what went where.

'Got it,' I proudly announced as I made my way back into the entrance hall. Quiff and Stinch had made themselves comfortable on my sofa and were having a cigarette. Terry had gone back to his flat to make some coffees. I could see by the flashing green arrow that the lift on the left-hand side was on its way back to ground level, hopefully with Terry and a tray of coffee in it. As the doors slid open, it wasn't Terry as expected. It was the RCM (Regimental Corporal Major) – forget colonels and other senior officers, this was the guy who ran the place. I hadn't seen Quiff and Stinch move so quick since we were in juniors as they did when they saw who emerged from the lift.

'Morning, gentlemen,' the imposing figure said as he studied my sofa. 'Which one of you is moving in?'

'Er, me, Corporal Major,' I replied, instinctively springing to attention.

'How's it going?' he started to continue, until a pinging sound from the other lift announced its arrival and a rather camp-looking Terry jumped out with a tray full of coffee, shouting 'ta-dah'. Luckily, the RCM found it amusing and continued on his way. Coffee drank, with the coffin door doing its job, the sofa just fitted in. I travelled with the sofa, while the others followed in the other lift. It was so tight in there that I was basically trapped. Where I was, I couldn't reach the button to stop the door from shutting when we reached our floor. What can I do, I thought, as the lift made its way skywards. Then I remembered something Terry did one night when we went back to his flat to get some cash – he just slipped his shoe off and left it to trap the lift door as it tried to shut. Like a contortionist with a combination of ballet-type moves, I managed to remove my left shoe and set in place on the lift floor, ready so I could push it into place with my socked foot when the lift doors opened. The only trouble was, every time the doors attempted to close, they made a loud thud sound which seemed to echo up and down the lift shaft. It was making so much noise that Pam came out from our flat to see what was going on.

'What are you doing?'

'What do you think I'm doing. Hold the "open" button down while I try to get out of here.'

I just managed to extract myself from my self-inflicted prison as the other lift arrived and the three musketeers stepped out. Thank the lord, within a few minutes we had the sofa in place alongside one of the long windows that surrounded the flat.

Pam was sad as we locked the door to our old flat in Penge for the last time. November was close approaching and the SIB thing seemed to have gone away. Nobody talked about it. I'm sure everyone just forgot about it and got on with their jobs. Little did we know what was being plotted a couple of miles away in Westminster.

Chapter 13

Kicked Out

CHRISTMAS CAME AND went. I had Christmas off this year, so Pam and I went back to Bristol for a few days. I was back on Queen's over the New Year. We spent New Year's Eve at the Paxtons with Terry and Liz. Everything was very normal. The up-and-coming summer season looked busy this year; along with the Trooping and various escorts, there was a musical ride taking place, so a good number of troopers and horses would be away for a large part of the summer.

Tuesday, 27 January 1976 was a pretty normal day, with watering order in the morning, grooming and kit cleaning after breakfast. I was listed for Queen's over the following weekend, so I was gradually getting my kit up to speed ready for a Friday guard. Pam was working overtime that day, so I knew she would be a little later home. In short, there was absolutely nothing that would cause me – or anyone else for that matter – any concern. No strange vehicles parked on the parade ground, no strangers in uniform wandering about – nothing. I'd taken Susie for her walk in the park after lunch and was making my way down for afternoon stables. The weather, for January, was good. The midwinter sun was shining as I walked in winter-order stable dress, down the ramp towards 3 Troop. Again, nothing strange going on, just the same old routine that kept the horses fit and well. The radio was playing music in each troop as I passed. Turning the corner into 3 Troop, Terry was studying the large blackboard which told us who was doing what this upcoming week. People say you get used to smells that you're frequently exposed too. I never did not love the smell of horses and stables; it calmed me in some sort of way. I looked along the troop room and took in the smells and sounds before going into the feed room to get a yard broom. The only thing that was intriguing me was who was going to be offered the posting to Germany that was on the cards. It was to look after the officer who ran the armoured regiment's horses – a doddle that I knew I was in the frame for. Six months in Germany, do a good job and get rewarded with a farriers' course. That was my thinking anyway.

Terry and I were just finishing sweeping the outside area of the troop stables when the telephone on the wall began to ring. I didn't realize it then, but all three troop telephones rang at the same time. Our troop three-bar came out of the cleaning room and answered it. A quick conversation that no one was paying much attention to resulted in him replacing the receiver and informing Terry and I that we were required on the parade square – pronto!

'I wonder what this is about?' I asked Terry as we grabbed our SD caps and made our way towards the square. As we walked, a bit like the pied piper we were being joined by other young troopers. Quiff came out of 1 Troop, Jarvo had run and caught us up from 3 Troop, and there were even a couple of lads who had not long passed out of riding school as we reached our destination, still oblivious to what was about to happen. As if by magic, senior NCOs began to appear, dressed in their dark blue one-dress and forage caps. We were in stable dress – green cotton trousers, KF shirts, heavy-duty jumpers with stable belt and SD caps.

As I sit here writing this now, it's not the first time I've written about it in recent years but the same chill flows through my body. Why didn't anybody sus out what was happening? Why were we so naïve? Why did I just line up as ordered and be marched in front of the commanding officer when told? Why? Because that's what we trained to do, that's why. We all had given our loyalty to the Queen and our regiment. As I became the next victim, I was aware that those that had gone before me didn't return to the parade ground. Totally confused by now, I found myself being marched into a busy colonel's office. The colonel sat at his desk. The same colonel that I'd stood up to a few months ago about the train being cancelled one morning. The same colonel that I'd played squash against two weeks before. The same colonel that was so angry that the PTI hadn't left the squash court door unlocked that he simply kicked the glass panel through to force entry. I didn't know it yet, but this colonel – the daddy of the regiment, as they were known – was about to ruin my life as I knew it, forever. Not only my life, as it turned out, but my wife's, my family's and seventeen other lives, all young, talented young men, each one destined – in my opinion – for greatness.

Here we were then. I could feel myself beginning to shake as I tried to take in what was in front of me. Colonel Dip-Shittington was pretending to read the sheet of paper in front of him, and behind him stood at least five officers, all dressed in their dark blue frock coats like dandies from many years ago. As he read out my destiny, as he took everything I'd worked so hard for away from me, one of them – a portly, clearly gay officer, Captain Roper – could be heard tutting under his breath. Everyone knew he was gay: bent as a hoof pick and camper than a row of tents were some of the expletives used to describe him. The hypocrisy was off the scale. I remember the colonel saying 'You're dismissed forthwith'. I remember him turning the piece of paper and ordering me to sign it. I also remember not being able to move, let alone sign anything, such was the surprise and shock. I remember the RCM leaning in towards me and whispering in my ear, 'Sign it, son, you're dismissed'. Then I was back in the fresh air and sunshine. Everyone there looked in total shock – Terry, Colin, Jarvo, to name but a few. Eighteen careers were unfairly ended that day. Not only that, all involved in what turned out to be 'placating the press' were responsible, in my opinion, for sacrificing eighteen young men's futures in order to save their own skins. From senior NCOs upwards, they were all weak, pathetic twats; twats that were not big or good enough to do the job they had been promoted to do. 'Simply following orders', they would weakly say. They didn't have the nuts to stand up for their men, the men they were tasked with looking after. A lot of us – , like Quiff, Jarvo and I – had served with honour since the age of 15½, giving our teenage years to serve the Queen. I was 19, with a new wife and a red discharge book which read, under reason for discharge, 'better suited to civilian life'. I can't tell you how that made me feel. I'd given my life to the army. I would have given my life for my country, and all they had done in return was to falsify so-say evidence, shame us and hang us out to dry.

As the shock calmed, the anger grew in me. We all knew the officers of this prestigious regiment were a bunch of over-privileged wankers. A lot of it was nepotism – 'daddy was in, you know, oh yes, he's useless but I served with his father'. I expect they all celebrated a job well done that evening, sat in their exclusive clubs in Pall Mall, while I contemplated the absolute shame of having to tell my father and family that Simon's fucked up again. Pam's parents advised her to leave me, but thank the lord she stuck with it. Love will always out, you know. It was clear in the days that followed that we weren't welcome there. From leaving the stables that afternoon, I never saw Pan Am again, wasn't allowed down there. I felt like kicking off, but what good would that do? My wife had her job in London, and she relied on me to keep a roof over her head. I couldn't do anything that might jeopardize that. I have to be honest, as the days moved on the feelings of shame grew. I had to tell my parents, which was not an easy conversation from a public telephone box outside Knightsbridge tube station. Of course, all my family thought it was my fault but didn't actually say so. Pam and I were on our own, so between us, Terry and Liz, Pam and I decided to stay in London. We would rent a flat large enough for the four of us, just get on with it. The flat we settled on was over two floors above a car salesroom opposite the Salvation Army on Balham High Road. It was a shithole, freezing cold and draughty. Pam and I occupied the top floor with Liz and Terry below. We shared a bathroom that was so small you had to climb over the toilet to get in the bath.

It was clear that Pam wasn't happy. What had I done to her? I'd lay on the bed while she was at work and wonder why, if we were so guilty, we didn't get charged with anything. If we were that bad, they would have all the evidence necessary to charge us. We'd get sent to 'Collie', the army prison in Colchester, and that would be that. My dad did his best. He sent a letter to the colonel, only to receive a thoroughly condescending reply. I didn't realize it then, but severe depression was sweeping over me. Life wasn't fun anymore. Pam and I weren't getting on as well as we did, and nothing in my whole life seemed to be as it was. I blamed myself. For forty-six years, I carried that shame. It forced me to have to lie during job interviews, to offer up pathetic reasons for my leaving the military – it wasn't for me, things like that – when I knew it was for me. It was my greatest achievement, taken from me by a bunch of over-entitled chinless wonders who didn't have the bottle to stand up for their men. If I sound 'anti-officer' in this book, that's not strictly true. I have great respect for some officers. Trouble is, the ones I respect had come up from the barrack room – 'Queen's commission', as it's known in the military. My brother Tony, for instance. I had and still do have huge respect for his achievements. And *Jacko*, Captain *Alex Jackson*. Of course there are many more I have to add to the list of those I do not respect. The senior NCOs at that time, who could have fought our corner but chose not to, for what reason I know not. All I know is that they all knew what went on under their command. Most were involved, but they chose to save their own skins and not look after their men, as we were taught to do at the depot. Shame on them; they know who they are!

Both Terry and I had to get jobs. We tried selling unit trusts door to door, cold calling. I found myself wandering around blocks of flats in Brixton – at the time it was a very dodgy area – in a suit carrying a briefcase trying to sell something that I didn't have a clue about! I got a job in the Mack market supermarket on the King's Road. My job was to keep the fruit and veg area stocked up. It was a doddle, and I was bored senseless within a few days. I moved my ambitions to working in a furniture store in Balham. I used to be on the road, helping the driver delivering beds and other furniture here, there and everywhere. I enjoyed that job, but I still wasn't satisfied with my lot. I was better than this, I thought. I didn't know it then, but I was slowly – very slowly – breaking out of my depression. After a few months in Balham, Pam had managed to secure a transfer back to Bristol, so we were on the move again, back to Baugh Farm, living in rooms at the front of the house.

Pam and I had our first child by now, Ben. I don't know how that happened, because we still weren't as close as we used to be. Anyway, I was extremely pleased and proud to be a dad. It gave me the impetus to get off my arse and get on with life once again.

Saturday evening sitting on our big sofa that somehow – I can't remember how – we had managed to get down to Baugh Farm from London, I sat flicking through *The Horse and Hound* and came across the jobs section. Maybe I could get a job running a yard. There were plenty of jobs offering accommodation as part of the package. Better not, I thought – what about references? What if they found out? Forget that. My eyes continued scanning the ads when 'Bloodstock Shipping' caught my eye. A bloodstock agency based in Windsor was looking for a horsebox driver. That sounds good, I thought. I'd recently passed my driving test, so it might be worth a punt. No time like the present, I thought, as I hunted for some writing paper and a pen that worked. I felt a little better just putting pen to paper. I wrote that I was ex-Household Cavalry. I had to be honest, as they'd find out anyway. I listed my experience and tried to convey my enthusiasm onto the paper. I really thought it would come to nothing as I put it in the post box and walked home. We were skint – couldn't even afford a beer. Something had to change. I was on the night shift at the chocolate factory next week. It was boring, although the money was alright. The only saving grace was that I was on a new chocolate bar line and it kept breaking down, so the other guys who worked on it and I had a fair bit of down time to explore the massive factory and sample all the sweets that seemed to be just hanging around.

It was around two in the afternoon when the telephone began to ring in the kitchen at Baugh Farm. Mum answered in the usual way. 'Wallington Baugh Farm', she politely informed the caller. You know what it's like when someone else answers the phone and you really wanted to. Pretty frustrating. 'Oh yes, he's here. Would you like to talk to him?' I'm hovering behind her now, contemplating physical intervention. 'Okay, hold on while I go and get him.'

'Hello, how can I help?'

'Good afternoon. My name's Ollie and I run Foxton's horse transport here in Newbury. Can you talk for a minute?' a rather posh voice introduced himself. I could hear voices in the background. He was clearly in an office of some sort.

'Er, yes. Nice to talk to you.'

'I've been given a letter that you wrote to Pedens bloodstock shipping agency last week. I noticed that you were in the Household Cavalry. Is this correct?'

'Er, yes, that's right,' I burbled, fully expecting this call to end at any second.

'When did you leave?'

'When? Oh, January 1976.'

'Good, good. I see you have a car driving licence – you would need a heavy goods licence if you worked for me. Don't worry, though, we can sort that out. When can you come and see me?'

'Whenever you want. Just say a time and I'll be there. Where's "there" by the way.'

'Newbury, just off the M4, about 60 miles from Bristol. You live in Bristol, don't you?'

'Yes, that's right. So when do you want me to come up?'

'Well, we've got to get on with it. We're very busy. Next Wednesday, late morning – is that alright?'

I was always told not to appear too eager in these situations. I probably did appear too eager, because I forgot to ask him where they were based – what their address was. I can't really explain how I felt, but I knew it was what I wanted. A chance; all I wanted was a chance. A chance to earn enough money to look after my family. A chance to work with horses again. A chance to at least to hold my head up again and do something I would be proud off. My next book, *Box to Box*, will follow what I did after finally passing my heavy goods licence and joining the fascinating world that is horse transport, and how – within two years of being kicked out – I was back in Hyde Park Barracks, back with my old regiment, as a civvy now, a civvy with quite a bit of influence, as it turned out!

Chapter 14

Justice

IT WAS A pleasant Sunday spring evening as we drove out of Bristol towards Chippenham. We were heading toward the Wiltshire village of Colerne, where our pub was situated. We had been there for twelve years, but decided to move back to Bristol and sell the lease on our pub. Our two horses were also stabled in the area, so we would combine our journey with a cheeky pint or two. I was studying a scrap of paper while Pam drove towards Marshfield. It was Quiff's mobile number that he'd emailed to me, and I'd quickly made a note of it before leaving. As I finished tapping the number into my phone, I turned the volume down on the radio and waited in anticipation, like you do, for it to start ringing. It didn't ring for long before a familiar voice from the past answered his phone.

'Alright dickhead, is Pam there?' he said.

'Yes, she is, so watch your language, dumb fuck.'

'So, what's happening? What are you up to?'

'We're going to see to the horses then we're going to our old pub for a pint.'

'Okay, well listen, now I've got your number I can pass it on to Skitmore and we can arrange a get-together.'

'Yep, that would be great. Give me a call.'

'That was Quiff,' I announced to Pam as she turned her small van into the long narrow lane that led to BJ and Indie's field. 'No shit, Sherlock,' she sarcastically replied as she pulled up outside the field. It was April 2016. I hadn't seen Quiff for a couple of years. I stayed with him once when I was in his location – Suffolk – working. Terry had visited us at the pub one Sunday lunchtime. Unfortunately we were so busy I barely had time to talk to him before he had to leave, so a catch-up was on the cards. Quiff suggested we all meet and stay at a holiday let that he looked after in Southwold at the beginning of July. We could use the place for a good price for a long weekend.

So at the start of July 2016, we piled our two deerhounds into the back of the car and began the four-hour-plus journey to Suffolk. The weather looked as though it was going to be good, so we were both looking forward to a couple of days' break. I drove past Quiff's road and went straight to the beach. The dogs needed a pee and I needed a pint before meeting up with him. An hour later, he was waiting on his doorstep as we turned into Seaview Road. 'I don't know why they called it Seaview Road,' I mentioned to Pam as we pulled up. 'Look, you can just see the tops of the beach huts about a mile away.'

'Stand by your beds!' Quiff's voice rang out as I got out of the car.

'How are you, mate? Is Terry here yet?'

'No, he's on his way. Come on, I'll show you where you're staying.'

The house was great, with plenty of room for all of us. I couldn't wait to see how Terry was, because he'd just been through a terrible few months after losing his long-term partner, Amin, to an horrific suicide. We were all concerned about him. Just seeing that familiar smile told me he was on the mend as he pulled up in his car. It had been many years since we'd all been together in the same room. A couple of days of much conversation, eating, drinking and walking were ahead of us. I was really looking forward to it. Saturday lunchtime found us sitting in a beach hut that Quiff had managed to blag, eating bacon rolls and drinking coffee. The conversation, inevitably, got around to January 1976.

'It was forty years ago last January, you know,' I mentioned as we sat there looking out over the deep blue North Sea.

'Forty fucking years. Oh, sorry for swearing, Pam,' Quiff noted in his usual fashion.

It took a while, mulling that fact over, before I suggested: 'Why don't we have a go at finding out why we were treated like that?'

'It would be tricky,' Terry replied. 'We all know it was a cover-up, and cover-ups are notoriously difficult to uncover. I'm going through a similar thing at the moment over Amin's suicide.'

Terry was right. It would be difficult – impossible maybe – but we all agreed to have a go. It was decided that I would arrange a meeting with my MP and gauge his reaction, then report back and we would collectively work out our next move.

A mixture of anticipation and excitement flowed through my body as I pulled into the car park of Severn Beach village hall the following Friday afternoon. I'd managed to secure a meeting with my MP, *Jack Lopresti*. Telling the story in an echoey village hall in front of this stranger and his assistant wasn't easy, I can tell you. Pam and I had only told our children a couple of years ago. We hadn't mentioned or talked about it to anyone else. What was to become familiar look spread across their faces as I recalled my career and our unjust ejection from the regiment. I've sort of got used to it now, having had to tell the story so many times. It starts with a furrowed brow of disbelief, then the eyebrows rise in questionable surprise. The head will normally start to shake, then there may be a tut or two as you finish.

'Well, I don't know what to say,' the man sat opposite me said in complete astonishment.

'Can you help us? That would be a good start.'

'Oh, yes, of course. Give me a week or so. I'll talk to the MOD – see what I can find out.'

As I drove back home, I called Quiff to inform him that was it, we were in now – shit or bust. We had to keep going. Following one or two meetings in the House of Commons, we kept getting the same answer: 'Sorry, but too many years have passed since the incident. You're out of time. You should have appealed your dismissal within two months of the act.' 'But we weren't given opportunity to appeal,' I would reply. 'Sorry, nothing we can do about it,' the response came. Door after door was shut in our faces until, one day, I was talking to my eldest brother, Tim, at a family party when he suggested that I contact our cousin Peter.

'Peter? Have I ever met him?' I asked.

'Probably. He's a barrister specializing in employment law. I'll give you his email address.' This whole journey was like a game of snakes and ladders: one minute you were up, the next the same old excuses sprung up and hit you back down. I contacted Peter Wallington, and he agreed to 'have a look' for us. To be honest, he didn't give us much hope. Getting money out of the MOD, he told us, would be close to impossible. I was living in Bristol now. Pam had retired and I was driving a 44-ton truck to Portsmouth every working day, on twelve-hour shifts. It gave me a lot of time for thinking – thinking of the next door to knock on. Peter did indeed 'have a look', and boosted our hopes when he found some *Hansard* records in his chambers. We applied for our army records, but mysteriously they had been destroyed. Quiff visited the National Archives at Kew, to no avail, in May 2017. Quiff, Terry and I met my cousin Peter in London. I was to meet him face-to-face at last. He was definitely a Wallington. We talked for a good hour about what we could do next. It's interesting how ideas you haven't had before just jump into your head when you're in that sort of company. He was, and has continued to be, a tremendous help. We truly couldn't have done it without him. We discovered that officers from the regiment had acted above their rank, and that our Red books (Certificate of Service) had been altered. In the military conduct grading, '5' (Unsatisfactory) was altered to read '1' (Exemplary), and my testimonial read: 'He has found it difficult to adapt to military life. Although he has no doubt got ability, I believe he's better suited to being a civilian.''

Some forty-nine years later, I still find it difficult to read. It's an insult; an insult to the work and dedication I'd given to my regiment, to the army and to the Queen. If you've read this book this far, you'll understand why!

Another significant step forward was a telephone conversation between myself and *Emma Norton* from the human rights campaigning group Liberty, whom Peter suggested I talk to. She in turn suggested we contact Fighting With Pride, the charity supporting LGBTQ+ veterans, where at last things began to change in our favour. Our first Zoom meeting with the group's founders, Craig Jones MBE and Caroline Paige MBE, was, quite frankly, a revelation. They supported our cause from the get-go, and guided us to our first really significant meeting with Lord Etherton – Terence Etherton, a former Chancellor of the High Court and Master of the Rolls – in The Cabinet Office in Whitehall. On 1 November 2022, the three of us made our way from Westminster tube station in the pouring rain towards the Cabinet Office in Whitehall, all suited and booted, ready to tell our stories. I was fascinated, first by the security and then by the amount of people who appeared to work there. Lord Etherton was late, but we decided to forgive him. While waiting for him in one of the COBRA (Cabinet Office Briefing Rooms) boardrooms, we gave our accounts of how we were treated on camera. I went first. I just wanted to get it over with; when you've shut something out of your mind for so long, even though over recent years you've relived it almost every day, it's still tricky when you've got a camera recording your every word. Terry was still being recorded as the Lord came through the large door in the corner of the room. I had been trying to work out, geographically, where we were. The net-curtained windows to my left looked out over other building close by, so that wasn't Whitehall. I was suddenly brought back into the room when I noticed Quiff to my right standing up. I thought at first it must be biscuits or some sort of food, because that's what makes Quiff move fastest. But no, it was a tall, thin gentleman wearing a slightly wet tweed overcoat. He was slightly stooped forward – if you picture an old judge in your mind, you've got him. I could imagine him having a black handkerchief placed on his wigged head before looking you in the eye and telling you your sentence!

'Good morning,' the Lord said. 'Sorry I'm late. Traffic around Regents Park was terrible. What's your name?'

'Oh, good morning, sir, your Lord – no, my Lord. I'm Simon, Simon Wallington.'

I felt like a right tosser as I sat back down. Terry was just as bad, nearly falling into my lap as he reached across to introduce himself to the Lord. As we started answering his questions, Quiff asked if he could address him as Terry, to which he peered over his spectacles and agreed that we could call him Terrence. Honestly, I was so embarrassed. If he had been in range, I would have kicked Quiff in the nuts.

The Lord wrote notes on what can only described as a threepenny jotter using an old chewed-up pencil. But notes he did write – lots of them. Even he raised an eyebrow when some of the events of forty-six years ago were described to him. This man, I was thinking, held the position of England's top judge. Imagine the cases he'd presided over, imagine the dreadful things he'd heard, and he looked shocked at our accounts of January 1976. Wow!

The meeting lasted an hour, and the Lord agreed to include our case in his government report into the treatment of LGBT military personnel that would be published in July of the following year. In short, we'd won. Six years of enquiring, begging, reliving everything, had come to a conclusion. Our regiment, the British Army, the MOD and of course the government of the time had acted incorrectly. In short, we had been kicked out to placate the press. Six trips to London, countless Zoom meetings, even more letters and emails later, we'd won. After our meeting, walking towards Trafalgar Square, the rain had stopped now. The Blues had just mounted the Queen's Life Guard. We decided to call in a pub for a drink. Terry and I had a glass of whisky, while Quiff had a girly coffee. There was no celebration; it hadn't sunk in yet, I guess. I just remember I felt quite empty, empty of any emotion or feelings. Forty-six years of that dreadful feeling of guilt and shame was gone now, but it didn't make me feel any better. There was no sense of elation. If anything, I felt worse. This would take some getting used to. As we all felt the same, we agreed that probably the best way to play this was to give it time, give ourselves time to process all that had just happened. We could forget being rejected by the Ombudsman in February 2018. We could forget the condescending letters from the regiment and MOD, and move forward.

For me personally, apologies count for nothing. Recognition was, and still is, my goal. Why should the current prime minister apologize for something a former prime minister sanctioned? Why should the Chief of the General Staff apologize for his predecessor's incompetence and weakness. However, we have all received both.

Thinking of the matter of recognition, sitting here at my desk after a lively Zoom meeting with Quiff and co, I thought I'd pen a letter to the current colonel of the mounted regiment. Firstly, I wanted to remind him of the regiment's conduct back in 1976 and also inform him of our victory regarding our now proven dismissal. I also wanted to ask that he might take a bit of time to either research or investigate this bit of regimental history, because whether the regiment likes it or not, it is history that should be recognized. Not the amazing history the regiment is famous for, but history all the same. To my surprise, the letter found its way to Whitehall and landed on the desk of the regimental adjutant, a polite man who seemed to understand my ranting. He agreed to my concerns and suggestions, so in June 2025, us three urchins and guests were guests of the regiment at one of the big parades on Horse Guards, followed by lunch in the officers' mess at Hyde Park Barracks. One of my suggestions was that they – the regiment and its associations – should assist us with trying to track down the remaining 'Cavalry Eighteen', as we are known. He agreed. The hunt goes on. If you have got this far in reading my memoirs and are one of the eighteen, why not contact me? I'll respect your confidentiality; that goes without saying, because I was there as well, remember.

At the time of publication of this book, we three of the Cavalry Eighteen have just received our first reparation payment from the government but are appealing our second impact payment offer.

Dedicated to Pam

With thanks

Peter Wallington

Kalvyn Friend

Terry Skitmore

The Cavalry Eighteen

Lt Col (Retd) RRD Griffin

Lt Col (Retd) Giles Stibbe OBE

James Wharton